The E-Mail Companion

Communicating Effectively via the Internet and Other Global Networks

John S. Quarterman

Smoot Carl-Mitchell

Texas Internet Consulting
tic@tic.com

Addison-Wesley Publishing Company

Reading, Massachusetts • Menlo Park, California • New York
Don Mills, Ontario • Wokingham, England • Amsterdam
Bonn • Sydney • Singapore • Tokyo • Madrid • San Juan
Paris • Seoul • Milan • Mexico City • Taipei

Library of Congress Cataloging-in-Publication Data

```
Quarterman, John. 1954-
     The E-Mail Companion:
     Communicating Effectively via the Internet and Other Global Networks /
  by John S. Quarterman, Smoot Carl-Mitchell.
       p.   cm.
Includes bibliographical references and index.
ISBN 0-201-40658-6
1. Internet (computer network).   I. Quarterman, John S.
II. Title.
TK5105.875.I57Q37   1994                              94-4910
384.3--dc20                                           CIP
```

Sponsoring Editor: Keith Wollman
Project Manager: Eleanor McCarthy
Production Coordinator: Lora L. Ryan
Cover design: Jean Seal
Troff Macro Designer: Jaap Akkerhuis
Copy Editor: Martha Hughes

1 2 3 4 5 6 7 8 9 –MA–9897969594
First printing, September 1994

Addison-Wesley books are available for bulk purchases by corporations, institutions, and other organizations. For more information please contact the Corporate, Government and Special Sales Department at (800) 238-9682.

To Gretchen

Contents

v

Preface

Frustrated by telephone tag? Tired of illegible faxes of faxes? Need to communicate with Tokyo or Paris without staying up until midnight? Electronic mail (or e-mail, email or just mail) may be for you. You can convert your computer or terminal from an isolated computing utility into a node in a global communications network. You can do this using very little additional hardware, not much more software, and the information in this book.

Electronic mail permits tens of millions of people throughout the world to communicate conveniently and quickly for work and play. Email among all these people, or between you and one other person, can be an interesting new toy or a powerful force, depending on how you use it. This technology can both broaden and simplify your life.

The Book

This is a book for people who want to use email today. It tells you not only how to use mail, but why you should want to, drawing heavily on examples from many different walks of life. This may not be the only mail book you need, but it is the first one you should read, and you will find it useful as a reference together with more specific publications about particular mail interfaces. You need to be able to type, or at least hunt and peck, but you can learn that quickly and little technical computer knowledge is required.

This book tells you how to use electronic mail to communicate with any of tens of millions of people worldwide without leaving your chair, picking up the telephone, or stamping a letter. Electronic mail travels through all the computers of the worldwide Matrix of computer networks, including the Internet, BITNET, UUCP, FidoNet, WWIVnet, CompuServe, GEnie, BIX, and many others.

Mail can be personal, when you address a message to just one person or to a small group of people who should read that particular message. Mail can also be used for group communications, when you address a message to an alias that causes the message to be distributed to many people; this is called a mailing list. You don't even have to know who all the people on a list are. Mail, whether sent to a single person or ten thousand, can be used for work or play.

In this book we focus on how to use this new method of communication. The point of the technology and of this book is not the mechanics of how mail is carried, any more than the point of television is the chemicals used in screen phosphors or the point of newspapers is the quality of the paper. Because mail is still relatively new, you do have to know something about the infrastructure that carries it, and we discuss that. The point is not the details of how to send, receive, reply to, and forward mail, although we spell out common mail operations such as those in detail. The point of the book is how to use mail to best effect, including dos, don'ts, context and etiquette.

In a few years the communication media of electronic mail and mailing lists will be as common as the telephone and newspapers. You can use this book to learn the communications of tomorrow today.

Electronic Mail

Electronic mail is a communication medium for both home and office. You will find it invaluable for business communications, and fun and fascinating for personal communications.

This book explains in clear and concise language:

- What email is and is not.

- It is a new medium; it has some similarities to older media, but is not exactly like any of them.

- How it differs from fax and telephone.

- Why it is more than just an electronic version of a paper memo or a paper letter.

- How it shares the immediacy and global reach of the telegraph, radio, and television.

- How it can be become one of your most valuable communications tool.

- How it is spreading rapidly throughout the world, for both business and personal use.

Learn how easy it is to get connected to the worldwide Matrix of interconnected networks that support mail.

This book does not describe details of specific mail user programs (that would take a much longer book). It does explain what to look for in a mail user program. For example, if it won't let you send a message to more than one person at a time, pass it by; if it can't even handle `Subject:` lines, ignore it.

This book does show you how to get the most out of mail by communicating with people and groups and by retrieving files and documents throughout the world. This may sound complicated, but is actually easier than you might think.

Organization

You can read this book from beginning to end, or you can look in the index and read just the section you want. It is both a tutorial and a reference. We hope you find it useful as well as amusing.

The first part of the book is about what you can do with mail, how it affects you, and the networks that support it. It includes concrete examples of how people use mail, and frequently asked questions and answers about mail.

The second part is about specific communication techniques, from basics such as composing and replying to messages, through routing mail through different networks, and dealing with errors.

The third part is about mailing lists, which are the newsletters, gossip columns, and trade journals of the online world. It begins with a chapter that shows you how to subscribe to a mailing list, send mail to it, and unsubscribe later, as well as how to retrieve information related to the list. The part continues with a chapter that explains many uses of mailing lists by comparing them to other media, such as newsletters and television. The part ends with a chapter on the etiquette of mailing lists.

The last part is about finding files, documents, and other information, including people's electronic mail addresses. It is also about retrieving or exchanging information in many formats, using a variety of mechanisms, including MIME. The information services discussed include ftpmail (file retrieval), archie (indexes to file repositories), WAIS (keyword searches of databases), and Gopher (browsing of those and other services using menus). For example, with WAIS you can search a list of names and descriptions of many mailing lists by keyword, so you can find a mailing list on a subject you want.

All chapters use concrete examples and discuss etiquette and ethics whenever appropriate.

Electronic Mail and the Networks

The Matrix of all computer systems worldwide that exchange electronic mail has many parts. These parts have different services. All of them have mail, or we wouldn't have included them here. Some have no services other than mail and lists. Others also have specialized databases, customized communication services, or sophisticated distributed information services. Each of these parts may have its own mail address syntax, charging methods, or rules of acceptable use. You need to be aware of some of these differences, so that you can send mail to best effect to people wherever they are in the Matrix.

Some of the systems we describe in this book, together with some of their distinguishing characteristics, include:

- Centralized Conferencing Systems such as CompuServe, BIX, GEnie: Many services, localized access, usage-based charging.

- Commercial Mail Systems such as AT&T Mail, SprintMail, EasyLink, and MCI Mail: These typically provide only mail.

- Global Networks such as the Internet, BITNET, UUCP, FidoNet, and WWIVnet: Some of these are very inexpensive (WWIVnet, FidoNet, and UUCP), but provide few services other than mail. One, the Internet, is very large and provides many services, but mail is still its most popular service. Most of these networks avoid usage-based charges.

- The Matrix which includes all of the systems previously mentioned, plus some others:
  Electronic mail is the most popular of all network services. The largest collection of networks that exchange electronic mail is called the Matrix.

Readers

Anyone with a computer who wants to use it to communicate with people should read this book. This book is especially for new users of electronic mail. However, even old hands at using mail may find useful tips here, since we present mail in an organized manner, combining practical examples with reasons for the practices we recommend.

You can reach any of approximately 30 million people throughout the world by electronic mail through the Matrix today. Most of the global networks, including the Internet, UUCP, FidoNet, and WWIVnet, are growing exponentially, with the biggest, the Internet, growing at about 100 percent per year. That means that if the Internet had 7 million users in 1993, and 15 million by the end of 1994, it will have 30 million in 1995, 60 million in 1996, and so on. This growth must stop eventually. But there are perhaps 60 million personal computers in the world already, and only a fraction of those are networked.

Terminology and Typefaces

Mail is mostly text, and there are many different textual terms to describe elements of mail. We use different typefaces to help you distinguish different types of terms.

- Hostnames such as tic.com are in a sans serif font.

- Mail addresses like mailbook@tic.com are also in a sans serif font.

- Headers used within a mail message, such as `Subject: hi there` are in the same fixed width font that we use when we show entire mail messages.

- User input, when we call attention to it in a mail message, in an example of using a program, or in the main text, as in *`I typed this!`* is in a fixed width italic font.

- Filenames and pathnames, such as **.signature**, are in boldface.

- Glossary items, such as *typeface*, appear in italics in the place in the main text where we first discuss them in detail. The same glossary item may appear in italics several times in the book, since it may be used in several different contexts. Each glossary items also appears, along with a concise definition, in the glossary at the back of the book.

Wherever we say *mail* in this book, we mean *electronic mail*, unless we explicitly qualify the word to mean something else, as in *paper mail*. The terms *e-mail* or *email* are also in common use, and we occasionally use them in this book. However, there is no consensus among mail users as to which of these terms to use. You will encounter all of them as you use mail, and we use all of them in this book. We do prefer mail, though, mostly because we think it sounds better.

Acknowledgments

We would like to thank Jon Boede, Brent Chapman, Heidi Chavez, Howard Coleman, Laura Fillmore, Martha Hughes, Eric McKinney, Kristin Kuntz, Matt Lawrence, Gretchen Phillips, John Rouillard, Eric Thomas, Glee Willis, Keith Wollman, and anyone else we have forgotten to name, for their contributions to this book.

1

What is Electronic Mail?

Electronic mail, often called e-mail, email, or just mail, is a fast and efficient way to communicate with your friends or colleagues using the ever expanding electronic highway. With just a computer and a modem, you, too, can send electronic mail to over 30 million users worldwide. You can communicate with one person at a time, or thousands. You can send a report or carry on one or dozens of simultaneous conversations. You can retrieve and send files and other information; not only text, but also graphics and other data. You can do all this from the computer or terminal you already have on your desk or lap, by whichever style of interface you prefer, whether by pointing and clicking or by typing commands.

But what is electronic mail? How does it work? Is it hard to use? Do you need fancy software or do you have to be a programmer? Let's start with some basics.

Communicating with a Person through a Computer

You can send an electronic mail message to another person in the same room or on the other side of the world. To do this, you need only fill in an address and type some text. Computers and software take care of the rest. The other person, who may be your business partner, spouse, employee, parent, child, friend, or a perfect stranger, can later read your message and send a reply by typing some text plus a few commands.

This is much faster than writing and mailing a paper letter. It's hard to find an electronic mail system anymore that takes more than a day to deliver mail anywhere in the world. Many networks deliver mail in hours or even minutes.

Electronic mail is also much easier than paper mail: no pen, no paper, no envelope, no stamp. Just keystrokes and data to connect two people.

Wherever we say *mail* in this book, we mean electronic mail, unless we explicitly qualify the word to mean something else, as in *paper mail.* The term *email* is also widespread, but there is no consensus among mail users as to which term to use, or whether to spell it out as *electronic mail.* Variety is the nature of mail.

An Example

A mail message looks something like this:

```
From: jsq@tic.com (John S. Quarterman)
To: smoot@zilker.net (Smoot Carl-Mitchell)
Subject: did you see the NYT article?

Liked the picture; wishe they'd spell my name right.
```

It looks much like an office memo, with `From:`, `To:`, and `Subject:` headers, followed by a blank line and the body of the message. But this message has only one line in the body, including a typo (`wishe`): you'd never send *that* as a paper memo! Such informality is common in electronic mail, which is often more like a telephone conversation than like a memo. Conversations of single lines exchanged within minutes are just as common in electronic mail as are lengthy formal messages. There are more examples of mail messages in Chapter 2, *Mail, Your Work, and You*. We discuss what sorts of things should go in mail messages in Chapter 5, *The Basics*. Answers to frequently asked questions appear in Chapter 3, *Common Questions*, but let's cover some of the most important ones here.

Mail Delivery

How does mail actually get delivered? Well, if you and the recipient both use the same computer, perhaps your mail message gets delivered by a single program appending data to a file (a *mailbox*) for the other person. More commonly, the recipient is associated with a different organization than the sender, as shown in the example. You can tell this by looking at the `From:` and `To:` lines. The parentheses indicate comments for human readers; the various programs involved ignore these comments. The real addresses are jsq@tic.com and smoot@zilker.net. The part to the left of the @ indicates the user. The part to the right indicates the system or organization. The organizations are different in these two addresses.

How different? In this particular case, down the hall in the same building, but you can't tell that from the addresses. Either address could indicate a location anywhere in the world. We discuss *the Matrix* of all computers and networks worldwide that exchange electronic mail and the main computer networks, such as *the Internet*, that compose it in Chapter 4, *The Networks*.

Even in the down-the-hall case the mail message will pass through four programs that explicitly handle it as mail, and four computers. In the across-the-world case, the number of programs and computers involved could be dozens or more. You will usually never know how many programs and computers are used or exactly where they are, and there is usually no reason you should care. See Chapter 6, *How Electronic Mail Works* for the mechanics of how mail works, Chapter 7, *Mail Addressing and Routing* for how your mail gets there, Chapter 8, *Error and Non-Error Messages* for when you have to care. The important point is that your mail usually gets there. You don't have to worry about how.

Mail, Fax, Telephone, and Memos

If mail is conversational, quick, and inexpensive, how is it different from calling someone on the telephone? To start with, mail is recorded, which makes it easy for you to quote parts of the other person's or your own messages for context. This makes it easy to keep track of conversations over long periods of time (hours, days, years), and to keep track of multiple conversations going on at the same time. Recording is also useful in business correspondence, since you can later check to see what tasks were agreed upon, or what motivations led to aspects of a contract. Some people realize this feature leaves a trail showing their previous actions, and avoid use of electronic mail because they do not want to be recorded. Such reluctance is easy to detect, and may give you a clue about what sort of person you are dealing with.

Fax has some of the convenience of electronic mail, but is slow, difficult to reuse because it's either on paper or in a binary image format, and usually expensive to send over long distances or to many recipients.

Paper memos may look like electronic mail, but they are generally more formal and have completely different etiquette. A paper memo is almost always a semi-public or public document, partly because it is distributed on paper, and more because of tradition. An electronic mail message is usually considered to be a private communication unless the participants agree otherwise. However, be aware that anyone may decide otherwise without asking you. It is prudent not to post anything you don't want to see on the evening news, unless you are sending it to only a very few people whom you know well.

Disadvantages of Mail

Electronic mail does have some disadvantages. Most mail is private only by convention, not by technology; it is easy to intercept or to forge. Of course, steaming open a paper envelope is also easy; societal conventions and laws are all that make this practice uncommon. Technical means of enforcing privacy of electronic communications are becoming more widespread. Some of them can protect your correspondence even from the government.

Traditionally, electronic mail only uses written words, and only in the Latin character set. Graphics, voice inflections, and background sights or sounds are all lacking. Sometimes this lack of context in mail messages can cause people to *flame,* that is, to send rude, irate, or otherwise inappropriate messages. We discuss flaming and how to deal with it in Chapter 11, *Mailing List Etiquette.*

Lack of visual or aural accompaniment to words can also be an advantage, just as using the telephone can be an advantage. The other party does not know if you are tired, have just gotten out of the shower, are wearing a suit, or have sixteen earrings in one ear. The conversation focuses on the content, not on trivia. Mail goes further than the telephone in this direction, and can be useful in forcing the other person to pay attention to what is actually being said, rather than to some imagined subtext derived from vocal inflections.

Mail Conventions

Nonetheless, conventions have been informally established for determining the mood of the remote party. If you see a *:-)* at the end of a sentence or paragraph, you know the remote party is "just joking." The character sequence looks like a sideways smiley face. In Chapter 11, *Mailing List Etiquette* we shall see that there are other similar conventions in use within the electronic mail community.

Fonts, Graphics, Images, and Sound

All the things that have been lacking in electronic mail are now being added. In Chapter 14, *MIME: Multipurpose Internet Mail*

Extensions we explain how you can send mail messages with italics, boldface, character sets for various languages, graphics, still images, moving images, and sound.

What Hardware and Software Do You Need?

To send electronic mail you need a computer or a terminal, either directly connected to a network or dialed up with a modem through the telephone system. Any kind of computer will do. Most computers are capable of running mail software locally, but many commercial services offer dialup mail connectivity. We discuss some of these in Appendix A, *Places to Connect*. For an extensive list of connectivity providers, see our other book, *The Internet Connection* (Addison-Wesley Publishing Company, 1994).

If you dial up, the biggest problem will be configuring your modem. After you succeed in dialing up, you will need to find a mail program that suits your needs and preferences. The mail program will provide you with some sort of user interface, perhaps using a mouse, perhaps using menus and function keys, or perhaps using textual commands. Some systems provide mail as just another part of a general menu interface, and give you no choice of mail programs. Since every mail interface is supported by some sort of mail program, and every mail program provides some sort of user interface, we sometimes refer to a mail interface, and sometimes to a mail program, but usually we refer to a mail program. For more on this kind of terminology, see Chapter 5, *The Basics*.

If the mail program on the system you are using doesn't have the features you want, your only choice may be to choose a different system to dial up. Other systems let you call a mail program explicitly, and often give you a choice of two or three programs, with different user interfaces. Some connectivity methods let you run a mail program directly on your own DOS, Windows, Macintosh, UNIX, or other computer system. In that case, you will need to get mail software to run on your system. Ask your connectivity provider for information about the mail interfaces they provide for your use. You want all the features described in Chapter 5.

Mailing Lists

Electronic mail is one of several *Computer Mediated Communication (CMC)* services. CMC sounds complicated, but all it means is that computers help people communicate. You'll occasionally encounter the acronym CMC because it has been used frequently in academic papers about networked communications. We'll just say communications services. Other communications services include mailing lists and USENET news. We say more about which networks provide which services in Chapter 4, *The Networks*. For the moment, what you need to know is that mailing lists are another communication service, like personal electronic mail in many ways, but different in others.

Multiple Recipients

Suppose you want to send the same message to many people at the same time. With paper mail you would need to copy the message, address each envelope separately, and then mail each message one by one. With electronic mail, the task is far simpler. You can send the same message to many people at the same time by simply adding each person's electronic mail address to the list of recipients. The participating computers make the necessary copies of the message and deliver them. You don't have to know how, any more than you have to know what trucks, roads, airplanes, and routes a paper letter takes to reach its destination. And with electronic mail, you don't even have to make copies; the electronic mail system handles that for you.

Local Aliases and Private Lists

In addition, you can send mail to a single name, such as bridgeclub, that causes delivery to a predefined list of recipients. You don't even have to type all their addresses; you only need to specify the single name, bridgeclub. This name is called an *alias*. Aliases save a lot of typing and typing mistakes. They make ongoing discussions easy. Most mail systems let you create your own aliases, either by selecting aliases in a menu, or by putting the alias in a file for the mail program to read.

System-wide Aliases and Mailing Lists

Most mail systems also support system-wide aliases, usable by everyone on that system, or on any participating network. The alias and the addresses on it are called a *mailing list*. Such a list is usually used for discussing a topic of interest to everyone who receives mail from it. People often subscribe to such a list in order to receive information or express views on a subject.

A mailing list is maintained on one machine, but the list members can be on different machines, possibly connected to several different networks. You simply send a message to the name of the list and the message will be automatically redistributed to everyone who is a member of the list. You don't have to wait for distribution, and none of the list members have to read it immediately, but they will all get the message. We discuss lists in much more detail in the chapters beginning with Chapter 9, *Mailing List Basics*.

Subscribing and Unsubscribing

Specific conventions have been developed for subscribing and unsubscribing to mailing lists. These conventions are similar to those for paper newsletters, as we will explain in Chapter 10, *Uses of Mailing Lists*, but mailing lists have their own rules, as we explain in Chapter 9, *Mailing List Basics*. We explain how to use lists without offending people and to best effect in Chapter 11, *Mailing List Etiquette*. For now, it is enough to know that mailing lists give you a way of communicating with many people who are interested in the same topics.

Files, People, and Things

Mail can also be used to transport files. Many mail systems are limited to plain text messages, but software is widely available to encode anything into plain text. You can send programs, data, or other information by mail. Of course, if you include non-text information when you send text, the receiving end has to be able to understand the format. Also, mail systems often impose limits on the size of mail messages, forcing large files to be broken into several messages. But mail can be used to send many types of data other than text.

Specialized programs scattered across the networks will return assorted information if sent appropriate mail messages. You can look up a book in a library catalog, fetch a weather report, or retrieve an article. You can find someone's address (postal or electronic), telephone number, or fax number. We discuss these capabilities in more detail in Chapter 12, *Finding Things*, Chapter 13, *Finding People*, and Chapter 14, *MIME: Multipurpose Internet Mail Extensions*. Here, it is enough to say that mail is not just text.

Summary

Mail is not just text, as we have just discussed, but most mail messages still do consist of text alone. Plain text mail messages, either alone or in mailing lists, are sufficient for conversations, reports, discussion groups, business deals, marriages, divorces, religion, politics, and just plain daily business. Mail is used by many people not only discuss these and other topics, but as a basic part of them. Many businesses use mail as their most basic communications technique, and quite a few marriages now depend on mail to alleviate separations of distance or time. Even on the most sophisticated networks, electronic mail is the most used service, and in some ways the most valuable service. This book explains how to use it.

2

Mail, Your Work, and You

Electronic mail can have an astonishing impact on your work habits and your productivity. Electronic mail can also be used to keep in touch with your friends and relatives. You will find it easy to learn and use.

You may ask, "Why should I use electronic mail? I can already get in touch with everyone by telephone. And besides everyone has a phone number and nearly everyone has a fax. Isn't the telephone more 'personal' than writing memos? Isn't electronic mail a throwback to written memos and letters? I used to do that, but writing seems old-fashioned and slower than picking up the phone."

Rather than explain why this isn't the case in some theoretical way, let's take a few concrete examples from our own and others' experiences of how electronic mail (also called email, or just mail) improved communications. Keep in mind, the people we will mention are not all technonerds or people with backgrounds in computer science, rather mostly working professionals and ordinary people. Some of them were at the outset skeptical or downright hostile about electronic mail. They did not believe us when we told them how electronic mail could inexpensively improve their business productivity and let them keep in touch with friends and family. Then they saw it for themselves.

Since mail is useful for both business and personal communications, these examples include some of each.

Case 1 — The Reluctant Editor

Back when we were writing one of our earlier books and it got behind schedule, we started getting frequent calls from our editor. We'll call her Karen. Almost without fail, Karen would call (we called it our editorial wakeup call) when we were out of the office or on the phone with someone else. Inevitably when we returned Karen's call, she was gone instead. To make matters worse, she had a voice mail system.

Funny thing about *voice mail.* Supposedly it is designed to allow two people to interchange useful messages. Well, we have found that most of the messages left on a voice mail system end up being the "call me back when you get in" variety that convey no information at all, except that a person called when you weren't in. The messages might as well be "call me back when you get in and I will most likely be gone, so you can leave me the same message on my voice mail box."

Because of the telephone tag we were playing, it often took us over a week to actually talk to Karen on the phone. Finally, we suggested she get an account on an Internet connected host system and start sending us email. Karen was very reluctant at first, but when she discovered (much to her surprise) that we would often respond to her messages within a few hours (and usually within a few minutes), she quickly began to see the virtues of email.

Karen quickly saw that mail is like the telephone in terms of responsiveness. She also learned how she could include parts of our messages in her responses without having to retype anything. She discovered this feature makes electronic mail more like the telephone with someone dictating the conversation and letting you play back selected parts of it later. Using these simple features we could keep a *thread* of email conversation going with her across hours or days.

Here is an example of our dialogue with her:

```
From: karen@bigpub.com (Karen Editor)
To: smoot@tic.com (Smoot Carl-Mitchell)
cc: jsq@tic.com (John Quarterman)
Subject: copyediting

Hi,

I found a copy editor for your book. We will be sending her
your last chapter drafts.

Thanks,

Karen


----


From: smoot@tic.com (Smoot Carl-Mitchell)
To: karen@bigpub.com (Karen Editor)
cc: jsq@tic.com (John Quarterman)
Subject: Re: copyediting

>I found a copy editor for your book. We will be sending her
>your last chapter drafts.

That's great. I'll put together an instruction sheet for
copyediting our work online, so she understands all the
formatter codes.

Smoot
```

```
From: karen@bigpub.com (Karen Editor)
To: smoot@tic.com (Smoot Carl-Mitchell)
cc: jsq@tic.com (John Quarterman)
Subject: Re: copyediting

>That's great. I'll put together an instruction sheet for
>copyediting our work online, so she understands all the
>formatter codes.

Okay. I look forward to getting it.

Karen

----
```

The lines starting with angle brackets (>) in the examples are the quoted parts of previous messages. Together with the repeated subject lines, these quotations permit an exchange of mail messages to carry a thread of conversation that is easy for all participants to follow. This single feature of email is unlike every other communications medium. It lets you keep a record of the conversation without retyping anything. It lets you compose a response quickly without a lot of repetition, but with enough information in the response that the original sender can quickly pick up on the thread of conversation and make a timely reply. This kind of dialog is similar to a telephone conversation, but it is in type, and it is recorded. Yet automatic quoting avoids typing errors by eliminating most retyping.

Strange as it may seem if you are new to electronic mail, we hardly ever talk to Karen on the phone anymore but we use email almost exclusively. How was our productivity increased? First of all, we avoided the expense and wasted time of telephone tag. We probably each saved around 100 phone calls per year. That is quite a few hours saved and a lot of frustration alleviated. And most of those calls were wastes of time for all of us, since they were of the "call me when you get in" type. The time Karen saved permitted her not only to coordinate our book more easily and quickly, but also to work more on other books. The time we saved permitted us to consult more and make more money.

Second, we ended up with more meaningful exchanges of information using email, since any of us could send a message whenever we thought of something worth saying, and we could all carry on threads of conversation over minutes, days, or months. We each kept important mail messages, which formed a record of the decisions we had reached.

Case 2 — The Time Zone Shuffle

Email is also very useful for working with associates who, by birth or circumstance, live many *time zones* away, without worrying about the difference in local time. Ever try to keep up with someone by telephone or paper mail in a foreign country? It can be tough for several reasons:

• the time zone difference itself

• the spoken language barrier

• the cost of international telephone calls

• the slowness of paper post

All these difficulties can be solved by using email. Let's use a concrete example to see how.

We did a report for a client in Japan (let's call him Minoru) last year and did almost all of our correspondence by email. Email let us work on the report with feedback from Minoru in a manner that would have been nearly impossible using other types of communication. The time zone difference between Austin and Tokyo is 15 hours. That, is when it is 9 A.M. in Austin, it is midnight in Tokyo. When it is 6 P.M. in Austin it is 9 A.M. the next day in Tokyo. There is virtually no overlap in ordinary working hours between the two cities, so telephone communication is inconvenient and nearly impossible, not to mention expensive. Paper mail is useful for background material, but even overnight courier services usually take two days between continents, and are expensive.

This is a case where email shows some of its real strengths and flexibilities. We would send Minoru email at around noon our time

(3 A.M. in Tokyo). Minoru would get to the office and reply around 9 A.M. (6 P.M. Austin time). If we were still at the office, we could mull over a response. If we had already left, we could pick up the reply the next day. Using this system, we could get any questions turned around within 24 hours. This would have been impossible using the telephone or even a fax machine. Using the same feature for quoting text that we described in the case of "The Reluctant Editor," we could quickly clear up problem areas and get questions answered rapidly.

Email also helped with the language barrier. The Japanese learn written English at a very early age, but their conversational skills in the language are often limited because of lack of practice and the emphasis on written skills rather than verbal ones. While it is not difficult to talk in English face-to-face, the language barrier can become insurmountable when talking over a telephone, especially if the connection is even slightly noisy. Because people in Japan are often quite good at written English, using email to communicate with them gives them a chance to compose a reply in proper English (oftentimes better than native English speakers!). The time zone difference actually helps in this case, since it gives both sides an opportunity to carefully construct a reply, understanding the potential language barrier.

You may wonder how we managed graphics. Quite well, thank you. This report involved several graphs and charts. We just sent them in PostScript, a common page description language used by many laser printers and onscreen previewers. We also sent the numbers we used to draw the charts, in case the client wanted to redraw them. It turned out they used at least one of our charts exactly as we drew it. We'll talk more later in the book about how to put graphics and other things that are not text into mail.

Needless to say, we got the report done in a much shorter time-frame than if we had relied solely on other means of communication. For making hotel reservations in Tokyo, we will occasionally use fax or the telephone. And we do like to go there ourselves. But for real work from here to there, we use electronic mail.

Case 3 — A Week's Work in a Day

Another editor (let's call him Bob) says he now gets a week's worth of correspondence with authors done in one day, now that he and all his authors have electronic mail. No printing, no envelopes, no postage stamps, and turnaround in hours or days instead of weeks.

Bob sends out email to his authors at least once a day. Because he does not have to bother with having a secretary type the correspondence, he can handle correspondence even when he is traveling. On the road, he simply uses his laptop to access his email system. He picks up the replies at least once a day and does not have to bother waiting to get his paper mail back at his office.

He tells us repeatedly that the whole arrangement is an enormous time-saver and his productivity has soared as a result. He gets a lot more done in a given period of time than he used to. Email has been a big time-saver, enabling him to reduce the amount of time he spends typing *postal mail* correspondence and playing *telephone tag.* Correspondence turnaround is in hours at most, rather than days.

He also often negotiates a contract by sending the contract document to a prospective author in an electronic mail message. So far, the final contract still must be signed in paper form, but that, too, may change. Meanwhile, knowing how to use electronic mail is a selling point for him and his publishing company in acquiring authors who are used to electronic mail. Such authors often don't want to deal with a publisher who can't use email.

Case 4 — Keeping in Touch Without the Telephone

Ever have one of those days when the telephone rings all day long? We have. It's especially annoying when you are trying to get work done on a deadline and the telephone constantly interrupts you. You could always take it off the hook, but that could cut you off from important calls. If the telephone is your major means of outside communication, you will find it impossible to leave. So you end up fielding a lot of calls (wanted or not) and returning calls that come in when you step out of the office for a moment, all inevitably leading to telephone tag.

We have found staying in touch with clients via email is much more effective than using the telephone. With one of our clients, we used email to plan an entire consulting visit beforehand. They told us about their specific consulting needs. We then proposed a schedule in a reply message. The specifics were hammered out around everyone's schedule. We kept their key people involved by sending each a copy of every message. This was all done online without a single telephone call. Given that more than two people were involved in the process, this avoided the hassle and expense of telephone conference calls, faxes, and Federal Express bills. This whole process took only a few days of elapsed time, and much less than that of actual work time. In between the email messages, we worked on other tasks.

We even use email to communicate between the two of us, even though our offices are only a few feet apart. We travel a lot, we work at home a lot, and many simple messages are too brief to be worth walking next door to ask. It turns out this was the original reason electronic mail over computer networks was invented, back in 1972: so people could communicate quickly without all having to participate at the same time.

Case 5 — Responding to Faxes

One of us recently wrote an article for a major computer trade journal. Submitting it was easy, since the editor has electronic mail. Strategy and changes involved some telephone discussions, and that's OK; we're used to that. The telephone still has its advantages for interactive discussions and for getting to know people. We mix media like that all the time.

The editor faxed copy back for us to correct, rather than sending it online by email. We're used to that, too, since we often need to correct formatted copy just before it's printed. There are usually few changes necessary, and we just stick comments on those in a mail message and send it off online. For anything before final formatted copy, we prefer to avoid faxes entirely.

This particular article involved quotations from a couple dozen people scattered over the world. Naturally, the editor had shortened the quotes to fit as many in as she could. But this meant we needed to check many of the quotes with their original authors, to see if the shorter forms still reflected what the authors had been trying to say. So we typed the quotes in again, and sent them off in email messages....

This editor said she would have mailed the copy electronically, but "our device was busy." In other words, she was sharing a single connection to a commercial mail service with a group of people. Unlike the book editors we mentioned, this magazine editor did not have access to email directly from the computer on her desk. We'll talk more later in the book about what to look for in mail access.

Partial electronic mail access such as she had is still better than none at all. The usual method of submitting an article to that trade journal is to send a paper copy and a floppy disk by express mail. This involves figuring out which kind of floppy (PC, Mac, or other) to send, which kind of word processor format, etc. But we just mailed the article online. Once we finished composing it, we gave the mail send command and our part was done. We didn't have to print it, stick it on a floppy, fill out paper address labels, pay ten dollars worth of postage, and wait a day for it to arrive. It just went, and it got there within a couple of hours.

Case 6 — The Virtual Office

So all your relatives are having a reunion, and they insist you come, even though you can't be away from *the office* long. This happened to one of our friends. She's the president of a small company, and she has to be sure everything is going well at the office, in addition to writing her own material and corresponding with people elsewhere. There is only one telephone at the rustic house her family uses for reunions, so she couldn't stay on it all day. Even if she could use the telephone most of the day, she would run up a very large bill, and she still couldn't transfer documents. If she had to rely only on voice over the telephone, she couldn't even go to the reunion for more than a few days.

Fortunately, she had just gotten a mail software package that allowed her to compose mail on her PC and then call a network carrier only when she wanted to actually transfer mail out or in. She was used to using this software at her office, and she could call the network carrier from her family's reunion house, so why not just relocate her office there temporarily? She didn't need to be on the phone all the time; just long enough to transfer mail. And people sending her mail didn't need to call that telephone at all. Software at the network carrier just saved her mail for her to pick up when she called. No need to interrupt the reunion, and she could get some work done.

The reunion was held in a rather old house, so she had to snake a telephone line into her bedroom, it's true. But lots of people know how to do that these days. Your house may already have telephone outlets everywhere they're needed. Have telephone, can mail.

Case 7 — Friends and Family

We have often stayed in touch with family members using email. It is like writing letters, but quicker and easier.

Smoot has two nephews in college. He corresponds with both of them electronically. Since almost every university and college in the U.S. (and many in other countries) have general email connectivity, corresponding via email is quick and easy. All Smoot needed to do was find out his nephews' electronic addresses. Smoot made sure they both had his business card before they left for school, so they would have his email address.

Smoot remembers having a running email conversation with one of his nephews, Rusty. They exchanged 8 to 10 messages in about half an hour. Smoot found out about Rusty's test in literature the next day and also what Rusty's course load was. It was a Sunday night in winter and since Rusty was going to school in New Hampshire, Smoot heard all about the fire in the fireplace and the snow outside. He has had similar electronic conversations with his other college-age nephew. This method of communication is a real boon for parents who want to stay in touch with their kids.

Students are more likely to write an electronic message than a paper letter, and mail costs less than telephone calls. You can also communicate with more people more easily, including people you wouldn't hear from otherwise.

Smoot has also used email to communicate with his sister. She discovered the medium when she went back to graduate school. She had never used email before and discovered it is an easy way to stay in touch with her non-letter writing brother. They found out that typing a quick email note is much less painful and much quicker than writing a formal letter. There are no stamps to mess with or envelopes to find or post offices to drive to. Smoot and his sister used email to arrange their parents' fiftieth wedding anniversary.

Smoot has also used email to send messages back to his spouse, Charlotte, when he was in Japan for 3 weeks several years ago. Charlotte is not technically oriented, and she had not used email before. But she picked up easily how to correspond using email, even using a rather primitive user interface. Here is how they corresponded:

She would drop messages to him by dialing up our office system locally. She would check her mailbox on that system periodically for messages from him. Since he was visiting computer systems people in Japan, he'd arrange to get access to a computer with Internet connectivity and log in to our system back at our office in Austin. In that manner they kept in close touch for the time he was gone. This was a lot less expensive and more convenient than the telephone, particularly with the time zone difference.

Similarly, John corresponds with both his brothers and assorted friends on four continents. They discuss everything from consulting to the family genealogy project to the health of elderly relatives. In addition to text, they exchange genealogical charts, scanned photographs, and computer programs. Since John writes paper letters so seldom recipients tend to frame them, most of this communication wouldn't happen without electronic mail.

Case 8 — Love on the Net

A friend of ours from Central America was attending graduate school at the local university here in Austin. She started corresponding with someone from her own country. He was then at a northeastern U.S. university. They exchanged electronic mail for months, and became close friends. Eventually they visited, each other, both here and back home. To make a long story short, one summer they honeymooned in Austin.

This is not a unique story. Text in glowing letters on the screen may seem a strange way to get to know somebody, but it works. In some ways it works better than direct personal contact. If words are all you have, you can learn more about someone than if you were distracted by other means of communication. Of course, words on the screen often lead to personal contact.

The Stages of Mail Use

Let's imagine Joyce is learning to use electronic mail by corresponding with Becky. Her stages of learning might look like this.

1. Ugh, it's a computer.

```
From: joyce@saddlebags.org
To: becky@rusk.com

Is thissxhxx^H^H  you do it?
```

```
From: becky@rusk.com
To: joyce@saddlebags.org
Subject: good, you're sending mail!

>Is thissxhxx^H^H  you do it?

Good, you've sent a mail message!

I'll come over to your office and show you
how to erase characters.
```

2. This is hard!

```
From: joyce@saddlebags.org
To: becky@rusk.com
Subject: Re: good, you're sending mail!

Thanks, that's better.
But there's so much to learn!
```

```
From: becky@rusk.com
To: joyce@saddlebags.org
Subject: Re: good, you're sending mail!

>Thanks, that's better.

Yes, you're getting the hang of it.

>But there's so much to learn!

Well, not so much.  Here, let me give you some ideas....
To start with, you can quote part of my message
back at me so I can see what you're responding to.
```

3. Initial Enthusiasm

```
From: joyce@saddlebags.org
To: becky@rusk.com
Subject: Re: good, you're sending mail!

You're right!
```

```
From: becky@rusk.com
To: joyce@saddlebags.org
Subject: Re: good, you're sending mail!

>You're right!

Um, I'm right about what?
I think I got your last message yesterday, but I've
handled 150 messages since then, and I don't remember
exactly what we were talking about....
```

4. Why don't you just pick up the telephone?

```
From: joyce@saddlebags.org
To: becky@rusk.com
Subject: Re: good, you're sending mail!

Oh, this is too hard to keep track of!
Why don't you just call me on the telephone?
```

```
From: becky@rusk.com
To: joyce@saddlebags.org
Subject: Re: good, you're sending mail!

>Why don't you just call me on the telephone?

Well, because I can send you a mail message in a few
seconds, when I can't take ten or fifteen minutes
off the job to call you....

Besides, I tried, and you didn't answer.
```

5. Why no reply yet?

```
From: joyce@saddlebags.org
To: becky@rusk.com
Subject: Re: good, you're sending mail!

Oh, all right.  Let's try it some more.
Now what was that about quoting stuff?
```

```
From: joyce@saddlebags.org
To: becky@rusk.com
Subject: Re: good, you're sending mail!

It's been hours since I sent you mail.
Where are you?  Why haven't you replied yet?
```

6. Initial panic.

```
From: joyce@saddlebags.org
To: becky@rusk.com
Subject: Re: good, you're sending mail!

I'm getting really worried!
I'd better come over there right now!
```

```
From: becky@rusk.com
To: joyce@saddlebags.org
Subject: oh, calm down

Really, nothing's wrong.  I just had some other things to do,
and I've only just now gotten back to my mail.
```

7. Backwards quoting.

```
From: joyce@saddlebags.org
To: becky@rusk.com
Subject: Re: oh, calm down

Really, nothing's wrong.  I just had some other things to do,

    Oh.  I'm so sorry.  I misunderstood.  I'll try harder.

    But look, I've figured out how to quote your message!
```

```
From: becky@rusk.com
To: joyce@saddlebags.org
Subject: Re: oh, calm down

>   Oh.  I'm so sorry.  I misunderstood.  I'll try harder.

Don't worry about it.

>   But look, I've figured out how to quote your message!

It's good you've been thinking about it.
But everyone will be confused if you quote like that.
I'll come over and show you how to use the > character.
```

8. From mechanics to etiquette.

```
From: joyce@saddlebags.org
To: becky@rusk.com
Subject: Re: oh, calm down

>From: becky@rusk.com
>To: joyce@saddlebags.org
>Subject: Re: oh, calm down

>> Oh.  I'm so sorry.  I misunderstood.  I'll try harder.

>Don't worry about it.
```

```
>> But look, I've figured out how to quote your message!

>It's good you've been thinking about it.
>But everyone will be confused if you quote like that.
>I'll come over and show you how to use the > character.

Oh, so that's how you do it!  That's easy!



From: becky@rusk.com
To: joyce@saddlebags.org
Subject: Re: oh, calm down

>Oh, so that's how you do it!  That's easy!

Well, yes, you're getting the hang of it.
But you usually don't want to quote the whole message,
headers and all.  Just the part you're responding to.

By the way, you probably also want to put in
a new Subject: header when you change subjects.
```

9. This is fun!

```
From: joyce@saddlebags.org
To: becky@rusk.com
Subject: oh, I get it!

Why, this is really easy!  I see it now!  All it really is is typi


From: becky@rusk.com
To: joyce@saddlebags.org
Subject: Re: oh, I get it!

>Why, this is really easy!  I see it now!  All it real
>ly is is typing and the computer does all the work.
>I'm so glad you showed me this!  What a timesaver!

Thanks, and I'm glad you're learning!
Next we'll show you how to keep sentences
to less than 70 characters and how to divide
messages into paragraphs....
```

10. Why doesn't everybody use mail?

```
From: joyce@saddlebags.org
To: becky@rusk.com
Subject: busy busy

I can't reach Joe today; his phone is always busy.
Why doesn't everybody use mail?

It sure would be easier if everyone uses mail
instead of the phone!
```

```
From: becky@rusk.com
To: joyce@saddlebags.org
Subject: Re: busy busy

>I can't reach Joe today; his phone is always busy.
>Why doesn't everybody use mail?

Well, maybe we can get him an account.  I'll
look into setting one up for him.
```

11. I get too much mail!

```
From: joyce@saddlebags.org
To: becky@rusk.com
Subject: so much mail!

Since Joe got an account and I got on all those
mailing lists and started getting mail from people
on them, I get dozens of messages a day!
How do you manage?  It takes so much time!
```

```
From: becky@rusk.com
To: joyce@saddlebags.org
Subject: Re: so much mail!

>How do you manage?  It takes so much time!

Well, the first thing is to delete most of them. :-)
```

12. Ugh, the telephone is ringing!

```
From: joyce@saddlebags.org
To: becky@rusk.com
Subject: you rang?

The message you left on my answering machine doesn't say
what you wanted.  Why didn't you just send me mail?
```

Not everybody follows the same stages in learning to use mail, but most who use it routinely now will recognize parts of Joyce and Becky's ongoing conversation as things they used to do. You'll find your own style as you use mail. The main thing is to use it.

Summary

We hope we have given you a flavor of what email can do for you, whether you are using it for business or personal use. With the rapid growth of the global networks, it is possible to exchange mail online with people both around the world and around the corner.

Mail is not (usually) a replacement for other communications methods, but it has a number of strengths. It is a proven and flexible system that can improve communication between people. We hope we have demonstrated that it is a useful tool to add to your communications repertoire.

3

Common Questions

Many new users of electronic mail encounter the same situations and the same problems, and many of them ask the same questions. We have collected some of the questions in this chapter with answers for you.

We've organized these questions and answers in general categories, starting with basic ones like people and mail, hardware and software, and reading, sending, and forwarding, to political and technical ones like privacy and security, through information overload, and ending with finding a mail connection.

People and Mail

Who would I send mail to?

Anyone you now send paper mail or faxes to, or whom you telephone. Some of these people will not be able to use electronic mail, but some of them will. As you use mail, you will discover many new people to communicate with.

How do I find someone's mail address?

The simplest way is to ask the person, just like you would for a paper mail address or telephone number. Call them on the telephone or talk to them in the hall and ask them. Various networks in the Matrix have sprouted more sophisticated techniques of finding people's electronic mail addresses. See Chapter 13, *Finding People*.

Why can't I just use the telephone?

Well, you can, but what if the other person isn't in, or you're collaborating on an article and want to send a draft, or you don't want to spend fifteen minutes on the telephone when you could send a mail message in fifteen seconds online. What if you want to communicate with ten people at once? A telephone conference call might work, but what if you need to discuss something with 100 people who are scattered all over the world? In that case, an electronic mailing list will work a lot better. Sometimes the telephone is the right answer for a specific communication, and sometimes electronic mail is. For more on which is appropriate when, see Chapter 10, *Uses of Mailing Lists*.

Why use mail when I have a fax machine?

To send a fax you have to compose a message. You'll often be using a computer anyway, especially for complicated messages. You have to print a traditional fax message on paper before running it through the fax machine. With electronic mail, you can send the message online without printing it first and without waiting for the fax machine to scan it. You also avoid playing telephone tag with the remote fax machine.

At an even more basic level, suppose you want to respond to someone else's message. With a fax, you have to compose a completely new message by hand or scribble on a paper copy. With electronic mail, you can quote any part of the other person's message in yours without re-keying any of it and without using paper.

In addition, electronic mail is often less expensive than fax because less data is sent, more messages are sent together on a single connection, and fewer long distance calls are involved.

For more comparisons of electronic mail and other media, see Chapter 10, *Uses of Mailing Lists*.

Will I be able to learn this stuff?

Yes. Anyone can learn to send and receive electronic mail. Not only that, but the more you use it, the more you will find it is convenient for all sorts of things you didn't expect. You may find yourself going from "Why don't you just pick up the telephone and call!" to "Oh, no! Not the telephone!"

I don't type. Do I need to learn?

Well, yes, you need to type. You don't necessarily have to touch-type, but you do have to hunt and peck. Sophisticated mail interfaces can simplify input for choices such as reading or replying so that all you have to do is point and click, but you still have to type the actual text of a message.

Fortunately, many electronic mail messages are, by convention, quite short. If you just want to agree with what someone said, you don't have to type a lengthy salutation, a chatty opening, a full paragraph of response, and a formal closing such as in Figure 3.1. Instead, you can send a brief message like the one in Figure 3.2. Not only that, but your mail program will put all the headers in for you, and it will quote the other person's message for you. All you need to do is delete parts of the quoted message that you don't want to respond to, and type in the one line of response at the end, as in:

```
I agree, having been among those doing so.
```

```
To: person@dream.co.uk
Cc: you@your.org
Subject: Re: Xanadu

A. Person
Dept. of Dreams
Porlock, England

Dear old A.,

It's been a while since our previous conversation,
the one about the poem.

I must say I do agree with your remark in the
Mongol history list about Kublai Khan.
He was certainly misunderstood, and I should
know, since I have been among those mythologizing him.

Yours ethereally,
A. Writer.
```

Figure 3.1 A Wordy Message

You could avoid typing altogether by dictating a response and having a secretary type it in for you. But you can do it more quickly yourself, even if you hunt and peck when you type.

What about pen computers and voice interfaces?

Pen computer interfaces may eventually let you write electronic mail longhand, and voice interfaces may eventually let you dictate it. Prototypes of such interfaces are commercially available, but the most accurate way to enter a mail message is still to type it. Once you learn to type, it's also faster than talking or writing longhand.

```
To: person@dream.co.uk
Cc: you@your.org
Subject: Re: Xanadu

> He was certainly misunderstood, and I should
> partly because he has been so mythologized by poets.

I agree, having been among those doing so.
```

Figure 3.2 A Brief Message

I'm an executive. Why should I have to type?

Perhaps you don't have to now. But in a few years you may find that all your competitors and colleagues do, because they needed to learn to send electronic mail. And once they can do that, they can communicate faster, more effectively, and with more people than you can.

How do I learn to type?

Programs are available for PCs and other computers that will teach you to type. Many of these programs are in the public domain and available for free. There are also commercial products. Many schools can also assist you: ask your local community college, technical school, or high school. The key to learning to type is simply to do it; practice makes perfect.

Hardware and Software

Before you need to worry about typing, list subscriptions, and online etiquette, first you need hardware and software. Fortunately, you probably already have most of it.

Can I use the hardware I have?

You can probably use the same computer or terminal you already have. Almost any kind of computer hardware can be used to send and receive electronic mail.

LAN connections If your computer or terminal is not already connected to a network that can handle mail, you will need additional hardware. If your company, university, or other organization has a *Local Area Network (LAN)*, your simplest option is probably to connect to that LAN. You will need some kind of local area network interconnection hardware; ask your organization's network administrator for the proper kind. If you don't know if the LAN has an external mail connection to the Matrix, ask your network administrator about that, too.

Modems If your organization doesn't have a LAN, if it's not connected to the Matrix, or if you want a personal mail connection to your own machine, your simplest option is dialup mail access. For this, you need a modem. A *modem* is a hardware device that translates digital signals from your computer into sounds that travel over an ordinary telephone line. Slow modems cost almost nothing these days. Even fast modems are not very expensive compared to a computer, so if you already have a computer adding a modem is a small incremental cost.

Why can't I send email with my fax machine? Because it doesn't have a keyboard. A fax machine has a sophisticated modem and, usually, a *CPU (Central Processing Unit)* as fast as the average personal computer. But a fax machine has been packaged so that all it does is send and receive faxes. Asking it to send electronic mail is like asking a microwave oven to compute a spreadsheet.

Can I send faxes with the modem I use for email? You can if you buy a fax modem, and most fast modems these days are also fax modems. You will probably need a bit of extra software, but most fax modems come with such software.

What if I don't have a computer? You may be able to use someone else's computer. Ask a friend, a university, or a public access network organization. However, if you plan to use mail much, you will need your own access point, and that usually means your own computer. You can make do with a cheap terminal and a modem. The main point is you need something that you can use when you need it.

What kind of software do I need?

If you use a LAN, workstation, or timesharing system in your company or university, or if you use a dialup login host account or a commercial conferencing system such as CompuServe, you can send and receive mail without any local software at your end, since the administrators of the system you use will have already installed appropriate software. Even in those cases, if you have a computer instead of a terminal, you may want some local software.

You need software to read and compose mail; this is called a *mail program* or a *UA (User Agent)*. Your UA will need software to transfer mail to another computer; this is called a *MTA (Message Transfer Agent)*. Often both functions are provided in a single software package. Many such mail software packages are available, some for free and some as commercial products.

You may also need software to handle underlying network protocols, such as the *Internet Protocol (IP)* or *UNIX to UNIX CoPy (UUCP)*. For more about these protocols and the networks they support, see Chapter 4, *The Networks*. Many software packages are available for such networking software, as well, some free, some commercial.

For which software you will need, see Appendix A, *Places to Connect*. For some types of mail connectivity you won't need any more software on your computer, because the connectivity provider has everything on its computer. For other types, you can get all the software you need from the provider. In other cases, you may want to collect your own software, for which see Appendix B, *Software*.

What should I look for in mail software?   First look for a mail software system that

- runs on your computer (PC-compatible, Macintosh, workstation, or other) and operating system (DOS, MacOS, UNIX, or other)

- connects to the kind of network you have available (UUCP, FidoNet, NetWare, VINES, the Internet, or other)

- has the kind of user interface you like (mouse and menu or command line).

For any combination of three items from each of these three categories you will probably find more than one mail system that offers all the features you need. Picking one mail system from among the choices available is the same kind of decision as picking any piece of software. For example, you must decide whether you want the cheapest one available or one with commercial support. If other people in your organization already have a particular mail system, you may find support easier if you pick the same one.

No matter what mail system you pick, it should be able to:

- prompt for a `Subject:` header

- handle long messages

- reply to all addressees of a previous message

- quote text included from previous messages

- let you intersperse your own text among quoted text

- let you incorporate a file into the message

- forward a previous message

- file messages in folders

For more detail on these and related points, see Chapter 5, *The Basics*.

Reading, Composing, and Forwarding

Once you have the hardware and software you need, how do you actually exchange mail messages with other people?

How do I read and compose mail?

The details depend on the mail program, but any good mail interface will implement common functions like reading a mail message, replying to one, or composing a new mail message. See Chapter 5, *The Basics* for details and examples based on a common mail program.

What if I get a "Command not found" message?

If you get the message

```
Command not found.
```

it usually means you mistyped the name of the mail program.

How do I delete old messages?

There are two ways of getting rid of old messages. One way is to actually delete them. The other is to file them in a folder by topic or by sender, so that you can find them later if you need to refer to them. We discuss these processes more in Chapter 5, *The Basics*.

How do I send a file?

If it's a text file, you can probably just incorporate it in a mail message and mail it. Any good mail user agent should permit you to do this. For text files, see Chapter 5, *The Basics*. For non-text files, see Chapter 12, *Finding Things*.

How do I send a binary program as a file?

Since most mail systems were designed to handle only simple text, you will probably have to encode the file before you send it. We'll talk about sending files, including compression and encoding, in Chapter 12, *Finding Things*.

How do I forward my mail?

Any good mail system can forward your mail automatically anywhere you like. On many UNIX systems, you do this by creating a file called **.forward** in your home directory (where you are when you first log in). In this file, you put one line containing the forwarding address. Some systems may have a menu item for forwarding your mail. Others may require you to ask a system administrator to do it. The details vary so much that the only general answer is to ask your system administrator.

How do I forward a message I received from someone else?

Any good mail program has a command for forwarding a message, permitting you to specify one or messages to forward and one or more people to forward it to. If your mail program does not have such a command, find another mail program. If your mail provider does not have a mail program that does have such a command, find another mail provider. For more on forwarding, see Chapter 5, *The Basics*.

Can I read mail on my Mac or DOS machine?

Sure. You can do this in any of several ways, depending on what kind of local network connection you have. One of the most popular is to use the *Post Office Protocol (POP)* to pick up mail from a system that serves as a mail hub. (Such a system usually runs a multiprocess operating system such as UNIX or VMS.) You can use a DOS or Macintosh user interface to read your mail. You don't have to leave your computer on all the time to accept mail; the mail hub system collects your mail and you pick it up whenever you're ready for it. When you want to send a message, you compose it on your local system and then use POP to deliver it through the remote system.

How do I get my signature appended to my messages?

On UNIX systems, you usually create a file called **.signature** and put your signature in it. Other mail systems have different methods of doing this.

Privacy and Security

Most mail systems have no security and therefore no privacy. You can get privacy by using encryption for security.

Is my mail private?

The first thing you need to know about mail is that personal is not the same thing as private. Most mail systems are not private because they have no security. You can make mail on your local computer somewhat private by carefully protecting access to that computer and to certain files on it. But to get the full value of mail, you need to be able to send messages to people on any of millions of computers on tens of thousands of networks in tens of thousands of organizations throughout the world. You don't know what systems your mail may pass through, and you don't know what systems other people's mail may pass through before you read it. Making any single network or computer secure won't help in general, because you don't usually know how mail will be routed.

How do I make my mail secure?

The only way to ensure privacy of mail is to encrypt mail when it is sent and decrypt it when it is read. Programs exist to do this, such as *Pretty Good Privacy (PGP)*. There are specific mail system enhancements for this purpose, such as *Privacy Enhanced Mail (PEM)*.

Does the system administrator read my mail?

Most good system administrators are ethical and do not read personal mail. However, some do, and you cannot stop all of them. In practice, this is usually not a problem, but be aware that it can happen.

Is there censorship on the mail system?

It can happen. Usually it is not a problem. However, your only real protection is encryption.

I get unwanted mail from a student I met. How do I stop this?

Tell the person sending the mail to stop, politely, but firmly. If that doesn't work, complain to the person's system administrator. You can also have a program automatically delete all mail from a certain person without you having to read it first.

Information Overload

With millions of computers and more millions of people using them to send mail from more than a hundred countries throughout the world, there is some danger of getting too much mail.

Will I get swamped with junk mail?

One of the few taboos that pervades almost all parts of the Matrix is that people do not send unsolicited advertisements to personal mail addresses. It still can happen, but in that case feel free to complain to the original sender. We'll discuss issues like this in more detail in Chapter 11, *Mailing List Etiquette*.

How can I easily send mail to a group of users?

There are several ways of doing this, and we discuss them in Chapter 5, *The Basics* and Chapter 10, *Uses of Mailing Lists*. Usually, you join a mailing list.

How do I join a mailing list?

By sending a request for subscription to a mail address related to the mailing list (but not the same address). Subscriptions to many lists are automated, so that you can subscribe to a list immediately by sending such a message. Other lists have manual subscriptions handled by a person on the other end, but the principle is the same. We discuss mailing list subscriptions in detail in Chapter 9.

How do I get off a mailing list?

The same way as you got on, except by sending a request for unsubscription instead of a request for subscription. We'll go into this in detail in Chapter 9.

How can I handle all this mail from mailing lists?

Partly, by subscribing only to lists you're really interested in or that you have to read for your work. Partly, by choosing a mail system and software that make it easy for you to delete unwanted messages. Partly, by more sophisticated methods such as those we describe in Chapter 9.

Folders   Some mail programs, such as Pine, can sort incoming messages into folders for you according to combinations of subject and sender that you specify. You can then read the messages in batches by subject or sender, rather than wading through unrelated messages by time of arrival. Some people find this approach useful. Others keep all incoming messages in one **inbox**, and simply plow through them in chronological order, or even in reverse chronological order, most recent first. For more on filing mail messages in folders, see Chapter 5, *The Basics*.

Pre-deleting   Some people take two passes through all incoming mail once a day. In the first pass, they look for and delete anything they don't want, such as certain subjects, mail from certain people, long messages, or flames. Some people go so far as to not read anything from anyone they do not know. In the second pass, they respond to everything left from the first pass, also filing anything that needs filing. This is somewhat like handling paper mail by picking it up once a day, throwing out all unwanted junk mail, and then dealing with the rest.

Reading mail in real time   Some people keep a window open in which their mail program notes each incoming message as it comes in. This way they can deal with each message in real time as it comes in. It's still possible to delete unwanted messages, but more time is involved because each message requires switching attention from some other task and back again. On the other hand, with this technique you can more readily keep a conversation going by mail, and people you communicate with this way are sometimes impressed by how responsive you are. This kind of event-driven approach works best if you are connected to an interactive network such as the Internet. If you are connected through a store-and-forward batch network such as UUCP, FidoNet, or WWIVnet, you will only get new mail each time your system polls another system.

USENET newsgroups   Finally, many large lists are gatewayed to *USENET newsgroups,* which are discussion topics for *news* articles (see Chapter 4, *The Networks*). Consider reading some of these lists as news rather than as mail. News doesn't pile up in your mailbox when you're away, and news reading programs have become very sophisticated about handling threads of conversation and deleting ones you don't want.

Time and taste   Whatever approach you choose for handling large volumes of mail, you eventually need to limit the amount of time you allow for it. Some people stick to a fixed interval, such as one hour a day. Others limit the time they spend on a single message.

You will have to decide which kind of approach works for you; it's a matter of taste. We discuss some more possibilities in Chapter 11, *Mailing List Etiquette*.

What is this daemon and why is it sending me mail?

When there is some kind of delivery problem with a mail message you sent, most mail systems send you a *bounce message* with indications of what the problem was. Since a bounce message comes from a program, not a human, it doesn't have an ordinary personal `From:` address. A common address is **MAILER-DAEMON**. A *daemon* is a program that handles some system function automatically. Daemons are common to most *multi-process systems,* including UNIX, VMS, etc. A *process* is simply a program that is running. Even *single-process systems* such as DOS can have a daemon, usually implemented in for that operating system as a *TSR (Terminate and Stay Resident)* process. The word daemon is Greek, and traditionally referred to a spirit, not necessarily a good or evil one. Mailer daemons are your friends; they tell you what happened to your message. For more detail on bounce messages, see Chapter 8, *Error and Non-Error Messages*.

Finding a Mail Connection

How do I find services in my area?

See Appendix A, *Places to Connect*. For what kind of connection you may want to find, see Chapter 4, *The Networks*. For a list of features you should ask any potential provider about, see Chapter 5, *The Basics*.

Summary

Once you decide to use mail, you will have to resolve some hardware and software questions, and find a place to connect. Fortunately, none of these steps are difficult. Then you will encounter many practical questions as you use mail, ranging from the first simple ones about reading and composing mail to more sociological ones about privacy, security, and information overload. Using mail is a never-ending learning process, but you can learn enough to communicate in a short time.

4

The Networks

To send mail to someone, you may need to know how to use various characters such as: at (@), period (.), percent (%), exclamation point (!), colon (:), underscore (_), or comma (,) in that person's address. This is because different kinds of systems that support mail have different kinds of mail addresses. Fortunately, many systems are now settling on Internet *domain syntax*, as in test@tic.com, with an @ in the middle, a local_part on the left indicating a user or alias, and a domain_part on the right indicating a computer or organization. However, you will encounter other address syntaxes.

To send and receive electronic mail, you need to use a computer that is connected to a computer network; such a computer is called a *host*. Some hosts charge for each message a user sends and receives, so it is polite not to send users of such systems too much mail. One host may provide a *menu interface* so that it users can select items that appear on the screen. Another host may provide a *command line interface* so that its users can type instructions. Some permit the user to choose among several mail programs, and some do not.

Different networks use different *protocols* (agreements for how to exchange information), much as some human communities shake hands in greeting and others bow. A new *implementation* of a network protocol, that is software that communicates with similar software across the network according to the rules agreed on in the protocol, may permit a network to expand to a new class of hardware, to a new operating system, or to a new variety of users. Each network protocol, and sometimes each implementation, has its characteristics of speed, flexibility, and most importantly the kinds of services it provides network users. For these and other reasons, you need to know something about the different networks that carry electronic mail.

Electronic mail crosses commercial conferencing systems and commercial mail systems, as well as distributed anarchic networks such as UUCP, FidoNet, and WWIVnet, enterprise networks entirely within companies, and the biggest network of all, the Internet. We define all these terms in this chapter. All these systems that exchange electronic mail are together called *the Matrix*. Many isolated systems that do not exchange mail with the outside world still exist, such as LANs, mainframes, and BBSes. We define these terms in this chapter, too. Many of those systems are joining the Matrix, which already has a pool of more than 30 million people who can communicate with each other by electronic mail.

Some networks restrict the line length or character sets that can be used in mail messages. You may receive a mail message containing features your mail system does not understand. Some systems do not understand features considered standard elsewhere, so you need to know which systems those are and make allowances for them. For practical and historical reasons, different networks have different conventions and cultures. Users of some networks prefer verbose messages with lengthy signatures, while others like pithy messages.

The fabric of the Matrix is not seamless, so you must know some of the peculiarities of the various networks to get mail there and back again. This chapter gives you a quick description of major types of systems you will encounter in your mail. We can't describe all of the differences among the networks in one chapter, but we can tell you the names and some major characteristics of the largest systems in the Matrix, so you will recognize them when you encounter them.

In addition, if you do not already have a mail connection to the Matrix, you will want to know some of the capabilities of the different kinds of systems in the Matrix so you can choose how to connect. We will list some places to connect in Appendix A, *Places to Connect*, but the information in this chapter will help you choose which type of system you prefer.

Commercial Conferencing Systems

The first exposure you may get to electronic mail is when you buy a modem or dialup software, and with it get a trial account on a *commercial conferencing system* such as Prodigy, CompuServe, America Online, GEnie, Delphi, TYMNet, or BIX. The systems just mentioned are based in the United States. Others exist elsewhere. For example, in Japan there are NIFTY-Serve, PC-VAN, ASCII-net, People, and Asahi-net. Each of these systems is made to seem like a single computer to its users, although many of them are actually tightly coupled networks of computers. Each of them provides a menu interface to its users, (as opposed to a command line interface), usually as the standard interface.

Most of these systems have more than one *Point of Presence (PoP)*, so that users may dial a local PoP and thus minimize telephone fees. However, most of them charge connect time by the hour. Many of them also charge per mail message sent or received, and sometimes by the size of each message, as well. What you get for these charges is reliable service.

These systems also offer local conferencing, in which users discuss topics of interest in forums dedicated to those interests. Most of these systems also have sophisticated databases and news services for information such as stock market quotations, airline schedules, weather, and many other topics. Often there is a surcharge for each such service, but many people find the value received worth the price.

Unfortunately, many of these systems do not provide sophisticated mail programs. Charging for mail discourages copying a mail message to several people or sending a message to a mailing list. Many such systems fail to understand facilities supported in most modern mailers, such as redirection of replies to an address specified in the message. Some such systems do not even permit labeling messages by subject. A few force the user to read all of a mail message, no matter how long it is.

Some major commercial conferencing systems do not even understand the concept of sending a carbon copy of a message to an additional recipient. One argument in favor of this situation is that group discussions are provided in the local conferencing facilities. This is true, but nonetheless those facilities are local to that system. Regardless of how good the system, everyone in the world is not going to subscribe to the same commercial conferencing system. Every major conferencing system has been forced to provide at least mail access to the outside world. Most of them are having difficulty adapting to that situation, since mail systems on the distributed networks tend to be more sophisticated, and messages from systems that do not charge to systems that do charge produce billing problems.

Commercial Mail Systems

Other commercial systems provide only electronic mail service. These include AT&T Mail, SprintMail, EasyLink, and MCI Mail. A *commercial mail system* may also provide conferencing or database services, and there is no easy way to draw a distinct line between commercial conferencing systems and commercial mail systems.

Distributed Global Networks

At least five networks connect more than 2,000 computers each: UUCP, FidoNet, WWIVnet, BITNET, and the Internet. These networks together reach almost 150 countries around the world. Some of them have somewhat selective users, whose participation is based on certain computer operating systems, such as DOS or UNIX, or based on certain networking protocols. The biggest network, and the most general, is the Internet.

Let's start with the least expensive networks, UUCP, FidoNet, and WWIVnet. They are primarily based on dialup connections, and do not support interactive services such as remote login. However, all three do support mail and some form of conferencing. Because USENET is often confused with UUCP (or with the Internet), we discuss it after UUCP.

UUCP

The *UUCP* network is named after the *UUCP (UNIX to UNIX CoPy)* protocol that it uses. UUCP implementations were distributed with every copy of the UNIX system for many years, and the corresponding network spread widely. Modern binary UNIX distributions often unbundle (leave out) UUCP, but free implementations are available. So, the main expense of UUCP, like FidoNet and WWIVnet, is the telephone bill. To connect to UUCP, you normally find a neighbor, friend, or colleague who will let you set up a UUCP link to their system. Because UUCP connections are still quite popular, finding one has become difficult in congested areas. For this reason, commercial UUCP providers have sprung up, and one of them may be your best solution for a UUCP connection.

If you're running UNIX and want an inexpensive mail connection, UUCP may be the answer for you. You don't have to run UNIX to use UUCP. There are several UUCP implementations for computers that run DOS and MacOS. The biggest network in Argentina still uses UUCP on DOS.

Finally, be aware that a connection to the Internet may actually be less expensive than a UUCP connection, and with the Internet you can use not just mail, but also many other services that UUCP, FidoNet, WWIVnet, and BITNET do not support.

USENET

USENET is a service, not a network. The service it provides is USENET *news,* which broadcasts information to millions of people worldwide. Unlike traditional broadcasting services such as radio or television, or mass paper media such as newspapers and magazines, any USENET reader can also *post* a message for everyone else to read. A USENET news message is called an *article,* and looks much like an electronic mail message, although it has a few more header lines. When you post a news article, you must specify a *newsgroup* to post it to. Newsgroups are organized according to general discussion topics. Computers participating in USENET may choose any or all of approximately 8,000 newsgroups to subscribe to. Any user of a computer that subscribes to a given newsgroup may also subscribe to that newsgroup. When you post a news article, you may also specify a *distribution,* which helps determine where your article will go. In any case, your article goes to each computer that accepts the newsgroup and distribution you specified, unlike electronic mail, which goes to each person you address in a mail message. A newsgroup can often reach a larger number of people than a mailing list because news distribution requires fewer copies of a message to be sent. For the same reason, newsgroups are generally less private than mailing lists, and often noisier. However, most of the etiquette of newsgroups is the same as the etiquette of mailing lists that we discuss in Chapter 11, *Mailing List Etiquette.*

There is no specific underlying protocol, software, or hardware required to carry news articles, so USENET isn't actually a network. It is a distributed conferencing service carried on top of various networks, including UUCP, BITNET, FidoNet, and the Internet. USENET started on UUCP, but most USENET news is now carried over the Internet. However, you may hear people talk about it as though it were a network, and you use it much like you would use a network.

You'll also hear people talk of *USENET mail addresses.* There's actually no such thing, since USENET is not a network, and doesn't even carry mail. However, every network that carries USENET news also carries mail, and people often reply to the *poster* of a news article by mail, rather than by posting a *followup* news article. USENET users are addressed according to the mail addressing style of whatever underlying network carries their mail and their news. Fortunately, you can use domain syntax to reach most USENET hosts. You usually don't have to worry about having to find a USENET user's mail address. You usually only need a user's address when you are replying to a USENET article posted by the user. In that case, the article itself includes the user's address in a `From:` header.

Many USENET newsgroups are gatewayed with mailing lists. A news article posted on such a newsgroup is automatically forwarded to the corresponding mailing list. A mail message posted to that list is automatically forwarded to the newsgroup. So the *gateway* that carries messages between lists and newsgroups permits you to participate in many discussions involving newsgroups without ever directly using USENET.

FidoNet

To many people, the word *network* implies a *BBS (Bulletin Board System).* A BBS is a single computer that users dial up with modems. BBSes almost always offer electronic mail for their own users, plus some kind of group conferencing system. Those BBS services are usually provided as items in a menu system. Many BBSes are connected together in a network called *FidoNet* that exchanges electronic mail and conference messages, called *echomail.* Echomail is organized in *echoes,* which permit a FidoNet user to post a message that is broadcast to all other FidoNet users who participate in that echo. Echomail is similar in principal to USENET news, and many USENET newsgroups are gatewayed with FidoNet echoes. The online culture is different, however, with echoes tending even more towards verbosity than newsgroups.

FidoNet is inexpensive, since it will run on a small machine with an inexpensive operating system (DOS), and the FidoNet protocol implementations are free, leaving telephone costs as the main expense. FidoNet is also very loosely organized; there is no centralized controlling organization, no set dues, no strict membership requirements. FidoNet was actually originally modeled somewhat after UUCP, and the informality of the network appears to be one of the features that was copied.

One disadvantage of FidoNet is its peculiar addressing syntax. Inside FidoNet, a FidoNet node (called a *fido* would have an address like 1:42/208, and a user is addressed by full name, for example: Jane Doe. From another network, you would typically address that user as Jane_Doe@f208.n42.z1.fidonet.org in domain syntax. Unlike native FidoNet addressing, this domain form at least looks like most other addresses you will use, although the fidonet.org domain does not actually work like most domains.

WWIVnet

Another BBS network is *WWIVnet*. The idea behind WWIVnet is similar to that of FidoNet, and WWIVnet was to some extent modelled on FidoNet. WWIVnet has mail. It also has *subs,* which are similar to FidoNet echos or USENET newsgroups. A WWIVnet user can post a message that is broadcast to all other users who read that sub. Some WWIVnet subs are gatewayed with FidoNet echoes.

However, the protocols of the two networks are different, and many users claim the organizational structure of WWIVnet is even looser than that of FidoNet. For example, WWIVnet does not have the hierarchical geographically organized address space that FidoNet does. If you are using a DOS system and want to connect to a BBS network, you could choose between WWIVnet and FidoNet by trying some of each network's software and seeing which user interfaces you like. More traditionally, you may choose by whom you know and what they are using. Don't forget UUCP is also an option for DOS.

BITNET, EARN, and relatives

BITNET (Because It's Time Network) uses a protocol called *NJE (Network Job Entry)* that essentially sends punch card images across serial links. That is, it imitates the information on the paper Holerith cards that were used with card readers and card punches. For this reason, each line of text in a BITNET mail message must have fewer than 80 characters. Lines longer than that in messages from other networks are usually truncated before being sent on to a BITNET user. Almost all BITNET hosts are now reachable using domain syntax and domain names.

BITNET is the name by which the network that uses the *NJE (Network Job Entry)* protocol is known in the United States and a few other countries. The NJE network in Europe is called *EARN (European Academic and Research Network)* and there are many others, such as *GULFNET* in the Persian Gulf region. Each of these NJE networks has its own administration, often supported by dues collected from member organizations. To join BITNET you have to be a member of one of the member organizations, or your organizations has to join one of the NJE network organizations. These NJE networks are all interconnected in a single worldwide NJE network, often also called BITNET. If you just want to send mail to a BITNET user, you don't have to worry about the administrative structures of the various NJE networking organizations.

BITNET was very popular in its time, especially in universities. Now, it is the only one of the networks mentioned in this chapter that is not growing. In fact, it is shrinking, because it is being absorbed by the Internet. Even many of the remaining hosts on BITNET are also connected to the Internet now.

Nonetheless, mail users will encounter a major BITNET facility, *LISTSERV,* a sophisticated mailing list handler. Since mail crosses network boundaries, many (perhaps most) LISTSERV users are not BITNET users. We'll discuss LISTSERV more in Chapter 9, *Mailing List Basics.*

The Internet

The biggest, fastest growing, and most capable network is the Internet. Mail on the Internet is generally faster than on any other large distributed network. Mail usually arrives within minutes or seconds, rather than hours or days, so you can carry on conversations by mail. In addition, the Internet supports many other facilities, such as remote login, file transfer, and browsing with menus, images, and sound.

The key to the Internet's success is that it is a distributed network of networks rather than a single network. It consists of tens of thousands of cooperating networks. Its networks, hosts, and servers are provided by thousands of organizations, ranging from the United Nations to individuals, in more than 60 countries, from Greenland to Antarctica, from Fiji to Bangkok, from Iceland to India. The glue that binds all these networks together is the *Internet Protocol (IP)*. IP supports a common address space and a suite of related protocols, such as *SMTP (Simple Mail Transfer Protocol), FTP (File Transfer Protocol),* and *TELNET* (remote login). Millions of computers connected to the Internet support more millions of Internet users. These computers run every known operating system, including MS-DOS, MS-Windows, MacOS, UNIX, OS/2, Windows-NT, VMS, CMS, MVS, and many others. Users and organizations connected to the Internet can be academic, commercial, governmental and nongovermental organizations, private homes, or still other types.

Methods of connecting to the Internet are legion. Many commercial conferencing systems, such as Delphi, America Online, and CompuServe, now provide their users Internet access. Other systems sell login accounts to their users for the express purpose of using the Internet, and each is called a *login host.* Some providers sell dialup IP connections for your computer, and others provide you with dedicated direct IP connectivity. There is even more variety within these broad categories of connectivity. For example, many login hosts are commercial. There is also an adamantly noncommercial kind of login host called a *freenet.* Some provide a command line interface unless the user requests otherwise. Others provide a menu interface to the user unless the user requests otherwise. We describe these and other types of connectivity in Appendix A, *Places to Connect*, along with contact information for connectivity providers.

Enterprise IP Networks

Many companies and other organizations have internal networks that are dedicated to support of company operations; we call such a network an *enterprise network*. Many enterprise networks use the same IP technology as the Internet; we call such a network an *enterprise IP network*. All major computer vendors, such as Intel, Apple, IBM, HP, and Digital have one of these, as do numerous other companies, ranging in size from GM and Exxon to TIC.

Because enterprise networks typically carry sensitive proprietary corporate information, the companies that own them usually do not want anyone but employees using them. Even an enterprise network that uses IP and thus could be connected as an integral part of the Internet may be deliberately separated by a *firewall* to prevent most Internet users from using most its services. Such a firewall will usually prevent you from using TELNET, FTP, or other interactive services through it into an enterprise IP network. Many universities use firewalls to limit outside use of some or all of their networked resources. Users inside firewalled networked can often connect from the firewalled network to the rest of the Internet, however. Users of firewalled networks can thus be users of Internet services.

Most enterprise networks, IP or not, firewalled or not, corporate or not, do exchange mail with the rest of the Matrix. So enterprise networks represent another large pool of people you can use electronic mail to communicate with. Many companies have set up electronic mailing lists for discussion of their products, for bug reports, or for direct product support. Sometimes you can even order products online. If you are a reporter or an academic, you will be able to reach many information sources or research colleagues through mail into enterprise networks.

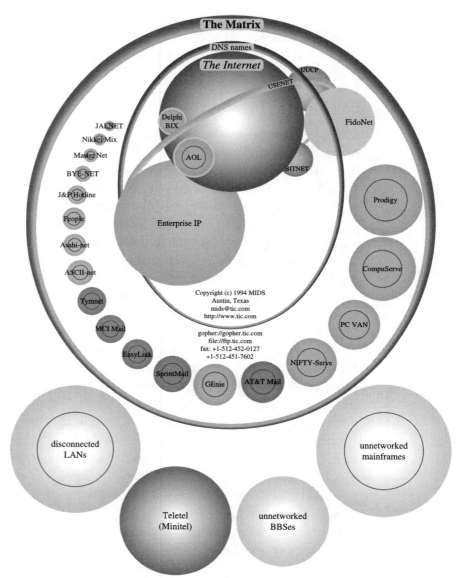

Figure 4.1 Inside and Outside the Matrix (Graphic: Matrix Information and Directory Services, Inc., mids@tic.com. Reprinted with permission.)

The Matrix

This book is primarily about *the Matrix,* which consists of all the networks and computers worldwide that exchange electronic mail. Some networks in the Matrix also provide other services, but mail is the most widespread service and usually the first to be exchanged when one network connects to another. Mail is the least common denominator of computer networks. It is the most popular service partly because it is one of the simplest to implement. However, it is also one of the most useful network services, and that usefulness accounts for most of its popularity.

Communication among users of the Matrix results in shared experiences, and often in perceptions of place and even of community. The social space that the Matrix supports is often called *cyberspace.* The two terms, the Matrix and cyberspace, are often used interchangeably, but we use the Matrix to refer to the hardware, software, and protocols, while cyberspace refers to what people experience while using the Matrix. Both terms were originally coined by William Gibson in a science fiction novel *Neuromancer* , (Ace, 1984). The use of the Matrix with a capital M to refer to the contemporary collection of communicating computer networks dates to the book *The Matrix: Computer Networks and Conferencing Systems Worldwide* by John S. Quarterman (Digital Press, 1990).

Figure 4.1 shows most of the largest networks and conferencing systems as spheres within the large ellipse of the Matrix. Systems that do not exchange mail with systems inside the Matrix, are shown outside the Matrix ellipse. The volume of the sphere for each system inside or outside the Matrix is proportional to an estimate of the number of users for that system. The Internet is the largest of all the systems.

The Matrix and the Internet

The Internet is not only the largest, but also one of the fastest growing of all the networks in the Matrix. It has doubled in size every year since 1988, as shown in Figure 4.2.

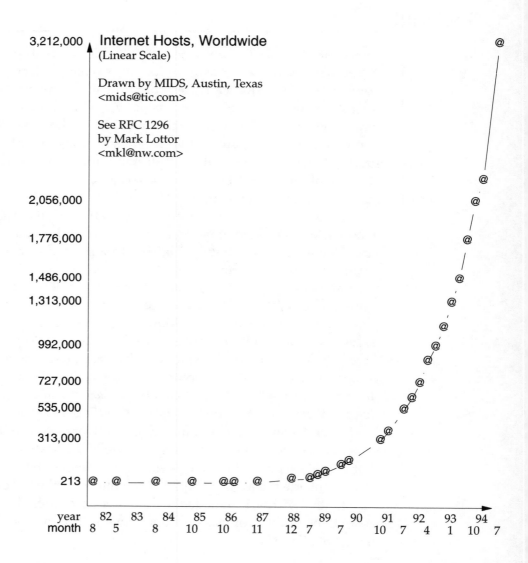

Figure 4.2 Internet Growth (Data: Mark Lottor. Graphic: Matrix Information and Directory Services, Inc., mids@tic.com. Reprinted with permission.)

You will hear the term, the Internet, used to refer to every computer or network that can exchange mail. People who use the term in this way usually do so because they don't want to leave out anyone who participates in the *Internet community*. But you can participate in that community by sending mail from anywhere, or for that matter by using the telephone or fax, or by going to meetings. If the name thus applies to every possible form of communication, the Internet is a meaningless entity.

So we choose a more strict but much more meaningful definition: *the Internet* is the largest group of computers and networks that use IP to provide direct interactive communication.

In other words, if you can use FTP to retrieve a file from rs.internic.net or some other node on the Internet, such as ftp.tic.com, you are on the Internet; otherwise you're not. If you can use FTP, you can also use TELNET and various other Internet protocols and services that are not supported by UUCP, FidoNet, or BITNET.

Don't let claims of *Internet access* made by many commercial conferencing systems, BBSes, and software vendors fool you. Many of them really only have mail and perhaps news connections to the outside world, often provided by UUCP or FidoNet. Look for FTP capability, at least, before believing that any service or product really provides Internet access.

Nonetheless, the service most used on the Internet is mail. Even if you are not on the Internet, you can use mail to access many other Internet services, as we will discuss in Chapter 13, *Finding People* and Chapter 12, *Finding Things*.

The Matrix and Academia

Many people think that most networks that support electronic mail are limited to research and educational use. Years ago this may have been true, but no longer. BITNET is still largely an academic network, but UUCP was partly commercial from its early days, and FidoNet was never primarily academic. The Internet originated with government-supported research and in academia, but it has long since outgrown the control of any government, or of any single organization, for that matter.

Outside the Matrix

Many systems outside the Matrix have mail, but do not exchange it with any system within the Matrix. We describe these systems only briefly because they are probably of only minor interest to you, since they do not exchange mail.

Unnetworked Bulletin Board Systems

BBSes almost always offer some form of electronic mail. A user can dial up a BBS and send mail to another user on the same BBS. But typically, neither user can send mail to a user of a different BBS, conferencing system, or distributed network. Tens of thousands of BBSes, with several million users, have only local mail and do not interconnect with any other system. Such BBSes are popular, but they are not really relevant to this book.

Unnetworked Mainframes

A typical large company or university will often still have a *mainframe* dedicated to payroll, accounting, manufacturing, or other specialized functions. Some of these mainframes include mail systems. Since each such system can have hundreds, thousands, or even tens of thousands of users, the total number of people using them is large. Many of these systems do not exchange mail with other systems. However, if you use such a system, you still may be interested in learning about how to use mail on the Matrix, because you may have an account on another system that can exchange mail with other systems.

Disconnected LANs

Companies often have LANs that include clusters of similar machines. AppleTalk LANs with Macintoshes. Novell NetWare or BANYAN VINES LANs with PCs. IP LANs with UNIX or other systems. Sometimes companies even tie together all their LANs (often using an IP network as the backbone), but still do not interconnect them to the outside world. There is a lot of potential in these isolated LANs for future interconnections.

Teletel (Minitel)

Finally, the largest isolated network we know of is the *Teletel* network in France, which is commonly known as *Minitel*. It is used by some seven million people. We have heard it is possible to send mail out of Teletel, but we know of no way to send mail in. Teletel is a universe unto itself, presumably with its own rules. It is not growing rapidly within France, but its owner, France Telecom, is now making concerted efforts to expand it outside of France.

Network Differences

The biggest difference among networks is whether they are part of the Matrix or not. A network within the Matrix offers its users online communication with tens of millions of other people. A network outside the Matrix can exchange mail among only a limited number of users. The Matrix is a huge pool of communicating and collaborating systems and people. Outside the Matrix are islands of electronic mail users, but they are disconnected from each other and from the Matrix.

The Matrix is defined by a common communication facility, electronic mail. Mail gives most users of the Matrix access not only to personal mail directed at small numbers of specific people, but also to mailing lists, which can support discussions among large numbers of people. Many parts of the Matrix also have access to USENET news or something like it (FidoNet echos, WWIVnet subs, etc.). Figure 4.2 summarizes the basic services of some major parts of the Matrix.

Among the networks that are included in the Matrix, the Internet is the most unusual. The Internet provides the same communications services of mail, lists, and news that we have mentioned for

	mail	news	databases	remote login, etc.
comconf†	yes	yes	yes	no††
commail*	yes	no	no	no
USENET	no	yes	no	no
UUCP	yes	USENET	no	no
FidoNet	yes	echomail	no	no
WWIVnet	yes	subs	no	no
the Internet	yes	USENET	yes	yes

†   Centralized conferencing systems such as Prodigy, CompuServe, America Online, GEnie, Delphi, TYMNet, or BIX.

††   Many of these systems are now connected to the Internet, and do provide Internet services including remote login to their users.

*   Commercial mail systems such as AT&T Mail, SprintMail, EasyLink, and MCI Mail.

Table 4.1 Networks and Services

other networks in the Matrix. However, it also provides fast, interactive, resource sharing services, such as remote login (TELNET), file transfer (FTP), and interactive communications. It also provides resource discovery services that enable its users to locate people and things. These services are not generally available on other networks in the Matrix, but many of them are indirectly available through mail interfaces. We discuss such interfaces in Chapter 13, *Finding People*.

Summary

Electronic mail is not only the most widely used service on the Internet and elsewhere in the Matrix, it is also one of the most useful network services. This book will help you use it to best effect.

5

The Basics

Context

Using electronic mail is generally quite easy and is analogous to composing a paper mail message or reading a paper message. However, there are some distinct differences between email and paper mail:

Email is faster than regular postal mail.   Email in the Internet today is received almost immediately after it is sent. Unless there is a network failure, an email message usually gets to its intended recipient within just a few minutes, or, at most, within an hour or two. This makes it much faster than postal mail and even faster

than overnight package delivery. Even on slower networks in the
Matrix, mail usually arrives within hours, or a day at the most.

Email is more conversational than its paper mail counterpart.
The simple fact of immediacy makes it possible to exchange a
whole series of email messages with someone in a very short period
of time. Because of this, email messages tend to be less formal and
more chatty in style. Also, email messages tend to be shorter and
more to the point.

**With email, you can keep a record of messages you send and
receive.**   You can easily include the text of a previous email message as part of your reply to the message. This lets you and your
email correspondents keep the context of replies sent in each message. Including context is polite, and also makes an email message
more immediately understandable.

Mail Programs

A mail program can be any one of several programs, depending
upon what kind of computer system you use and what your personal preference is for reading mail. Mail programs exist for just
about every type of computer hardware and operating system, all
the way from PCs to supercomputers and mainframes. Please note
that some commercial systems, like CompuServe or Prodigy, may
integrate the mail program into a larger and more comprehensive
user interface. Access to the mail program may be through a menu
choice, rather than explicitly executing a standalone program.
However, underneath the covers it is a mail program doing the
work, no matter how it is packaged.

Mail programs range from very simple line-oriented programs
to packages with full screen displays or those that use pointing
devices such as a mouse and run on bit-mapped displays. Regardless of the type of mail program you may use, they all share some
common features.

At its heart, a mail program consists of a mail reader and a mail
composer. The mail reader retrieves incoming mail messages from

your own personal mailbox and displays them for your perusal. Suffice it to say a mailbox is usually just a computer file. The mail composer lets you compose new mail messages and reply to received messages. It usually consists of a simple text editor or has a way to use your own favorite text editor.

Most mail programs also have some message management functions that let you organize and file your mail messages away for future reference. These management functions range from those that simply allow you to file messages in alternate files to sophisticated search and retrieval functions to those that help you organize and cross-reference large volumes of mail messages.

Many mail programs also let you manage lists of commonly used mail addresses much like an address book. This lets you conveniently look up and reuse sometimes hard-to-remember mail addresses with the click of a mouse or a few keystrokes.

Composing and Sending Mail

Composing an email message is as simple as typing a paper letter, and sending it is much easier. Let's look at some examples that use a simple mail program called *Pine* to send messages. Pine runs on practically all UNIX systems. We have selected Pine for our examples because it is simple, yet it incorporates most of the features typical of any common *mail program,* also sometimes called a mail *User Agent (UA),* or just a *mailer.* By whichever name, a mail program is the software that lets you receive mail messages, reply to them, and compose new ones. Pine happens to be screen-oriented, as are many mail programs, but being screen-oriented is not a requirement for mail programs. Some mail programs are command-line oriented; others use bit-mapped displays with a mouse or other pointing device. All mailers share the same features as Pine for both sending and receiving email messages. To start Pine, enter the Pine command at the UNIX shell prompt ($):

```
$ pine
```

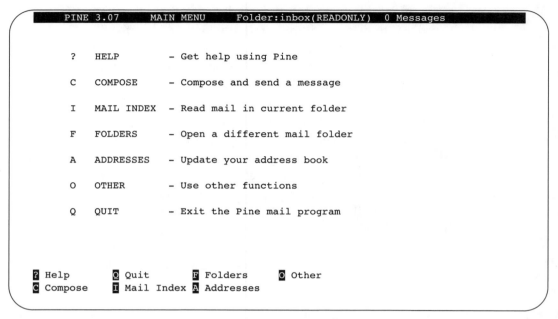

Figure 5.1 Pine MAIN MENU Screen

Note that the name of the command as you type it, *pine*, is in all lowercase letters.

If you're using a computer system that has a menu-oriented interface, to start your equivalent mail program you will need to find a menu for mail and select items from it. That computer system will run an underlying mail program for you.

Figure 5.1 shows the initial Pine MAIN MENU screen. The Pine MAIN MENU screen gives you a number of different options. We will use the COMPOSE option to send a new email message. Type the letter *c* to bring up the COMPOSE MESSAGE screen, as in Figure 5.2.

The COMPOSE MESSAGE screen gives you a template for typing a new message. The template is divided into two parts: some headers that look like an office memo and an area in which you enter the message text.

The header lines give the basic addressing information, and a brief description of the contents of the message. To send a message,

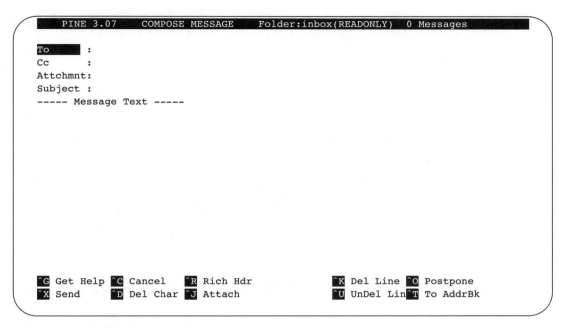

Figure 5.2 Pine COMPOSE MESSAGE Screen: Composing a Message

you simply supply the electronic address of the recipient. Usually, you also provide a subject so that the recipient can easily see what the message is about. The message itself is free-form text.

In Figure 5.2, Pine is asking you to fill in who to send the message to. Pine does this by highlighting the various fields. When you finish with one field, press the Enter key and Pine moves the cursor to the next field.

The Cc: (carbon-copy) line is for additional recipients. This lets you send the message to more than one person at the same time, that is, to the person addressed in the To: line and also to the person addressed in the Cc: line. You can send a message to more than two recipients by putting more than one address in the Cc: line, separating the addresses with commas.

The Attchmnt: line lets you attach other documents to your basic message. These documents can be just plain text or they can be bit-mapped pictures or other encoded information. We will discuss this further when we talk about the MIME extensions to

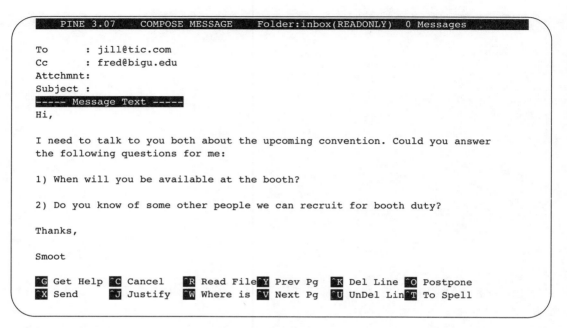

```
  PINE 3.07     COMPOSE MESSAGE     Folder:inbox(READONLY)   0 Messages

To      : jill@tic.com
Cc      : fred@bigu.edu
Attchmnt:
Subject :
----- Message Text -----
Hi,

I need to talk to you both about the upcoming convention. Could you answer
the following questions for me:

1) When will you be available at the booth?

2) Do you know of some other people we can recruit for booth duty?

Thanks,

Smoot


^G Get Help ^C Cancel    ^R Read File^Y Prev Pg  ^K Del Line ^O Postpone
^X Send     ^J Justify   ^W Where is ^V Next Pg  ^U UnDel Lin^T To Spell
```

Figure 5.3 Pine COMPOSE MESSAGE Screen with a Message

electronic mail in Chapter 14. For now, we will just send a plain text message.

After you fill in the header fields, you can compose a message. Figure 5.3 shows the Pine COMPOSE MESSAGE screen after a message has been typed. In this example, a simple text editor provided for the purpose is used to compose the message. Some mail programs let you use a mouse to select text to delete, or to point to a place in which to insert text. Other mail programs may use cruder line-oriented editors or let you use your favorite screen editor. Regardless of the mail program you use, the principle is the same: you compose a text message to send.

Sending the message is simple. In Pine, just press the ^x key combination (Ctrl X; hold down the control key and type the x key). The message is then sent on its way to the intended recipients. In this case the message goes to jill@tic.com and fred@bigu.edu. The message usually takes only a few minutes to reach its destination. (Sometimes it can take a few hours, depending on the system which the message is sent to.)

You may have noticed that you did not have to fill in the address of the person sending the message (your address). The mail system does this for you automatically. The mail system also dates the message and adds information that makes it easier to track down lost messages. You only need to supply the recipients' email addresses and the contents of the message.

Receiving and Reading Mail

Receiving and reading mail is as simple as composing and sending it. Most computer systems with mail support notify you when you receive a new message. The notice may appear on your screen as a line of text or, if your system uses a graphical user interface, as a popup icon. When you receive the notice, you can call up your mail program to read the incoming message. You do not have to be at the computer in order to receive mail messages. Since most computers on the Internet operate 24 hours a day, incoming mail messages are queued up for you, so you can display them when you use your mail program.

This doesn't mean that you have to leave your computer on 24 hours a day. When you turn your computer on, it can check the network for any mail for you. One of the computers that does operate 24 hours a day will keep your mail for you and your computer will pick it up from there. If you get your mail through a dialup network such as FidoNet or UUCP, or through a dialup conferencing system such as CompuServe, when you have your computer dial up you can tell it to pick up your mail for you. If you are using a dialup connection to the Internet, your computer can use the *Post Office Protocol (POP)*, to pick up your mail which was designed for this purpose, and which we describe in Chapter 6, *How Electronic Mail Works*.

In Pine, you use the `MAIL INDEX` command to view messages. Why `MAIL INDEX`? Because this command indexes your previously received messages, as well as new messages. It provides an overview of all your current mail messages, that is, ones you haven't deleted or filed elsewhere.

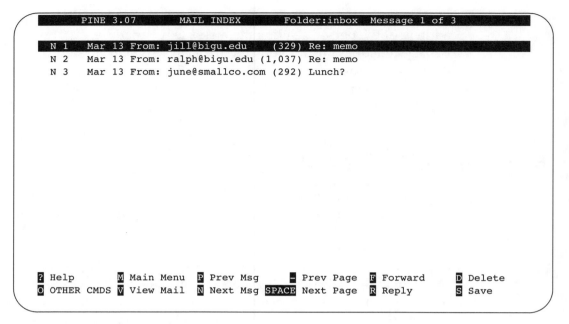

Figure 5.4 List of Messages to Read

Other mail programs have similar capabilities. All let you read messages you receive from other people. Some go into a reading mode immediately when you start up the mail program.

Figure 5.4 shows the Pine MAIL INDEX screen. Notice that this screen gives you a list of messages you have received since the last time you checked your mail. The N prefix means the message is *new* and you have not read it yet. Following this prefix are:

• Number of the message in the index

• Date the message was sent

• Identity of the person who sent the message

• Length of the entire message in characters

• Subject of the message.

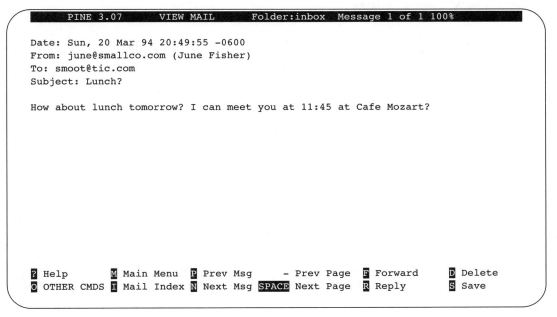

```
      PINE 3.07        VIEW MAIL        Folder:inbox  Message 1 of 1 100%

Date: Sun, 20 Mar 94 20:49:55 -0600
From: june@smallco.com (June Fisher)
To: smoot@tic.com
Subject: Lunch?

How about lunch tomorrow? I can meet you at 11:45 at Cafe Mozart?










? Help          M Main Menu  P Prev Msg     - Prev Page  F Forward     D Delete
O OTHER CMDS  I Mail Index  N Next Msg  SPACE Next Page  R Reply       S Save
```

Figure 5.5 Reading a Message

This message list is typical of most mail programs. The list lets you select the messages of most interest to you first, even though other messages may have arrived earlier. Think of this process as the electronic version of sorting your paper mail.

To select a message to read, move the highlighting to the message you want to look at. With Pine, you do this by pressing the keys on the keyboard that move the cursor (typically, the arrow keys). When the message is highlighted, press the Enter key to display the message text. Other mail programs have similar facilities for selecting a message to read.

Figure 5.5 shows how a selected message is displayed. In this example, we selected message 3 from the message list. Pine displays the message's header lines, followed by a blank line, and then the body of the message.

Replying to Messages

Composing and reading messages are two fundamental mail program operations. Replying to a message is another fundamental operation. Sending a reply is such a common operation that Pine has a reply option as part of both the MAIL INDEX (Figure 5.4) and VIEW MAIL (Figure 5.5) screens.

Figure 5.6 shows a reply to the previous example message. Replying to a message is similar to composing and sending a new message, with one important difference: you don't have to re-type the recipient's address when replying to a message. This simple, but powerful, feature makes email even easier to use. More importantly, it allows you to reply quickly to messages. In fact, it is such a time saver, you and your correspondent can virtually carry on a conversation, sending and receiving messages almost immediately (especially on a relatively fast network like the Internet). You can send and receive many messages an hour with a willing correspondent.

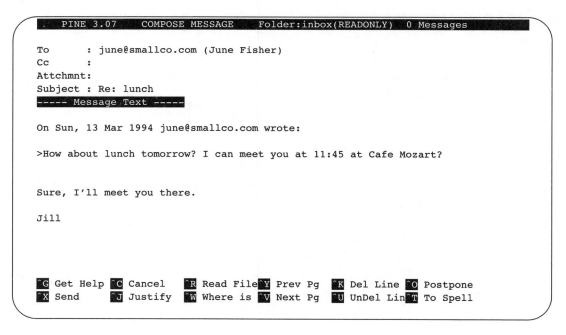

Figure 5.6 Replying to a Message

Another useful feature of the reply option is its ability to include the text of a previous message in the body of the reply message. When you select the reply option, Pine asks if you want to include the message text in your reply. The example shows the reply message being composed with the text of the previous message included. Notice that the text of the previous message is set off from any new text with the > character. This is a common convention and many mailers do this automatically for you. Pine also adds a line telling who wrote the text. This is especially useful when you send a message to many recipients.

Including previous text in a new message helps retain the context of a mail conversation, which can be important when answering questions. Sometime it is clear from a reply what a question means; sometimes it is not. A reply that includes both the question and the answer to the question provides a thread that makes it easier for the recipient to keep track of the conversation. Don't quote all of a long message, though; delete all but the part you are replying to.

When you select the reply option, Pine places you in the same message composer used for creating an original message. You edit and send the message in the same way you compose and send an original message. Pine also automatically fills in the reply address for you.

Notice that the `Subject:` line contains the original subject preceded by a `Re:` (Regarding). This is another common convention used by many mail programs.

Forwarding Messages

Most mail programs allow you to forward a mail message to another person. This process is similar to replying, but the entire message is sent to the recipient. Pine's `VIEW MAIL` screen includes an option to forward a message. When you press the *f* key, Pine places you in the `COMPOSE MESSAGE` screen with headers for you to fill in as shown in Figure 5.7.

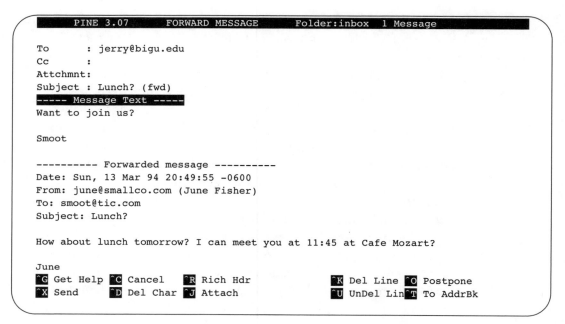

```
      PINE 3.07        FORWARD MESSAGE       Folder:inbox   1 Message

To      : jerry@bigu.edu
Cc      :
Attchmnt:
Subject : Lunch? (fwd)
----- Message Text -----
Want to join us?


Smoot


---------- Forwarded message ----------
Date: Sun, 13 Mar 94 20:49:55 -0600
From: june@smallco.com (June Fisher)
To: smoot@tic.com
Subject: Lunch?

How about lunch tomorrow? I can meet you at 11:45 at Cafe Mozart?

June
^G Get Help  ^C Cancel    ^R Rich Hdr        ^K Del Line ^O Postpone
^X Send      ^D Del Char  ^J Attach          ^U UnDel Lin^T To AddrBk
```

Figure 5.7 Forwarding a Message

The screen includes the entire message to forward, including the message's original headers. (Notice that the forwarded message is identified as such.) At this point, you can add any annotation you want to the forwarded message. Think of it as scribbling on an office memo or sticking a Post-It note with comments on a message you received that you want someone else to see. Once you finish composing the message, you send it the same way you send any other mail message.

Filing Messages in Folders

Another useful mail program feature is that it lets you file away mail messages for future reference. Almost all mail programs, including Pine, incorporate this feature. In Pine it is handled by the FOLDER command. A mail folder is just a file in which you can store mail messages for future reference.

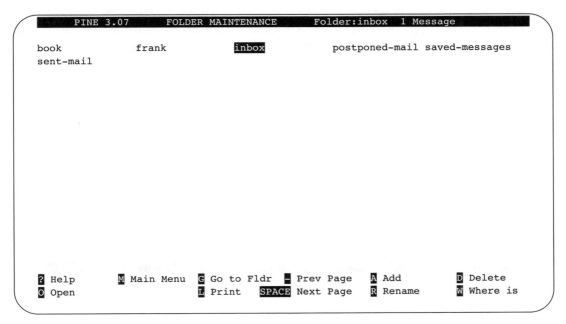

Figure 5.8 Pine Folder Listing

You can have many mail folders. Pine's folder scheme is relatively simple. Other mail programs include elaborate indexing schemes or the ability to nest folders under folders. If you receive a large volume of mail, these more elaborate schemes may be more useful. For most users Pine's simpler method usually suffices.

Figure 5.8 shows the Pine FOLDER MAINTENANCE screen. You get to this screen by typing an *f* in the MAIN MENU screen. This screen has a list of folder names. Several folders are predefined by Pine itself. The **inbox** folder is where incoming mail is stored. This folder is the default folder when you start up Pine. The folders **postponed-mail**, **saved-messages**, and **sent-mail** are also predefined by Pine. These folders are used to save a partially composed message, any generic messages you want to save, and any mail you send from Pine. The last folder is a particularly nice idea, since any message you send is saved to this folder by default.

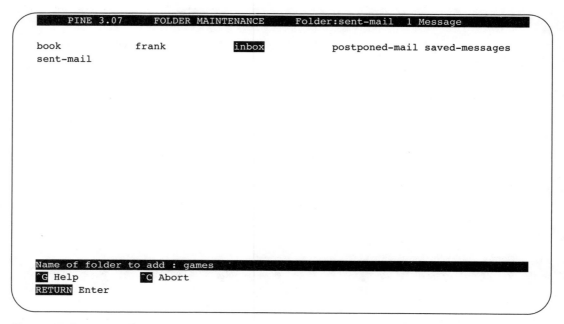

Figure 5.9 Creating a Folder

Figure 5.9 shows the folder screen after you type the *a* command to add a folder. Pine asks you the name of the folder to add. Here the name *games* has been already typed. Pressing the Enter key adds the folder to the list, as shown in Figure 5.10.

You can place a message in a folder from the screen you use to read the message. After you've read the message, you can save it to a folder by pressing the *s* key. Pine asks you which folder to save the message in. Unless you type in another folder name, Pine saves the message in the **saved-messages** folder.

You can also use the FOLDER MAINTENANCE screen to retrieve messages that you've saved in folders. When you get to the FOLDER MAINTENANCE screen, you can set the current folder to the one you want to look at by highlighting the folder name. Pressing the Enter key selects the highlighted folder as the current folder and places you in the MAIL INDEX screen where you can read and review any message in the folder. Any of the messages can be replied to or forwarded just like any other message.

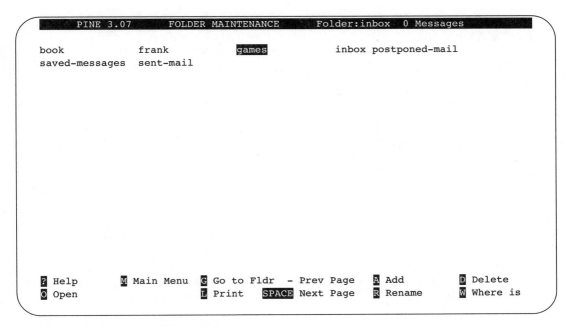

Figure 5.10 Screen with New Folder

Address Books and Aliases

Most mailers let you keep a private list of commonly used addresses. This is usually called an address book, and is a convenient way to recall electronic mail addresses you use frequently. In most cases, the address book lets you enter short names that represent long and hard-to-remember mail addresses. Such a short name is called an *alias*. In Figure 5.11 we see an example of the Pine ADDRESS BOOK screen. This screen is displayed when you press the **a** key in the MAIN MENU screen. The example shows an address book that contains 3 addresses. Each address book entry contains a short name for the address, the full name of the addressee, and the mail address.

To use an address in the address book, just use the short abbreviation as the recipient address when you, compose a message. To send a message to Jane Brown, you would simply type *jane* in the COMPOSE MESSAGE screen, as shown in Figure 5.12.

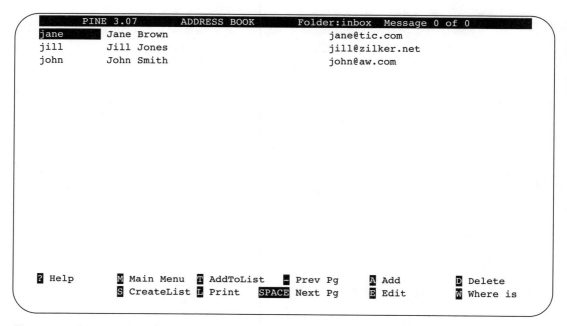

Figure 5.11 Address Book Screen

When you got the next field the full address for Jane Brown is displayed and used in the message (Figure 5.13).

Adding an entry in the address book is also simple. To add an entry, press the *a* key in the ADDRESS BOOK screen. Pine then prompts you for the email address, name and nickname of each entry. Each user can set up their own list of aliases. Your list is your own private list, and is available for your use only.

Some mail systems also have global aliases which are known to all users of the system. These global aliases are set up by your system administrator and are accessible to all users. You can also ask your system administrator to forward your mail to another address. This is convenient if you have multiple accounts on several systems and want all your mail to be received at a single location. If you are using a UNIX system, you can also forward your own mail to another location. To do this, place the forwarding address in the **.forward** file in your home directory.

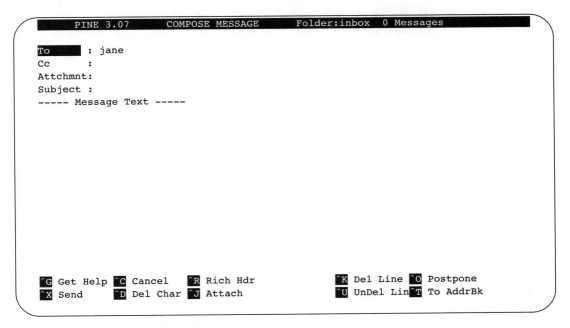

Figure 5.12 Using an Address Book Address

For example suppose Joe has an account on the UNIX system ivy.bigu.edu, but wants to receive all his mail at the address joe@tic.com. He can do this by putting the following text in the **.forward** file on ivy.bigu.edu:

```
joe@tic.com
```

The mailer on ivy.bigu.edu will forward any mail sent to joe@ivy.bigu.edu to joe@tic.com.

Including a File in a Message

Most mail programs also let you include text from a file as part of the message. This saves you from having to re-type a long document to make it part of a message. In Figure 5.14 we show the Pine COMPOSE screen with part of a message composed.

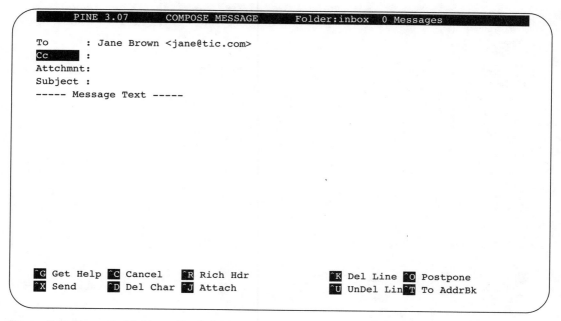

Figure 5.13 Expanded Address Book Address

The user has pressed the Ctrl-R key which prompts for the name of a file to add to the message body. Here the contents of the file **texttoadd** will be included as a part of the message.

Email Etiquette

The electronic postal system has no hard and fast rules about what you can say in a message. However, since all this correspondence goes out over a shared resource, some general rules of etiquette have generally been adopted.

Try to be brief and to the point.   Just like a long letter is hard to wade through, a long email message is also difficult. On the other hand, if you are corresponding with someone who expects you to have a lot to say, go ahead and say it. Most email messages are short, though, since the message turnaround time is short.

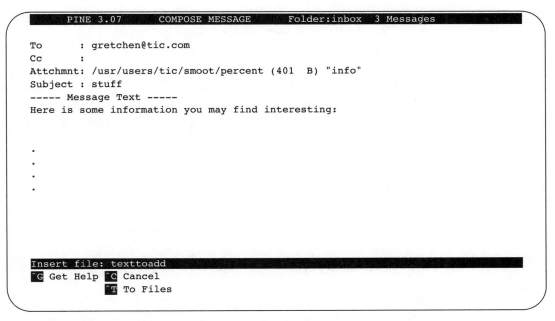

```
        PINE 3.07        COMPOSE MESSAGE       Folder:inbox   3 Messages

To      : gretchen@tic.com
Cc      :
Attchmnt: /usr/users/tic/smoot/percent (401  B) "info"
Subject : stuff
----- Message Text -----
Here is some information you may find interesting:


  .
  .
  .
  .




Insert file: texttoadd
^G Get Help  ^C Cancel
             ^T To Files
```

Figure 5.14 Including Text in a Message

Include the context of the previous message when you compose a reply.   If you get a lot of email correspondence from someone and they do not include any context, replies can be misunderstood. You can gently prod someone who does not include context by including your own context when you reply.

Send messages only to those with a "need to know."   It is not polite to send a message to hundreds of people when just a few will do. It is particularly inappropriate to send *junk mail* to hundreds of recipients unless you have their prior approval. It also uses network resources unnecessarily. Because sending to hundreds is no harder than sending to a few, sending to hundreds is often very tempting.

Be sure you are not misunderstood (as much as you can).
An electronic message is just words. It does not convey body language or speech inflection that provide clues to your mood when you speak to someone face to face. Since email tends to be less

formal than paper mail, people are not as careful about what they write. A number of conventions have been adopted to convey mood when you write. Here are a few of them:

- Put emphasis on words you want to emphasize. Doing this with just ASCII text can be tricky. A good way to show emphasis is to use an asterisk (*) to set off words. The asterisk usually implies the text should be in italics. The phrase

```
I *need* you to pick that package up today.
```

is much clearer than the same phrase without emphasis.

- Use boldface to convey even stronger emotions. Usually boldfacing means you are angry and shouting. While this should not be used often, it can get the point across at times.

- Use some commonly understood symbols to convey other moods. Most of these are variations on the sideways smiley face. The symbol:

```
:-)
```

means the person is just kidding or the previous phrase or sentence was a joke. Notice it looks like two eyes, a nose, and an upturned mouth with the bottom of the face facing right. Other symbols in the same vein are:

```
;-)   winking smiley face
:-(   frowning face
:-)>  smiley face sticking its tongue out
```

You may also see abbreviations of commonly used phrases. Examples of these are:

- *IMHO (in my humble opinion)*

- *FYI (for your information)*

- *FAQ (frequently asked questions)*

- *BTW (by the way)*

You may not use any of these variants in your message, but you commonly see them in many email messages.

Since it is easy to be misunderstood when you send email, be sure to give a correspondent the benefit of the doubt when you are unsure about their mood. If a message's meaning is ambiguous, ask your correspondent for clarification before jumping to conclusions.

For still more etiquette, especially for communicating with many people through mailing lists, see Chapter 11, *Mailing List Etiquette.*

Summary

If you've tried all the commands in this chapter, and you've read the material on etiquette, you now know enough to use mail in your daily activities of business and pleasure. This is a good foundation to learn many more things.

6

How Electronic Mail
Works

In this chapter, we deal with some of the more technical issues surrounding electronic mail in order to give you a better idea of how the distributed electronic postal system really works. We will explain:

- how electronic mail works in a networked environment.

- the structure, both seen and unseen, of a typical mail message.

- the general structure of the software systems that make up the underlying structure of the electronic mail system.

Figure 6.1 Message Delivery

The Distributed Electronic Postal System

After you send a mail message, it seems to arrive at your electronic pen pal's computer as if by magic. But what really happens to your message? How does it get delivered? We will see that, although most of the technical wizardry that makes email possible remains hidden from you, it is important that you understand how the email system works. If you understand how the system works, you'll know what to do when your message does not get delivered or when the underlying system occasionally breaks down.

An Example Message Delivery

Let's take a look at how a typical message gets delivered. In Figure 6.1, we show a message composed by a user on the machine xfr.tic.com. This particular message is being sent to a user on another machine ws.aw.com. After the sender composes the message, it is handed off to a program on the machine *xfr.tic.com* . When this program receives the original message, it looks at who the message is being sent to and deciphers the recipient address to determine where the message should be delivered. Delivering the message directly to the recipient machine may be impossible, or may not be the most optimal delivery route for the message. So, the message goes from where it was composed to where it eventually is delivered in a hop-by-hop fashion from one machine to the next. We see in the figure that the message first passes through the machine akasha.tic.com. Next it gets sent to a machine called aw.com. And finally it gets delivered to the recipient's machine called ws.aw.com. Here it is placed in a file called a *mailbox* where the recipient can later retrieve and read the message.

For the time being, we will ignore how the message gets from one machine to another. Suffice it to say, it could be over a high-speed network like the Internet, slower-speed telephone lines, a NetWare LAN, or any one of many other networking systems. The important point is that the bits that compose the message get transmitted from one machine to another in a *store-and-forward* manner. That is, when akasha.tic.com receives the message xfr.tic.com transmitted, it stores the message on disk, then transmits it to the next machine, which also stores it on disk, and so on.

This hop-by-hop approach to mail delivery may seem at first glance to be awkward and inefficient. Why not just send the message directly to its final destination and avoid all the intermediate steps? There are several reasons for not taking that approach.

The biggest reason for not delivering mail directly is that the sending machine would need to know where all the machines are that everyone reads email from. This is an impossible task due to the enormous number of possible recipients. Instead of every computer having to know where everyone's mailboxes are, the hop-by-hop enables a computers to pass the mail message to smarter gateway machines that have more information about where the final destination is. You could say the message is sent from an email *relay machine* to a computer that is closer to the final destination.

Another reason direct delivery is not practical is that your electronic pen pal may use a computer that you cannot send the message to directly. Suppose your machine is on the Internet and sends mail using the TCP/IP protocol suite, and your pen pal uses a Macintosh that only speaks Appletalk. Although your machine cannot talk to the Mac directly, it can send the message to a machine that understands both TCP/IP and Appletalk, which then relays the message. The hop-by-hop approach to mail delivery ties together the entire electronic mail community, even though different parts do not speak the same underlying network protocols. The hop-by-hop approach lets you exchange mail with millions of people without having to know either where their computers are or how they communicate with the rest of the email Matrix.

Another good reason for the hop-by-hop approach is its greater reliability. Suppose, in our example, the machine aw.com is out of commission for some reason or the network link from akasha.tic.com to aw.com is not operating. With the hop-by-hop approach, akasha.tic.com holds the message until it is able to successfully transmit it.

Mail System Architecture

As you may have guessed already, the postal system is composed of many different hardware and software systems. Far from being just a hodgepodge of systems, there is a common architectural model that holds these sometimes divergent pieces together and lets the electronic mail system function, for the most part, very smoothly. There are two major components to the email system: the *UA (User Agent)* and the *MTA (Message Transfer Agent)*, as illustrated in our example, which shows many of each.

User Agents

A UA is a fancy name the mail program we described in the previous chapter. It is the program visible to you, the end user, which you use to compose, send, and receive mail messages. In our message delivery example, the user used a mail program to send the message. This is the only part of the overall system you actually see and use directly.

Message Transfer Agents

The other, more hidden, piece of the mail system is the MTA. An MTA is a software system which does all the dirty work of routing and transporting a message to its final destination. An MTA runs on each computer system that exchanges mail messages from another host system. Think of an MTA as the program that performs the store-and-forward operation to deliver each mail message. An MTA also determines what the next hop should be on the delivery path. MTAs are generally very complex programs, but at their heart, they perform the store-and-forward operations that deliver every electronic message.

The whole system of MTAs is closely analogous to the regular postal system. In that system, you compose a letter and drop it into a postal box. From there, the postal service picks up the letter and routes it, possibly through many post offices, to its destination. At that point, a mail carrier places the letter in a mailbox. Some time later, the receiver of the message takes the letter out of the mailbox and reads it.

You may ask, how does an MTA know where to send the message next? Essentially, an MTA looks at the addressing information contained in each electronic message. Just like the regular postal system has addresses, so does the electronic postal system. But before delving into how an MTA uses the addressing information, we need to understand the structure of a mail message.

Mail Message: Header, Body, and Envelope

The thread that holds the mail system together is the common *mail format* adopted for all mail messages. A mail message is made up of three distinct parts, which are analogous to a paper mail message:

- message header

- message body

- message envelope.

The message header and body take their formats from the conventional office memo. We will talk about the envelope later on in this section. First, let's examine the header and body.

Message Header

Figure 6.2 shows an example *message header* and body. In fact, this is the message sent in the delivery example earlier in this chapter. The header consists of a series of lines, each with a keyword followed by a colon. The value of each keyword follows the colon.

```
From: smoot@tic.com
To: keithw@aw.com
Subject: book schedule
Date: Mon, 3 Jan 94 10:50:11 CST
Received: from xfr.tic.com by akasha.tic.com (5.65/1.8)
    id AA21661; Mon, 3 Jan 94 12:18:58 -0600
Received: from akasha.tic.com by aw.tic.com (5.35/main.1.6)
    id AA22781; Mon, 3 Jan 94 13:20:10 -0500
Received: from aw.com by smtpgate  id: 2D3E9536.454
        (WordPerfect SMTP Gateway V3.1a  04/27/92)
Message-Id: <9401031650.AA27058@xfr.tic.com>

Hi,

We need to talk about the book schedule.  Let me know when you are
available.

Thanks,

Smoot
```

Figure 6.2 Example Message Header and Body

These header lines have specific meanings. They are called *RFC822 header* lines because they are defined in a document called *RFC822 (Request for Comments Number 822),* which describes the Internet standard format for electronic mail messages. Fortunately, this standard has become widely adopted and is understood by almost every electronic mail system, regardless of whether or not that system is a part of the Internet.

The meaning of each header line is sometimes obvious. For example, the `Subject:` header line contains an explanation of the contents of the message. This is supplied by the sender of the message. The `To:` line tells who the recipient of the message is. This is also supplied by the sender of the message. The `From:` line tells who the sender is. This line is usually added automatically by the sender's mail program. In addition to identifying the sender, it provides an address the recipient can use to conveniently send a reply to the message. Most mail programs have a facility you can use to generate a reply to a message. These facilities automatically put the address of the sender in the `To:` field of the reply. This saves you from having to manually re-type the address, which can be prone to error.

The meanings of the other header lines in this example are not quite as obvious. They are typically generated by the mail delivery system itself and placed in the header as the message is sent. The `Received:` line tells when the message was received by a particular MTA along the path the message was sent. In this example, we show several `Received:` lines. The MTA on each host the message passed through adds a line to the message header. Each `Received:` line contains a `by` phrase and, possibly, a `from` phrase . The `by` part shows the name of the host system that received the message. The `from` part tells the name of the host system that sent the message. Also, in most cases this line includes the date the message was received.

The `Message-id:` line contains a unique network-wide identifier for the message. This identifier is enclosed within angle-brackets. For a user this line is not very interesting. Mail system administrators use this line as a debugging aid when a message is returned due to an error.

These lines are closely analogous to the postmarks found on the envelope of a paper letter. We will have more to say about these lines and how to interpret them when we discuss bounced messages in a later chapter. Notice that when any header lines continue to the next line, the continuation line starts with whitespace (tabs or spaces). Any header line can continue across multiple lines by following this convention.

There are other header lines, but the ones we described are the most common one found in mail messages.

Message Body

The *message body* follows the header lines. The body is separated from the header by a single blank line. The body can contain just about any printable ASCII text. Like an office memo it is composed by the sender. In a later chapter, we will see how the MIME protocol transports non-ASCII and binary data. Most messages sent today are plain ASCII, so we will stick with just ASCII messages in our discussion.

When a message is sent from one host to another, the email system treats the header and body as a series of lines that contain ASCII characters. Although this format must be strictly followed a mail program may present you with quite a different interface. For example, some mail programs may prompt you for header lines such as `Subject:` and `To:`. Others may present you with two different windows: one to collect these lines, and another in which to compose the message body. Regardless of how a mail program gathers the information contained in a mail message, it formats the header and body as shown for transport.

Different computer systems do use different sequences as line terminators, however. DOS systems use carriage-return <CR> followed by a line-feed <LF> character. Macintosh systems use just <CR>, while UNIX systems use just <LF>. The mail system rule is that when a message is composed, the composing system's line terminators are used; when the message is received, the recipient system's line terminators are used. We will see how this translation occurs when we talk about message envelopes, next.

Message Envelopes

Conceptually, the *mail envelope* is what a message is placed inside of when it is transported via the system of MTAs. You can think of an electronic mail envelope as the equivalent of an envelope for a paper letter. Like a paper envelope, an email envelope contains a recipient address and a return address. Although you may think that the message header `From:` and `To:` lines make up the envelope of the message, this is incorrect. The envelope of the message does contain this information, but is kept in a different place. Think of the envelope as separate information conveyed to an MTA by the mail program that composes the message.

A good way to illustrate this is with a message sent to multiple recipients, such as the message shown in Figure 6.3. Note the `Cc:` line which says to send a carbon copy of the message to jane@smallco.com. This single memo is actually sent as two separate messages. The first is sent to keith@aw.com and the second is sent to jane@smallco.com. Both envelopes have the same sender

```
From: smoot@tic.com
To: keithw@aw.com
Subject: book schedule
Cc: jane@smallco.com

Hi,

I've gotten the third chapter finished.

Thanks,

Smoot
```

Figure 6.3 Carbon Copies

address, but different recipient addresses. The sending MTA sends two separate messages with the same contents.

Envelope addresses are found in a variety of ways. For example when you use one common UNIX UA to send a message, you might type something like

```
$ mail smoot@tic.com
.
.
.
```

This command runs a program called **mail** with a single argument of smoot@tic.com. The "$" is the command line prompt character. The argument smoot@tic.com becomes the envelope recipient address. The UA derives the sender's address by checking which user on the local system is sending the message. Both of these pieces of information are then transmitted to the first MTA which uses it as the envelope of the message.

There are other ways to convey envelope information between two MTAs. The most commonly used transport mechanism for moving mail from one MTA to another in the Internet is *Simple Mail Transfer Protocol (SMTP)* SMTP is as its name implies a simple protocol for transferring a mail message. SMTP follows the *client/server paradigm of computing*. A *client process* on one machine contacts an SMTP server on another machine. In the case of SMTP, the *server process* waits for a client to send it a mail message. The movement of the mail message is unidirectional from the client to the server.

```
(1)    220 akasha.tic.com Sendmail 5.65/1.8 ready \
           at Mon, 3 Jan 1994 12:18:35 -0600
(2)    HELO xfr.tic.com
(3)    250 akasha.tic.com Hello xfr.tic.com
(4)    MAIL FROM:<smoot@tic.com>
(5)    250 <smoot@tic.com>... Sender ok
(6)    RCPT TO:<keith@aw.com>
(7)    250 <keith@aw.com>... Recipient ok
(8)    DATA
(9)    354 Enter mail, end with "." on a line by itself
(10)   { message header }
       .
       .
       .
       { message body }
(11)   .
(12)   250 Mail accepted
(13)   QUIT
(14)   221 akasha.tic.com closing connection
```
Figure 6.4 SMTP Example

The client and the server follow a strict dialog.

We show an example SMTP dialog in Figure 6.4. This dialog is the one used to send our example mail message from xfr.tic.com to akasha.tic.com. In this case the SMTP client is the MTA on xfr.tic.com and the SMTP server is the MTA on akasha.tic.com.

The SMTP dialog is a simple *send/receive protocol*. Each line of the dialog is terminated with <CR><LF>. Here is a brief explanation of the example dialog.

1. After the client connects with the server, the server displays a banner explaining who it is. Each server reply is prepended with a 3-digit code. These codes are the only part of the reply the client uses. The coding scheme tells the client whether the command was successful or not. The client ignores the rest of the response from the server, but records (in a human-readable format) whether or not the response was accepted.

2. The client identifies itself with the HELO command. The argument is its own host name.

3. The server sends back a message saying it is okay to proceed.

4. The client identifies the sender of the message with the MAIL FROM: command. The sender envelope address is enclosed within angle-brackets.

5. The server acknowledges the address of the sender.

6. The client uses the RCPT TO: command to identify the envelope recipient address.

7. The server acknowledges the recipient address.

8. The client issues the DATA command to tell the client that what follows is the message header and body.

9. The server acknowledges that it is ready to receive the message header and body.

10. The client sends the message header and body. Each line of the message is terminated with <CR><LF>, regardless of the native line terminator used by the client system. This allows two MTAs with different line terminators to agree on a standard canonical format for the message.

11. The client signals the end of the message header and body by sending a line with a single period on it. If a line in the message has a single period, the client doubles the period, so it won't be interpreted by the server as the end of the message. The server understands the double period as a single period and puts it correctly in the message text as a single period.

12. The server acknowledges receipt of the message. At this point the server on akasha.tic.com stores a copy of the message along with the envelope information. Using the envelope information, it forwards the message on to the next hop at aw.com. Once the client on xfr.tic.com sees the acknowledgment from the server on akasha.tic.com, it can safely assume the server has gotten the message. The MTA on xfr.tic.com then removes its own copy of the message and notes that the message was successfully forwarded.

13. Although the client can start the dialog all over again and send another message, the client more commonly sends a single message to a server, then sends the QUIT command to tell the server it is finished.

14. The server issues a final farewell and drops the connection.

In this dialog, the MTA conveys the envelope information explicitly in the dialog itself. How each MTA stores the envelope information is its own business. The important point is that each MTA uses a specific and well-defined protocol to convey the information to the next MTA. We use SMTP in this example, but two MTAs can use any commonly agreed upon protocol to communicate. As an extreme example, an MTA could store mail messages for another MTA and then copy the messages to a tape. The tape could then periodically be physically moved to the other MTA's machine and read in. As long as the tape formats are compatible between the two MTAs, this system, albeit slow, is a legitimate mail transport protocol.

Although SMTP is the standard Internet mail transfer protocol, most of the time the dialogue we have explained here is hidden from you. It is mostly used between the computer programs that are the MTAs in the mail system. However, a message that is not delivered correctly is usually returned to the sender, along with an explanation of the failure. Sometimes this explanation contains parts of a failed SMTP dialogue, so it is important to at least be able to recognize this in a returned message. We will show you more details on how to use this information in Chapter 8.

Mail in the Matrix

The Matrix connects many different types of mail systems into a somewhat heterogeneous whole. While we focus on Internet mail in this book, you should realize that because all MTAs use a store-and-forward protocol, mail messages can be sent to sites without direct Internet connectivity. You can send mail messages to networks such as the UUCP mail network and Fidonet. These networks do not use SMTP to transport mail messages. Other host-based mail systems such as Prodigy, CompuServe, MCIMail, and ATTMail are also interconnected for mail traffic with the Internet. For example, if you are on CompuServe, you can send a mail message to an Internet user, as well as to a Fidonet user. The Internet, in a real sense, serves as an interchange network for these diverse mail systems. Even internal corporate mail systems that do not directly support SMTP, such as those based upon, say, Novell's proprietary mail system system, can exchange mail with the Internet. The Novell system must support a gateway MTA that speaks SMTP to other Internet sites. SMTP transports a mail message coming in from another Internet site. The Novell system's own mail transport protocol forwards the message within the Novell environment.

Summary

We have seen how electronic mail works in a networked environment, including the way the structure of a message is related to the structure of the software systems that deliver it. As we shall see in the next chapter, the only thing necessary to get the mail to its destination is a reliable way to address the mail so that it gets to the gateway, and from there on to its final destination. This process is called addressing and routing.

7

Mail Addressing and Routing

Like its paper counterpart, electronic mail uses addressing to get mail to its destination. Electronic mail address syntax can be rather mystifying at times. What does an *address* like

widget1!ralph%gateway@bigco.com

really mean? How does the mail system interpret the address in order to get the message to its final destination? More importantly, why does it have, at first glance, such a strange and obscure *syntax*? Fortunately, most mail addresses are much less complicated than this example. However, you will run into addresses like the example from time to time. In this chapter, we explain some of the mysteries of electronic mail addressing and how they are used to get a message to its destination.

Some clear mail address standards are emerging, so some of the confusion is at least lessening. Addressing today is generally a lot simpler than it was five or even just a few years ago. There are still some ad hoc and only partially understood standards. Generally, you use the ad hoc standards to route mail across mail gateways linking heterogeneous mail systems.

General Addressing Conventions

The general convention for most mail addresses in use today on the Internet and many other mail networks divides a mail address into a series of *tokens*. A token is a funny word for what is just a string of *alphanumeric* characters or a single non-alphanumeric character. Our example address is divided into nine distinct tokens. Here they are separated by spaces to make it clear to you what each token comprises:

```
widget1 ! ralph % gateway @ bigco . com
```

In a real email address, *do not* put spaces between tokens. The meaning of each of the tokens depends on the nature of the mail system which interprets the address. Complex addressing syntax is generally used to route or to gateway mail between different mail systems. Also, various systems use a number of ad hoc conventions to forward mail from one mailing address system to another. A mail address which, at first glance, may appear incomprehensible can often be understood better once it has been divided into tokens.

Fortunately, in this seeming mishmash of addressing and routing conventions there are some emerging and commonly used standards. We will explain the most widely used standard first — domain addressing.

Domain Addressing

Perhaps the most common addressing syntax in use today is what is called *domain addressing*. A *domain address* is simply two sets of tokens separated by a single at sign (@). For example the address

> smoot@tic.com

is a simple domain address. The string to the left of the @ is called the *local_part* of the address. The string to the right of the @ is called the *domain_part* of the address. You read this address in the following way: this address belongs to a user called smoot at the company *TIC (Texas Internet Consulting)*, which has the domain tic.com. If you read this address aloud, you say "smoot at tic dot com." When we explain how domains are defined, we will see why tic.com refers to a particular company and no others.

Domain addressing evolved from a similar syntax in the early ARPANET, the precursor to the Internet, where addresses like:

> smoot at ut-sally

> or

> smoot@ut-sally

were both perfectly legal mailing address and meant exactly the same thing: this address belongs to a user smoot at a host called ut-sally connected to the ARPANET. The first address with the word at is now an obsolete form and is no longer supported.

However, these days, the domain_part of a domain address may or may not correspond to a host name. It does in some cases, but only rarely. In our example and for most mail addresses, it corresponds to an organization. Also, the domain_part in a mail address has its own internal syntax. Note that this part has several alphanumeric tokens separated by periods. The domain_part in a mail address originates from the *Domain Name System (DNS)*, which is the distributed naming system used by the Internet community. Before delving further into mail addressing, we need to explain a little about DNS.

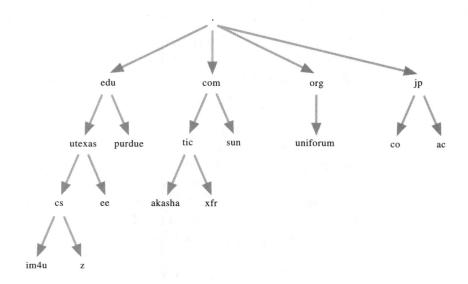

Figure 7.1 Part of the DNS Naming Tree

The Domain Name System

A *DNS name* is a series of tokens separated by periods. Each domain name maps to a unique node in a tree-like naming structure. Figure 7.1 shows a very small part of the *DNS tree.* The real DNS tree has millions of nodes. Each DNS name refers to a specific node in the DNS naming tree.

A DNS name is read from right to left starting at the root of the tree. The top-most node is called the *root node.* (For some unknown reason, computer scientists like to display trees upside down with the root of the tree at the top.) Note that the root node is designated by a single period. However, when used as part of a mailing address the final period is dropped from the name. Notice also that each node may have many children, but only a single parent. So the DNS name in our example, tic.com, corresponds to node (1) in the figure. The DNS name cs.utexas.edu refers to node (2) in the figure.

DNS names have no intrinsic meaning assigned to them. However, the commonly understood context is the name tic.com is a commercial company (the com node is associated with commercial companies) called tic (the abbreviation for Texas Internet Consulting). The name tic is an arbitrary name. It could have been anything. The only rule about a node name is it must be unique with respect to its single parent node. That is, each sibling node must have a unique name. This uniqueness is guaranteed by a registry system. Whenever an organization gets a domain name, it must register the name with the parent node's registry. In the case of Texas Internet Consulting, we decided the initials of our firm would be a nice short and easy node name. We submitted the name to the registry for the com domain. If some other organization had already taken the name tic, then we would have had to come up with an alternative. This is very similar to how business names are registered, and it guarantees the name to be unique.

As shown in Figure 7.1, underneath the node labeled tic.com are child nodes called akasha.tic.com and xfr.tic.com. These names are unique across the entire DNS tree. We can add nodes under the tic.com part of the DNS tree without interfering with other parts of the tree. This allows us to keep our own data for our little corner of the DNS tree and add and delete nodes under tic.com any time we want to. Other subtrees can do the same thing. This allows us to dynamically add names that are guaranteed to be unique across the entire DNS tree. It also lets the maintenance of DNS names be distributed among the thousands of organizations that make up the Internet community.

Just adding domain names to the DNS tree is not terribly interesting. What *is* interesting is what the names can refer to. It turns out the DNS tree works in a way very similar to the telephone book *White Pages,* except on a much larger scale. Software exists that lets you look up information stored under any node of the DNS tree. Think of the name of a node as a unique key for any information stored there. The information associated with each node is called a *resource record.* A resource record is simply a value stored under a domain name. It is very similar to a record in a database. Just as you can look up someone's telephone number and address in the

White Pages of the phone book if you know the person's name, you can look up information associated with a domain name. We can illustrate this with an example using the domain tic.com and its children.

The most common resource record in use by the DNS is an *IP address*. An IP address is simply a unique 32-bit integer that is assigned to each host attached to the Internet. Most nodes in the DNS tree are names of hosts. So, if you look up the information under the node akasha.tic.com you find an IP address of 192.135.128.129. If you look under the node xfr.tic.com you find the IP address 192.135.128.132. The IP address of a host is used in a similar way to a telephone number for a person in the phone book. To send information to a host, an MTA must have a way of finding out the IP address of that host, just as you must know the telephone number of a person if you want to call them on the phone. But as we shall see in a minute, an IP address is not the only information that can be associated with a domain name.

Looking at a domain name, you might ask: "How does the mailing system know where to deliver a message with an address of smoot@tic.com?" And you might guess that the mail system looks for and finds the IP address associated with tic.com and delivers the mail to that machine. This is a good guess, but it is incorrect.

In the ARPANET mail address we discussed, smoot@ut-sally, the token to the right of the @ is a host where the mail message is received. On the ARPANET, the sending system used SMTP to connect to the remote system and delivered the message. The receiving system then simply interpreted the local_part of the address and delivered the message to the appropriate mailbox.

Domain addressing is not necessarily this direct. Although this makes the delivery system more complex, it also adds a great deal of flexibility to the addressing system. In addition to an IP address, a node in the DNS tree can have data called an *MX (Mail Exchanger)* record. An MX record associates a domain name with another domain name that is the name of a real host. For the domain tic.com there are two MX records. They point to the host akasha.tic.com and xfr.tic.com. A message sent to smoot@tic.com is delivered to the host that is the target of one of the MX records.

When there are multiple MX records, each MX record has a priority value associated with it. If the first host cannot receive the mail, delivery is attempted at the next host. This mechanism lets a single domain have redundant mail servers. It also disassociates the domain_part of a mail address from any specific host system. This is a good thing, since hosts tend to come and go and a mail address should be more permanent.

Using our example, a message to smoot@tic.com is actually sent to the host akasha.tic.com. This is because the target of the MX record for the domain tic.com is the domain name akasha.tic.com, which is the name of a real host.

Use of MX records is a useful indirection. We will see later in this chapter how the MX facility lets mail systems that are not a part of the Internet use domain addressing.

With domain addressing you can send mail to any user with a mailbox on any one of the millions of hosts in the Internet. Aided by MX records and the DNS, the mail system on the Internet can quickly locate the machine and send your mail message.

Local Addressing

Since networked electronic mail lets you send mail to recipients on different machines across a variety of networks, it is convenient to distinguish a purely *local address* from one that is clearly for a recipient on another machine. Generally speaking, a mail address that is simply a string of alphanumeric characters, like ralph, is considered a local address. That is, the recipient of the message has his mailbox on the same machine from which the message is sent. A local address allows the mail system to locate where the local user's mailbox is.

A *mailbox* is the place where incoming mail is stored so the reader can later use a mail program to read it. On a computer system, a mailbox is simply a file on a disk drive. Usually, a simple mapping is done between a local address and the name of the mailbox. For example, on some UNIX systems, a mailbox is given the login name of the local user and stored in the directory

/var/spool/mail. Other *multi-user systems* employ similar strategies. On a PC or Macintosh, a similar mapping is done, but since these systems are typically *single-user systems,* a less elaborate scheme is employed. Usually, you configure the location of your mailbox when you install the mail software.

Needless to say, mailbox location issues are usually handled by your system administrator. For the most part, you do not have to worry about this kind of low-level detail.

One thing you should note is that when a mail message gets to its final destination, the mail system must recognize this and inter-pret the address as a local address. For example, a message with an address of **smoot@tic.com** eventually gets to its final destination. At that point the mail system recognizes any address with a domain_part of **tic.com** as local. The mail system then interprets the local_part of the address to determine the location of the mail-box for the user **smoot** and deposits the message in that mailbox.

Some systems employ more elaborate local addressing syntax. A local address can consist of several alphanumeric tokens sepa-rated by periods (.). In MCI Mail, the local address is a number (or two numbers) separated by a dash. With CompuServe, the local address is a number or two separated by a period. Also, some sites have adopted the convention of allowing local addresses of the form **First_name.Last_name**. These various conventions are purely a matter of taste and are sometimes set up for the convenience of the local administrator (not always for the user). There is no single standard local address format.

UUCP

UUCP addressing is another addressing method that is quite com-monly used in the Matrix. A *UUCP address* is often called a *bang-path address* because of the use of the exclamation point (!) to sepa-rate alphanumeric tokens in the address. The address **radish!carrot!sam** is an example of a UUCP address. A UUCP address is used to send mail among a set of hosts that make up the *UUCP Mail Network.* This network primarily consists of machines that use the UUCP protocol to exchange mail, hence the name of the network. UUCP is an old method for using modems to transfer files from one UNIX system to another over ordinary telephone lines. There are gateways between the Internet and the UUCP Mail Network, so mail can be exchanged between the two.

A UUCP address is semantically different than a domain address. A domain address defines an absolute address, while a UUCP address defines a relative address. Let's illustrate this distinction with a few examples. The address smoot@tic.com means the same thing and points to the same location regardless of where it is used in the set of systems that support domain addressing. Someone on the machine im4u.cs.utexas.edu can send mail to smoot@tic.com and someone on the machine world.std.com can send mail to smoot@tic.com. Both people use the exact same domain address. The mail is routed differently depending on the source of the message, but it ends up in the same place. The routing details are completely hidden from the sender.

On the other hand, the UUCP addresses cypress!redwood!ralph and pine!oak!redwood!ralph both point to the same mailbox. The syntax is different because the address depends on the relative locations of the sending and receiving systems. In the first case, the address causes the message to be sent to a UUCP host called cypress, which forwards it to the UUCP host redwood, which delivers the message to the recipient, ralph. The message with the second address follows a path to the host pine through the host oak and finally to redwood.

Note that UUCP host names, unlike DNS host names, do not form a hierarchy. Instead, they are a flat address space. In fact names of hosts may be duplicated. So the above two addresses might point to a different user on two hosts with the same name. Confusing? Yes, it is.

Fortunately, there is a *UUCP registry* which guarantees unique host names to those who bother to register. The registry solves the duplicate host name problem. However, to send mail with UUCP addressing requires the sender to know the full path to the destination system. This is rather cumbersome, so several programs have been developed to help automatically generate paths to hosts, at least for hosts in the UUCP registry. One of the most popular is **pathalias**. If a system uses **pathalias,** it is possible to specify a partial path to a destination mailbox. Using our example, a host with **pathalias** support would allow you to use the UUCP address redwood!ralph to send a mail message, rather than the full UUCP path. This simplifies UUCP addressing syntax considerably. However, the **pathalias** database must be generated on every host which uses it from the full set of UUCP hosts. Given the dynamic nature of the database this solution is less than optimal, since information in the database changes periodically.

Other Addressing Styles

Other addressing styles also exist. BITNET, for example, uses the old-style ARPANET syntax of a local_part with a BITNET host name: i.e.

user@bitnethost

This is easily confused with domain addressing, but it is not the same. Many Internet mailers also accept the following pseudo-domain syntax for sending mail to a BITNET site:

user@bitnethost.bitnet

The name bitnet is not a real domain name, but it serves to distinguish a domain address from a BITNET address. Most Internet sites understand this format, but be aware that it is not universally supported and is not a standard address format. Novell's mail system follows the same syntax as BITNET. Also, DEC VMS systems have their own addressing syntax with the local_part of an address separated from the host name by two colons (::), as in:

host::user

This looks a lot like a single-path UUCP address, with the exception of the separator character. DECNET host names like UUCP names are not guaranteed to be unique.

X.400

X.400 is an international standard method for transporting mail messages, and has its own address syntax. In most ASCII based mail systems you will see an X.400 address written in ASCII like:

S=smith/PRMD=attmail/O=bigcorp/C=uk

This is not the real X.400 format used in a mail message, because when X.400 transports a mail message, it uses a binary representation of the ASCII shown.

Mixing It Up

Having to learn all the different addressing forms is bad enough. However, it gets worse, since the above formats can be combined, often in very ad hoc ways of *mixed addressing*. The reason for combining addressing formats is to allow the gatewaying of mail from one network to another. Let's look at an example of why you might what to do this.

As illustrated in Figure 7.2, suppose a machine called backfire sets up a UUCP mail link to the machine akasha.tic.com, which is connected to the Internet. If you are on a machine connected to the Internet, you send mail to jill on backfire with the address backfire!jill@akasha.tic.com. As in our previous discussion of MX records, you could also use the address backfire!jill@tic.com. This address is interpreted as follows: send the message to akasha.tic.com via SMTP. From there, send the message via UUCP mail to the machine backfire, which delivers it to jill.

Conversely, if jill wants to send mail to jim@cs.utexas.edu she uses an address like akasha!cs.utexas.edu!jim on backfire. This address means: Send the mail to akasha (this presumes the UUCP hostname for akasha.tic.com is akasha. It could be something quite different) and from there send the message on to jim@cs.utexas.edu. In the UUCP mail network, you need to write domain addresses like jim@cs.utexas.edu as cs.utexas.edu!jim. The address akasha!jim@cs.utexas.edu might work, but as we shall see shortly, this address is ambiguous.

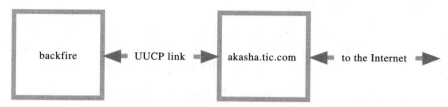

Figure 7.2 UUCP to the Internet

So, mixed addresses are often used to gateway mail to other networks to and from the Internet. The gatewaying is explicitly laid out in the address itself. The previous example shows how mail addressed to a UUCP mail host is explicitly gatewayed through an Internet mail gateway.

A fairly standard way for doing explicit routing through a mail gateway is to use the percent sign (%) in the local_part of a mail address. In fact, it is a standard on mail systems on certain networks in the United Kingdom, but it also appears widely on other networks. Take the address jill%smtpgate@aw.com This is a domain address, but the local_part has a percent sign (%) in it. In this case, it probably means the mail is sent to the mail gateway for the domain aw.com, but is then further processed at that gateway machine, which uses a specific internal gateway named smtpgate to send the message on to the user jill You really do not know where the mail message will end up or what happens to the message once it reaches the host aw.com. In fact, the mail message may end up being passed to a proprietary mail package such as *cc:Mail.* So, the ad hoc gatewaying convention lets you glue together disparate mail systems. What makes this kind of addressing even more confusing is that the *percent sign convention* is an ad hoc one and is not necessarily supported on all sites. However, it is widely adopted and is used to help construct many mixed addresses.

Domain Addressing Outside the Internet

Mixed addressing is both difficult to read and to understand. Domain addresses are generally much more straightforward to understand. Within the Internet domain addressing is the standard mail address format. It is possible to use domain addressing outside the Internet. In fact, many hosts connected to an Internet host via a UUCP link use only domain addressing. How is this handled? Let's go back to our example with the host **backfire** linked via UUCP to the Internet site **tic.com**.

Suppose the administrator of **backfire** registers a domain called **offnet.com**. Now, this domain has no hosts directly connected to the Internet, so no hosts need be registered. Suppose the DNS node **offnet.com** has an MX record associated with it which points at **akasha.tic.com**, the gateway machine on the Internet. If mail is addressed to, say, **sam@offnet.com** from any Internet host, the mail is forwarded to **akasha.tic.com**. From that point, the MTA on **akasha.tic.com** can be smart enough to relay the mail via UUCP to the UUCP machine **backfire**. The MTA on the machine **backfire** then can recognize the domain address and deliver the mail to **sam**.

In this manner, the actual transport used to get the mail to its destination is hidden. Also, the addressing is greatly simplified. All the users on **backfire** can use domain addressing. If a message has a domain address, but does not include a domain_part of **offnet.com**, the system uses UUCP transport to forward the message to **akasha.tic.com**. With this system, the actual UUCP transport is completely hidden from view.

Mail through the Matrix

The Matrix is the set of all interconnected mail systems. The Matrix includes a diverse set of systems, ranging from traditional single-site mail systems like *MCI Mail CompuServe* and *Prodigy,* all the way to distributed anarchies like *FidoNet* and *WWIVnet.* The core of the Matrix is the Internet and, for mail, the DNS mail system, as we saw back in Chapter 4, *The Networks.* You can use domain addressing to get to most mail systems interconnected to the Internet, even though those systems may not use such addressing internally.

Table 7.1 shows some common addressing formats used for sending mail from the Internet to these systems. There are far more

System	Domain Gateway	Local Format	Example
Applelink	applelink.apple.com	u	joe@applelink.apple.com
AOL	aol.com	u	jill@aol.com
BITNET	none	u%host.bitnet	u%rice.bitnet@cunyvm.cuny.edu
CompuServe	compuserve.com	nnnnn.nnn	75432.234@compuserve.com
FidoNet	fidonet.org	u	tim@f555.n123.fidonet.org
MCI Mail	mcimail.com	nnnnnnn	2345678@mcimail.com
UUCP	none	host!u	thumper!carol@uunet.uu.net
		u%site	carol%thumper@uunet.uu.net

u: user mail address

Table 7.1 Example Addressing Formats

systems in the Matrix than are listed in the table, but most of the others use some variation on the example formats listed in the table.

Summary

We have discussed addressing conventions, ranging from the general, to the most widely used (DNS addresses), to those specific to particular networks. You will encounter some or all of these types of addresses as you use mail, and now you will recognize them and know what they mean. Let's move on to even stranger things in the next chapter: errors and bounce messages.

8

Error and Non-Error Messages

Much like the postal system, the electronic mail system occasionally fails. In this chapter, we will explore how you can decipher why a message failed to get delivered and give you some hints about how to deal with messages that get returned. In this book we do not try to tell you how to configure a mail system; for that, see *The Internet Connection* or *Practical Internetworking with TCP/IP and UNIX*. However, you do need to be able to interpret messages the system generates when common problems occur, and know how to deal with such problems.

```
Return-Path: <Mailer-Daemon>
Received: by xfrsparc.tic.com (5.65/sub.1.6)
    id AA21143; Fri, 11 Feb 94 08:58:22 -0600
Date: Fri, 11 Feb 94 08:58:22 -0600
From: Mailer-Daemon (Mail Delivery Subsystem)
Subject: Returned mail: User unknown
Message-Id: <9402111458.AA21143@xfrsparc.tic.com>
To: <smoot@tic.com>

    ----- Transcript of session follows -----
>>> RCPT To:<frd@tic.com>
<<< 550 <frd@tic.com>... User unknown
550 <frd@tic.com>... User unknown

    ----- Unsent message follows -----
Return-Path: <smoot@tic.com>
Received: by xfrsparc.tic.com (5.65/sub.1.6)
    id AA21141; Fri, 11 Feb 94 08:58:22 -0600
Message-Id: <9402111458.AA21141@xfrsparc.tic.com>
To: frd@tic.com
Subject: hello
Date: Fri, 11 Feb 94 08:58:21 -0600
From: smoot@tic.com

Hi,

How is life treating you?
```
Figure 8.1 Unknown User

Bounce Messages

Much to your horror, you may get a message that looks something like the message in Figure 8.1. This looks at first glance like something out of your worst nightmare. What does this message mean? Why did it get sent to me? The first thing to do is: don't panic.

Look at the From: line in the message header. This message is from the user *Mailer-Daemon.* This is not some malevolent entity out to get you. Instead, it is the ordinary name of the mail system itself. Note what is in the commentary section of the From: line (between the parentheses). The message comes from the delivery system itself, which automatically sends this message when a failure to deliver a message occurs. Since a machine is generating the message, it is not very chatty. Think of it as the equivalent of all those marks you see stamped on a paper mail message that gets returned. Also, don't bother replying directly to Mailer-Daemon, since the message you got was sent automatically by a program that won't read mail you send to it.

Also look at the `Subject:` header line, which tells you the reason the message was sent. In this case, the message was returned because the mail system did not know the recipient of the message. The rest of the message contains a bunch of strange looking information. The message looks like it has multiple message headers. However, bounce messages actually follow a rather uniform structure. The real message headers end at the first blank line. In this example, the last header line before the blank line is `To:` `<smoot@tic.com>`. After that, the message body is divided into two parts. Each part starts with a line that begins with a header enclosed in dashes. The second part is the entire header and the body of the original message as they were sent earlier. This part starts with the line

```
----- Unsent message follows ----- .
```

This part is usually not very helpful in figuring out why the message got returned, but it does contain all the original information in the message, including the message header lines as generated in transit and as received by the remote mail system. You can use this part to actually resend the original message text once you figure out why it got returned in error.

The first part of the body which starts with the line

```
----- Transcript of session follows -----
```

is where you look to see what went wrong. This is the session transcript. Remember our discussion about SMTP in an earlier chapter. This transcript shows an actual SMTP dialog between two mailing systems. It says that the sending system tried to send a message to the recipient frd@tic.com. The 3-digit number 550 indicates that the receiving system rejected the recipient address because the recipient was unknown. Here is what happened to this message: The sending system sent the receiving system an SMTP RCPT TO line. The receiving system could not find a user with that address and sent back an error reply message.

Error replies always start with the digit 5. Note that the receiving system is usually the final destination of the message, since only the final system in a chain of MTAs knows whether an address is unknown. These two lines start with right and left angle brackets. Think of the right angle brackets as what the sending system sent as part of the dialog and the left angle brackets as what the receiving system sent back. The final line in this section restates the reason the message transmission failed.

When SMTP is used as the transport protocol there is almost always a transcript of the SMTP dialog at the point the message transfer failed. So, when a message bounces, always look for a line starting with a 5 to find the transcript of the SMTP dialog. In most cases the reason the message bounced is a mistyped user name. In this case the user name **fred** was mistyped as **frd**.

The example message shown in Figure 8.1 is a common format for a bounced message. However, it is not the only format, since there is no uniform way bounced messages get returned to the sender. (We explain another format in Chapter 14, *MIME: Multipurpose Internet Mail Extensions*). However, all returned messages give some indication of what went wrong when the message delivery was attempted.

Carbon Copy Bounces

Message bounces can be more complex when you send a message to several recipients at the same time. Figure 8.2 shows a message sent to two recipients where one delivery succeeded and the other delivery failed. In this case, the transcript of the session just shows the failed message and not the message that presumably got delivered. Remember, a message sent to more than a single recipient is treated like two separate messages.

How can you tell where the message failed? That is, which system is returning the failed message? You can tell this because the system where the message failed is the last one in the sequence of `Received:` lines in the header of the returned message. In this example, the message was returned by the system on akasha.tic.com.

```
Return-Path: <Mailer-Daemon@tic.com>
Received: from akasha.tic.com by xfrsparc.tic.com (5.65/sub.1.6)
    id AA15647; Sun, 13 Feb 94 21:14:59 -0600
Received: from xfrsparc.tic.com by akasha.tic.com (5.65/akasha.m4.1.15)
    id AA29203; Sun, 13 Feb 94 21:14:54 -0600
Date: Sun, 13 Feb 94 21:14:54 -0600
From: Mailer-Daemon@tic.com (Mail Delivery Subsystem)
Subject: Returned mail: User unknown
Message-Id: <9402140314.AA29203@akasha.tic.com>
To: <smoot@tic.com>

    ----- Transcript of session follows -----
>>> RCPT To:<joex@aw.com>
<<< 550 <joex@aw.com>... User unknown
550 <joex@aw.com>... User unknown

    ----- Unsent message follows -----
Return-Path: <smoot@tic.com>
Received: from xfrsparc.tic.com by akasha.tic.com (5.65/akasha.m4.1.15)
    id AA29201; Sun, 13 Feb 94 21:14:54 -0600
Received: by xfrsparc.tic.com (5.65/sub.1.6)
    id AA15639; Sun, 13 Feb 94 21:14:53 -0600
Message-Id: <9402140314.AA15639@xfrsparc.tic.com>
To: smoot@aw.com
Cc: joex@aw.com
Subject: bounce testing
Date: Sun, 13 Feb 94 21:14:52 -0600
From: smoot@tic.com

This is a test of a message bouncing off a carbon copy addrerss.
```

Figure 8.2 Carbon Copy Bounce

The message transcript can also contain parts of the dialog that may confuse you. Let's look at another example to see this. In Figure 8.3, a message is sent to two addresses, one of which, smuot@aw.com, is mistyped. The other, good, address, sam@vtel.com, is found on a host whose mail system is not responding at the current time. Because the MTA that tried to send the correctly addressed message, to sam@vtel.com, did not get a response from the remote SMTP server within a timeout period, it put the message in a queue of messages it will try to send again later. The remote system might not respond for any of a variety of reasons. For example, it may have been down, or there may have been network difficulties somewhere between the two systems. The

```
Return-Path: <Mailer-Daemon>
Return-Path: <Mailer-Daemon@tic.com>
Received: from akasha.tic.com by xfrsparc.tic.com (5.65/sub.1.6)
    id AA02479; Mon, 14 Feb 94 08:57:59 -0600
Received: by akasha.tic.com (5.65/akasha.m4.1.15)
    id AA06257; Mon, 14 Feb 94 08:57:55 -0600
Date: Mon, 14 Feb 94 08:57:55 -0600
From: Mailer-Daemon@tic.com (Mail Delivery Subsystem)
Subject: Returned mail: User unknown
Message-Id: <9402141457.AA06257@akasha.tic.com>
To: smoot@tic.com

    ----- Transcript of session follows -----
>>> RCPT To:<smuot@aw.com>
<<< 550 <smuot@aw.com>... User unknown
550 smuot@aw.com... User unknown
421 vtel.com.tcp... Deferred: Connection timed out \
    during user open with vtcsub.vtel.com

    ----- Unsent message follows -----
Return-Path: <smoot>
Received: by akasha.tic.com (5.65/akasha.m4.1.15)
    id AA06242; Mon, 14 Feb 94 08:54:48 -0600
Date: Mon, 14 Feb 94 08:54:48 -0600
From: smoot (Smoot Carl-Mitchell)
Message-Id: <9402141454.AA06242@akasha.tic.com>
To: sam@vtel.com
cc: smuot@aw.com

Testing.
```

Figure 8.3 Extraneous Transcript

message with the mistyped address, to smuot@aw.com, got
bounced back because the recipient was unknown on the destination system.

The confusing part is that the bounce message shows both the
unknown recipient as well as the timed-out connection. The connection timeout is shown by the line starting with 421. SMTP dialog lines starting with a 4 indicate recoverable errors, such as in this
one in which a remote host is either down or is temporarily
unreachable. The word "Deferred" in the error message about the
connection timeout also indicates that the error message is simply a
warning; that mail message is still queued for delivery and will be
sent at a later time.

The unknown user message indicates a real and unrecoverable error. You will need to resend the message to the unknown user, smuot@aw.com, after you correct the address to read smoot@aw.com. Since the bounce message includes a complete copy of the entire original message, you can, if you like, pick the original message out of the bounce message and resend it. However, not all bounce messages contain the entire original message, so sometimes you will need to find a copy elsewhere. This is one reason it is a good idea to copy yourself on outgoing mail messages, or to have your mail UA record outgoing messages for you.

Common Errors

Here are the most common kinds of errors you will find in bounce messages.

Deferred

A *deferred bounce message* is just a warning, so unless they persist the best thing to do with these bounce messages is to delete them. They do let you know that the addressee hasn't received your message, however, so at least you know why you haven't received a response. You might also want to double-check the domain name, just to be sure you didn't accidentally send the message to the wrong domain.

Unknown user

The most common type of serious bounce message is an *unknown user message*. You can usually correct such an error by typing the recipient's correct mail address.

Unknown host

Another common type of bounce message is the *unknown host message*, as shown in Figure 8.4. Instead of tic.com, the original message had toc.com in the destination address. There is no toc.com domain, so the message bounced. This kind of bounce not only

```
Received: by akasha.tic.com (5.65/akasha.m4.1.16)
    id AA00827; Sun, 24 Apr 94 15:59:34 -0500
Date: Sun, 24 Apr 94 15:59:34 -0500
From: Mailer-Daemon (Mail Delivery Subsystem)
Subject: Returned mail: Host unknown
Message-Id: <9404242059.AA00827@akasha.tic.com>
To: jsq

    ----- Transcript of session follows -----
550 smoot@toc.com... Host unknown

    ----- Unsent message follows -----
Return-Path: <jsq>
Received: by akasha.tic.com (5.65/akasha.m4.1.16)
    id AA00825; Sun, 24 Apr 94 15:59:34 -0500
Date: Sun, 24 Apr 94 15:59:34 -0500
From: jsq (John Quarterman)
Message-Id: <9404242059.AA00825@akasha.tic.com>
To: smoot@toc.com
Subject: Meeting next week.
Cc: jsq

What time is the meeting next week?
```

Figure 8.4 Unknown Host

looks very similar to a user unknown bounce, but can be fixed the same way. You can re-type the hostname and send the message again.

unknown mailer error

Look at the bounce message in Figure 8.5. The format of the bounce message is similar to the previous bounce messages, and the transcript contains an error line that starts with 554. The error message says *unknown mailer error* 1 You may ask: What is an "unknown mailer?" The message is a bit ambiguous. It is really saying that an unknown error occurred when the system tried to send the message to parish@tpoint.com.

What is the error? The error is not that the recipient's address is bad or mistyped, but rather that the mail system failed. This is usually due to a configuration error on the system that generated the message. If you examine the line above the line that starts with 554, the system gives you a clue, but not much of one. This line

```
Return-Path: <Mailer-Daemon@tic.com>
Received: from akasha.tic.com by xfrsparc.tic.com (5.65/sub.1.6)
    id AA09161; Mon, 21 Feb 94 18:34:51 -0600
Received: from netcomsv.netcom.com by akasha.tic.com (5.65/akasha.m4.1.15)
    id AA01888; Mon, 21 Feb 94 18:34:48 -0600
Received: from localhost by netcomsv.netcom.com with internal (8.6.4/SMI-4.1)
    id QAA11758; Mon, 21 Feb 1994 16:35:23 -0800
Date: Mon, 21 Feb 1994 16:35:23 -0800
From: Mailer-Daemon@netcom.com (Mail Delivery Subsystem)
Subject: Returned mail: unknown mailer error 1
Message-Id: <199402220035.QAA11758@netcomsv.netcom.com>
To: <news@tic.com>

The original message was received at Mon, 21 Feb 1994 16:35:03 -0800
from cactus.org [192.207.27.4]

    ----- The following addresses had delivery problems -----
<parish@tpoint.com>  (unrecoverable error)

    ----- Transcript of session follows -----
uux failed ( -1 )
554 <parish@tpoint.com>... unknown mailer error 1

    ----- Original message follows -----
.
.
.
```

Figure 8.5 A Different Kind of Error

```
uux failed (-1)
```

says that an error occurred when trying to run a command known
as **uux**. This means the remote system was trying to use UUCP to
forward the message, and failed.

It is more important that you know *where* the error occurred,
rather than why it occurred. You find out where the error occurred
by by looking at the `From:` line to see what system generated the
bounce message. In this case, it is from the system netcom.com.
That is where the unknown error occurred.

Informational Errors

Occasionally you get a message that looks like the one in Figure 8.6.
This message is not really an error message, but is only an *informational message.* Before taking any action, such as sending the

```
Return-Path: <MAILER-DAEMON@isl.rdc.toshiba.co.jp>
Received: from akasha.tic.com by xfrsparc.tic.com (5.65/sub.1.6)
    id AA04263; Sat, 30 Apr 94 09:56:26 -0500
Received: from tsbgw.isl.rdc.toshiba.co.jp by akasha.tic.com (5.65/akasha.m4.1.
    id AA26066; Sat, 30 Apr 94 09:54:43 -0500
Received: by tsbgw.isl.rdc.toshiba.co.jp (8.6.9-KCONV/8.15) with UUCP
    id VAA18383; Sat, 30 Apr 1994 21:36:36 +0900
Received: by mailhost.isl.rdc.toshiba.co.jp (8.6.9-KCONV/1.4) with internal
    id XBE20772; Sat, 30 Apr 1994 23:34:33 +0900
Date: Sat, 30 Apr 1994 23:34:33 +0900
Subject: Returned mail: warning: cannot send message for 12 hours
Message-Id: <199404301434.XBE20772@isl.rdc.toshiba.co.jp>
From: MAILER-DAEMON@isl.rdc.toshiba.co.jp (Mail Delivery Subsystem)
To: mm-dist@tic.com


    **********************************************
    **       THIS IS A WARNING MESSAGE ONLY      **
    **   YOU DO NOT NEED TO RESEND YOUR MESSAGE  **
    **********************************************

The original message was received at Sat, 30 Apr 1994 10:42:41 +0900
from uucp@localhost

    ----- The following addresses had delivery problems -----
saisho@eis.rdc.toshiba.co.jp  (transient failure)

    ----- Transcript of session follows -----
saisho@eis.rdc.toshiba.co.jp... Deferred: Host is unreachable
Warning: message still undelivered after 12 hours
Will keep trying until message is 1 week, 3 days old

    ----- Original message follows -----
```

Figure 8.6 Informational Error Message Example

message again, read the body of the message. It explicitly states that no action is required and that the message is simply informational. It is not necessary for you to take any action or to resend the original message The message is giving you information about a temporary condition in the mail delivery system that prevents the message from being delivered. Usually there's nothing you can do about the condition the message warns you about. You may want to delete such messages, or perhaps file them for reference in case further mail problems occur with the same host or user.

Bounces Caused by Unqualified Domain Names

In this section we discuss an unfortunate, but common, type of mail system error. We go into some detail on this because it can produce some rather mystifying error messages, especially if you are sending a message to multiple people at the same time. The solution to this particular problem is relatively simple, but mail systems in the Matrix that are configured incorrectly continue to cause this type of error.

Local vs. Fully Qualified Addresses

As a general convenience, mailers on many systems let you specify a local user by using the user's mail address without a domain suffix. For example, if you are sending mail to jack@tic.com and you are sending the message from a machine within the tic.com domain, you can simply address the message to jack. You could have used the address with the domain part appended: jack@tic.com. The domain part of the address (to the right of the @ sign) is known as a *fully qualified domain name (FQDN)* in network mail parlance. An address with an FQDN is guaranteed to be unique within the entire Matrix, while an address with an unqualified domain name is only guaranteed to be unique within a specific domain. For example, there could also be a jack@utexas.edu or a jack@bigco.com. It is the domain part of the address that distinguish all these "jacks" from one another.

In general, most mail systems know that an address without a domain part should be delivered to a user within the local system. This is a convenient shorthand and saves having to type the entire, and much longer, FQDN address. It is just like sending a paper memo to one of your officemates. When you do that, you rarely have to specify the full postal address of your office. Instead, you just specify the local address, which is usually a room number or perhaps a departmental mail drop. This shorthand saves time, but can lead to some perplexing problems if a mail system is badly configured.

```
From: smoot
To: jill@bigu.edu
cc: jack
Subject: meeting scheduled for tomorrow

There is a meeting scheduled for tomorrow at 11:00.  Please be
there on time

Smoot
```

Figure 8.7 Carbon Copy Message

Carbon Copies to the Rest of the World

Now suppose you send a message to jill@bigu.edu. and a carbon copy to jack. The message is shown in Figure 8.7 as it is originally sent. As explained in an earlier chapter, the mailer may add some other headers, such as `Received:` lines. For brevity, these are not shown in this discussion; only the pertinent address headers are shown.

This message, when sent to Jack, will leave all the addresses in the header just the way they are in the original message. When Jack receives the message and then later tries to reply to the message, the system can use all the header addresses just the way they are to generate correct addresses for the reply message, A message sent back to Smoot will be sent to smoot@tic.com, since both Jack and Smoot are both within the tic.com domain. A message sent to Jill is sent to her FQDN address jill@bigu.edu.

Now when this message is received by Jill, the unqualified header address smoot will not work from Jill's point of view outside of the tic.com domain. Neither will the address jack. Each of these header addresses must be fully qualified when the message leaves the tic.com domain.

This problem is similar to that of mailing an office memo to someone outside your organization. When the person outside the organization reads the memo and the list of people it was sent to in the memo header, that person cannot just reply to the addresses in the memo, but must understand whether all the addresses are internal to the company, division, etc. Usually this information can be derived by knowing where the sender sent the memo from. For a

```
From: smoot
To: jill@bigu.edu
cc: jack
Received: from akasha.tic.com by cc.bigu.edu (5.65/bigusendmail.1.9)
    id AA13974; Thu, 17 Mar 94 16:52:15 -0600
Received: by akasha.tic.com (5.65/sub.1.6)
    id AA01370; Thu, 17 Mar 94 16:52:12 -0600
Subject: meeting scheduled for tomorrow

There is a meeting scheduled for tomorrow at 11:00.  Please be
there on time

Smoot
```

Figure 8.8 Carbon Copy Message

paper mail reply, we are usually smart enough to figure out the addressing context. But mail programs are not quite as smart, so a properly configured mail system rewrites unqualified header addresses by adding the correct domain to them, thus making the context clear and unambiguous. The address **smoot** gets turned into **smoot@tic.com** and the address **jack** gets turned into **jack@tic.com**. Most mail systems do this kind of address rewriting.

Now, suppose the system does not rewrite header addresses. No harm is done when the message is sent to Jack; all the addresses are still correct because Jack receives the message within the **tic.com** domain. Poor Jill, on the other hand, gets a message with unqualified addresses and will not be able to successfully reply to the message. At best, she will get an unknown address error message when she sends a reply. Worse, suppose there is a legitimate user with a mail address of **jack** within the **bigu.edu** domain. When Jill replies to the message, it will be sent to the incorrect Jack! With the unqualified address, Jill's mailer thinks the message should be sent to a local user with a name of **jack**.

The only way to really tell where a message with unqualified headers came from is to carefully examine the `Received:` lines in the mail header. Figure 8.8 shows the message as received by Jill. As you can see, the received lines indicates that the message was sent from a machine within the **tic.com** domain. This gives you a clue that the sender is not local and the header addresses have not been fully qualified. At this point Jill should complain to the

```
From: smoot
To: jency@smallco.com
Subject: another message
cc: jack
```

Figure 8.9 Two Hop Message as Sent

Postmaster within the tic.com domain, saying the mail system is not doing header address rewriting correctly.

Intermediate Hops

The previous example of a bounce created by incorrect header addresses is generally fairly easy to track down. To add a bit of complexity to the issue, suppose the message without fully qualified addresses passes through an intermediate mail gateway. This is commonly done to forward mail to another mail system that is not a part of the Internet. Suppose the message in Figure 8.9 is sent to jency@smallco.com, and that smallco.comhas mailgate.com, This message, like the one in the previous example, is sent without fully qualified addresses. Suppose the mail system on the gateway within the mailgate.com domain does fully qualify any unqualified addresses. The message will be sent to Jency, and will look like Figure 8.10 when it arrives. Now things are even more confused! When Jency sends a reply to Jack, it goes to jack@mailgate.com.

To make matters worse, some mail software adds the domain part to an address in the `To:` header line, but not in the `cc:` header line. In this case messages sent without carbon copy recipients work just fine, but those with carbon copy recipients are incorrect! This causes all reply messages sent to the carbon copy addresses to bounce. Hence the generic name for this type of mail system problem.

```
From: smoot@mailgate.com
To: jency@smallco.com
Subject: another message
cc: jack@mailgate.com
```

Figure 8.10 Two Hop Message as Received

Most mail systems on the Internet are properly configured to rewrite header addresses so that systems at any other location can reply to them. You should be aware of this problem, since it is an error system administrators of new sites commonly make when they first get their mail system connected. If you ever receive mail messages that look like any of these examples report them to the appropriate Postmaster. That is, send mail to the postmaster of the original domain from which the message came. Be sure to include a copy of the erroneous message.

Most mail systems on the Internet do not have this FQDN problem, but some do, and you will encounter it. Examining this problem also gives you a practical feel for the distributed nature of mail transfer on the Internet and in the Matrix.

Mailing Lists and Errors

Some errors may seem rather mysterious. In all the examples we have shown so far, you can find the actual mistyped recipient address in the header of the original message. Take a look at Figure 8.11. Here the message was sent to what seems like a single address: eff-austin. However, the message bounced with several bad addresses. These addresses are not anywhere in the original message header. What is going on here? In this case several errors occurred when delivering the message. Two recipient addresses failed and two were deferred. But where did these mail addresses come from?

You can surmise that the original recipient address, eff-austin is really an alias for a larger list of addresses, as we will discuss in Chapter 9, *Mailing List Basics*. So, the system tried to send a message to each of the recipient addresses in the larger list in turn, and several of them failed to be delivered. Whenever the original address in the message header is different than the addresses shown in the error transcript, you can assume that the original address is an alias.

```
Received: from akasha.tic.com by xfrsparc.tic.com (5.65/sub.1.6)
    id AA09454; Mon, 21 Feb 94 18:42:09 -0600
Received: by akasha.tic.com (5.65/akasha.m4.1.15)
    id AA01769; Mon, 21 Feb 94 18:30:53 -0600
Date: Mon, 21 Feb 94 18:30:53 -0600
From: Mailer-Daemon@tic.com (Mail Delivery Subsystem)
Subject: Returned mail: Deferred: Connection timed out \
    during user open with s_bridge.rehab.texas.gov
Message-Id: <9402220030.AA01769@akasha.tic.com>
To: owner-eff-austin-list@tic.com

    ----- Transcript of session follows -----
421 zero.cypher.com.tcp... Deferred: Connection time out \
    during user open with zero.cypher.com
550 Greg Walker <walker@asc.slb.com>... Host unknown
>>> RCPT To:<jthiebes@selway.umt.edu>
<<< 550 <jthiebes@selway.umt.edu>... Addressee unknown
550 Joseph J Thiebes <jthiebes@selway.umt.edu>... User unknown
421 s_bridge.rehab.texas.gov.tcp... Deferred: Connection timed out \
    during user open with s_bridge.rehab.texas.gov

    ----- Unsent message follows -----
Received: by akasha.tic.com (5.65/akasha.m4.1.15)
    id AA01762; Mon, 21 Feb 94 18:30:53 -0600
Date: Mon, 21 Feb 94 18:30:53 -0600
From: riddle@is.rice.edu (Prentiss Riddle)
Subject: Carpool from Houston to Austin for Robofest? (ORGANIZER WANTED)
Message-Id: <1994Feb22.003045.1707@tic.com>
To: eff-austin

Robofest 5, the Austin Robot Group's annual extravaganza, will be held
.
.
.
```

Figure 8.11 Redistribution Error

How to Complain

Some errors you can deal with directly. You can correct a mistyped
mail address and resend the original message. But who do you
complain to when the mailing system itself fails? Fortunately, most
sites have a well known mail address called appropriately,
postmaster. This address is usually aliased to the real person in
charge of maintaining the mail system at that site. So if a message
bounces (for any reason other than that of unknown user), send a
copy of the bounced message to the postmaster at the site that

bounced the message. You can delete the body of the original message to shorten the message and to delete private correspondence you really do not want others to read. The postmaster needs only the header of the original message in order to track down mail system errors. Always try to send the message to the postmaster at the bounce site first, but if the message to that postmaster fails, send the bounce message to your local postmaster, if you have one. He or she may be able to track down the person responsible for the mailing system more easily than you can.

Sometimes you may even want to tell the remote postmaster about an unknown user error. For example, someone may have told you their electronic mail address over the telephone, and you may have mistranscribed it. The remote site's postmaster may be able to help you find the correct username. See also Chapter 13, *Finding People*.

You can handle an unknown user or unknown host error in one of two ways, depending on the type of error.

1. If you are responsible for knowing the mailing address of the recipient, try to solve the addressing problem yourself, as we have already discussed.

2. If you get an unknown user or unknown host error when sending a message to a mailing list, forward the bounce message to the list owner. This is usually the name of the list followed by the string -owner. So, a bounce message when sending to the list biglist@somesite.com should be sent to biglist-owner@somesite.com.

If this does not work, the list is not set up in accordance with standard Internet conventions. (We explain some other list conventions in Chapter 10, *Uses of Mailing Lists*). Try sending the message to the postmaster at that site with an explanation of why you sent the message. Most lists are set up to send bounce messages to the person responsible for the list. However, there are some circumstances in which the system sends the bounce message to you instead of to the person who maintains the list.

Summary

Now you know not to panic when you hear from MAILER-DAEMON, and how to interpret bounce messages. You even know what to do to fix the most common mail delivery errors, namely, retype a mistype user name or host name and resend the message. You can interpret some rather complicated error conditions, and you know when to forward a bounce message in a complaint, and which ones to ignore. Now that you know the practical details of using mail to a single person or a few people, the next chapter will introduce you to mailing lists.

9

Mailing List Basics

How do you subscribe to a mailing list? How do you post a message to it? And how do you get off it once you are on it? Conventions or customs for these and other common operations on mailing lists have evolved over the years. We prefer to call them conventions rather than customs, because if you violate a custom you usually just get laughed at, but if you don't follow list subscription conventions, usually you don't get on the list. But don't worry: they're easy to learn.

In this chapter, we describe common conventions for mailing lists. We start with the simplest but least recommended method of distributing a message to many people, and end with the more sophisticated methods you will usually use.

Pseudo-Lists

In addition to real mailing lists, there are also at least three ways of sending a mail message to many people. We discuss these methods first in order to explain why they are not appropriate for most mailing lists.

Multiple Addressees

You can send a mail message to many people by putting all their addresses in `To:` or `Cc:` headers, as shown in Figure 9.1. This method produces ugly mail, because every recipient sees all those addresses cluttering up the screen.

It is also messy, because people will (count on it!) reply to the message without looking to see where the reply goes. Such a reply may go to the original sender only, but it might go to everyone listed in the original message, with everyone listed again in the `Cc:` header of the reply. However, some of those people may not get the reply message at all, because the respondent's local mail user agent may not be able to handle that many addresses. Also, some of the addresses may not be fully qualified domains.

Worse, even domain addresses may have to be spelled differently depending on the local network, host, MTA, and UA. For example, if you are sending from a DECNET network, you may have to add a prefix, and maybe quotation marks, as in IN%"interesting@zilker.net" or SMTP%"interesting@zilker.net",

```
From: mememe@bigcom.com
To: joe@bigco.com, jane@smallu.edu, kali@sariswati.co.in,
    toru@there.co.jp, another@whoever.oz.au,
    somebody@southpole.aq, etc@informatik.uni-dortumund.de,
    "xyzy::phlugh"@dechost.digital.com, a!b!yo@forward.sf.ca.us,
    Speaker.Mort@f1.n13.z23.fidonet.org,
    long!boring!list!of!hosts!jill@gateway.berkeley.edu,
    boris@success.msk.ru, else@northpole.gl,
    123-5678@compuserve.com,876-1234@aol.com,
    jack@tic.com,jane@fumar.rtp.nc.us
Subject: Important News for January

Continuing our story from last month....
```

Figure 9.1 Multiple Addresses (Not Recommended)

depending on the UA or MTA you are using on your host. And some MTAs on the Internet *still* don't know how to handle the *MX records* that permit domain addresses to refer to hosts outside the Internet, even though that facility was specified in 1986. So, even a perfectly good domain address may fail from some machines.

Finally, you don't want to have to type in all those addresses every time you send a message to all those people.

A Local Alias

In Chapter 5, *The Basics*, we discussed how to create a local alias. A local alias really should be used to provide you with a brief mnemonic for a single address. But you can also put a list of addresses in a local alias, as in the example shown in Figure 9.2. Then when you send mail to that alias, your message will be sent to all the addresses listed in the alias.

But when you use a local alias, all it does is put the whole list of addresses in the outgoing mail headers, just as if you had typed them all into the headers. So if you send mail like this:

```
To: busypeople
Subject: more time saving hints

Use a local alias to avoid typing!
```

The alias in Figure 9.2 will simply produce a message just like the one seen in Figure 9.1. A local alias can save you some typing, but it still has all the defects just mentioned for long lists of addresses. Therefore we don't recommend using local aliases to construct mailing lists.

```
busypeople: joe@bigco.com, jane@smallu.edu, kali@sariswati.co.in,
    toru@there.co.jp, another@whoever.oz.au,
    somebody@southpole.aq, etc@informatik.uni-dortumund.de,
    "xyzy::phlugh"@dechost.digital.com, a!b!yo@forward.sf.ca.us,
    Speaker.Mort@f1.n13.z23.fidonet.org,
    long!boring!list!of!hosts!jill@gateway.berkeley.edu,
    boris@success.msk.ru, else@northpole.gl,
    123-5678@compuserve.com,876-1234@aol.com,
    jack@tic.com,jane@fumar.rtp.nc.us
```

Figure 9.2 A Long Local Alias (Not Recommended)

Sending Many Times

Another method of distributing mail to many addresses is to write a small program that takes a list of addresses and simply sends a separate message to each one. This kind of distribution is useful for sending out membership mailings or newsletters, because each message can have a `To:` header referring to a specific recipient.

In addition, replies will not go to the whole group, since the message copies do not contain addresses for the whole group. Instead, replies typically go only to the address in the `From:` header, and perhaps also to the original recipient. You may also choose to add further headers to the outgoing message copies. For example, putting in a `Reply-To:` header can help ensure that responses go to the right place.

This option of using a program to send an individual copy of a mail to each person is, of course, only available to users whose systems have facilities for writing programs, which many systems with menu-driven interfaces do not. It is not an approach you would want to use for most mailing lists, anyway. For example, you want many responses to go to everybody; you just don't want everybody's addresses in the headers. A real mailing list solves these problems.

Mailing Lists

Real mailing lists avoid typing everybody's addresses or having to have them in the headers of each message. Yet a real list permits anyone to respond easily to the whole list. Here are the major features of mailing lists and how to use them.

Subscribing and Unsubscribing

See Figure 9.2 for the two most common conventions for posting and subscription addresses, which are those of the Internet and of BITNET. No matter where you are in the Matrix, whether on UUCP, FidoNet, WWIVnet, a commercial mail network, a commercial conferencing system, a local LAN, or elsewhere, you can subscribe to Internet and BITNET lists.

the Internet	BITNET
To post:	
To: info-nets@think.com	To: INFONETS@BITNIC.BITNET
Subject: a new idea	Subject: a new idea
Not heard before!	Never before heard!
To subscribe:	
To: info-nets-request@think.com	To: LISTSERV@BITNIC.BITNET
Subject: subscribe info-nets	Subject: subscribe INFONETS
Please subscribe me.	SUB INFONETS Joe R. User
To unsubscribe:	
To: info-nets-request@think.com	To: LISTSERV@BITNIC.BITNET
Subject: unsubscribe info-nets	Subject: unsubscribe INFONETS
Please unsubscribe me.	UNSUB INFONETS

Table 9.1 Mailing List Conventions

Most electronic mailing lists have these components:

- a name, such as interesting

- a distribution address, such as interesting@zilker.net
  You send a message to this address to post to the list, and software distributes the message to an associated *distribution list.*

- a subscription address, such as interesting-request@zilker.net, or
  perhaps majordomo@zilker.net or listserv@zilker.net
  You send a message to this address when you want to join or
  leave the list. If you don't know which of the various possibilities
  of subscription address to use, use the `-request` form, since it's
  the most likely to work.

The subscription alias is almost never the same as the posting
alias. Many new users find it difficult to grasp the concept of two
aliases for the same mailing list. If there was only one alias, all subscribers to the list would have to see every request from a user to
join or leave the list. There is no point in anyone but the person (or
program) responsible for handling subscriptions seeing all these

requests. For this reason, the functions of distributing messages to a mailing list and of maintaining the distribution list are visibly separated into two different mail aliases, so you have to remember which address to use when sending mail related to a list.

Types of Lists

Every list has a *list owner,* who is responsible for maintaining the list. The list owner keeps the basic mechanics of the list working. This may involve updating informational messages, tracking down problems with addresses on the list, and removing bad addresses if necessary. Many other properties of lists are optional. Many of them are listed in Table 9.2 and discussed in this section.

Most lists are *autoposted.* Submissions are automatically forwarded to the list by software, without human intervention.

A list may instead be *moderated.* When you send a message to a moderated list, it is not automatically distributed to the list. Instead, it is sent to the *moderator,* and it is called a *submission.* The moderator may *accept* your submission and post it to the list for all subscribers to see. The moderator may also annotate your submission before posting it. Or the moderator may *reject* your submission. In this case, the moderator typically sends the message back to you with a reason for rejection.

Most lists are *open* and anyone may subscribe. Some lists are managed manually, and when you subscribe to such a list there may be a delay of hours or days until the list owner (or, for a moderated list, possibly the moderator) adds you. Other open lists have software to handle subscription requests, and if you subscribe to such a list, you will be added automatically, although there will still be a time lag, however brief, while your subscription request gets to the list management software and its reply returns to you.

Other lists are *closed,* and subscription requests must be approved. The list owner typically performs that function, although for a moderated list the moderator may do so.

Many lists are *public,* and anyone may retrieve information about the list, including the addresses of its subscribers. Other lists are *private,* and only subscribers can retrieve information about

Type	Description
autoposting	postings are distributed automatically by software
moderated	postings must be approved by the moderator
open	anyone can subscribe, perhaps automatically
closed	subscriptions must be approved by the moderator or list owner
public	anyone can see who subscribes
private	only subscribers can see who subscribes

Table 9.2 Types of Mailing Lists

them. Some lists are so private only subscribers can post to them. This idea of public and private lists is unrelated to the idea of open and closed lists.

A summary of these types of mailing lists is shown in Table 9.2. A list may be moderated regardless of whether it is open or closed, private or public. A list always has a list owner, regardless of whether it has a moderator, and even if it is open. If a list is moderated, the moderator and the list owner may be the same person, but don't have to be. With a moderated list, the moderator decides which submissions to accept for distribution to subscribers. If the list is closed, the list owner typically decides which subscribers to put on the list, although if the list is moderated the list owner and the moderator may agree for the moderator to handle subscriptions. You don't have to worry about most of these details. The main thing is that someone is performing the functions of the list owner, and if necessary of the moderator.

Using Lists

Here, in detail, is how you subscribe to a list, send mail to it, unsubscribe from it, get information about it, and set options related to it.

Using Internet Lists

The Internet convention for creating a subscription alias for a list is to add -**request** to the local part of the list's posting alias. For example, the subscription alias for the list interesting@zilker.net is interesting-request@zilker.net. To unsubscribe from the interesting list, you would send a message containing an unsubscribe command to the same -**request** address, interesting-request@zilker.net.

Many lists have subscriptions handled by a human. For those, it is standard practice to include in the body of the request a message for the person who maintains the list, as in the examples in Table 9.2.

Many Internet lists now use software to handle subscriptions. Some of them use the -**request** convention, and others use a special alias at the same machine, such as majordomo@zilker.net. *Majordomo* is a program that automatically handles mailing list subscription requests. Most lists managed by Majordomo have a -**request** alias associated with them, but that alias just sends you information on how to use Majordomo. (Although Majordomo version 1.90 permits using of the -**request** alias to subscribe or unsubscribe from the list, as well as to perform some other commands.) When in doubt about what address to use to subscribe or unsubscribe to a list, always try the -**request** address first.

Here are the most common Majordomo commands, using the mailing list interesting@zilker.net as an example. We present the commands in complete examples of the mail message you would send to Majordomo, followed in each case by a description of the command.

help

```
To: majordomo@zilker.net

help
```

Tell Majordomo to send a helpful message listing its commands. The returned message also includes the version number for the responding Majordomo.

subscribe

```
To: majordomo@zilker.net
```

```
subscribe interesting
```

Subscribe to the list named **interesting**. For an open list, Majordomo handles subscriptions automatically. For a closed list, Majordomo forwards the subscription request to the list owner for approval.

```
To: majordomo@zilker.net
```

```
subscribe interesting jane@fumar.rtp.nc.us
```

Subscribe to the list using an address different from the one in the `From` header of your request. Note that the extra information is an electronic mail address, not a person's real name. If the address is different from that of the sender (this is a slight oversimplification), Majordomo forwards the subscription request to the list owner, even for an open list.

post

```
To: interesting@zilker.net
Subject: what's so interesting about this list?
```

```
I've read a dozen messages from it now, and none
of them were interesting!  What's so interesting?
```

The most basic function of a list of a mailing list is to distribute messages to its subscribers. Majordomo proper isn't directly involved in this function, and you don't send postings to Majordomo, rather to the posting address for the list, in this case, interesting@zilker.net. However, some software from the same package as Majordomo may be involved in rearranging headers in messages before they are posted, for example by adding:

```
Reply-To: interesting@zilker.net
```

For a moderated list, the list owner usually arranges for Majordomo to be involved in sending submissions to the moderator for approval, and in handling postings approved by the moderator.

When you post a message to a moderated list, you don't see any of the mechanics of how your message gets shuttled between Majordomo and the moderator; you just post to the usual address.

unsubscribe

```
To: majordomo@zilker.net

unsubscribe interesting
```

Unsubscribe from the list.

```
To: majordomo@zilker.net

unsubscribe interesting jane@fumar.rtp.nc.us
```

Unsubscribe a different address from the list.

info

```
To: majordomo@zilker.net

info interesting
```

Retrieve the general introductory information for the list. If the list is private and you are not a subscriber, Majordomo will send you an error message similar to that in Figure 9.3.

```
Return-Path: <majordomo-owner@zilker.net>
Date: Wed, 1 Jun 94 08:10:16 -0500
Message-Id: <9406011310.AA08034@oak.zilker.net>
To: you@bigco.com
From: majordomo@zilker.net
Subject: Majordomo results
Reply-To: majordomo@zilker.net

--

>>>> who interesting
**** List 'interesting' is a private list.
**** Only members of the list can do a 'who'.
**** You aren't a member of list 'interesting'.
```

Figure 9.3 A Private List

which

```
To: majordomo@zilker.net

which
```

Have this Majordomo server check the lists it runs and tell you which you subscribe to.

```
To: majordomo@zilker.net

which jane@fumar.rtp.nc.us
```

Find out which lists another user is subscribed to. Unlike for the who command , if the list is private and you are not a subscriber, Majordomo does not send you an error message. Instead it silently ignores that list and does not mention it in its report to you.

lists

```
To: majordomo@zilker.net

lists
```

Find out which lists are served by this Majordomo server.

who

```
To: majordomo@zilker.net

who interesting
```

Find out who is on the list. If the list is private and you are not a subscriber, Majordomo will send you an error message similar to that in Figure 9.3.

end

```
To: majordomo@zilker.net

help
end

Jane R. User
jane@fumar.rtp.nc.us
```

Tell Majordomo not to read further in the message past the *end*, so it will ignore any signature that follows. In this example, Majordomo will read and obey the *help* command, and then read and obey the *end* command.

Using BITNET Lists

A BITNET list has a posting alias, for example this one: INFONETS@LISTSERV.NET. However, the subscription alias is not directly related to the posting alias, and may not even be on the same machine. Instead, you send mail to a pseudo-user named LISTSERV, such as LISTSERV@LISTSERV.NET. *LISTSERV* is a program that automatically handles subscription requests. In addition, LISTSERV also supports the Internet convention of appending -request to the list name to form a subscription address, such as INFONETS-REQUEST@LISTSERV.NET. When in doubt about how to subscribe or unsubscribe, always try the -request address first, regardless of whether you know the list is run by LISTSERV, Majordomo, other software, or manually.

Some people, especially in academic circles, use the term LISTSERV as a synonym for a mailing list of any kind. We find that usage confusing, and when we write LISTSERV we mean the BITNET program that handles some mailing lists.

You can actually send your subscription or unsubscription message to any of several BITNET hosts running LISTSERV, such as UGA.UGA.EDU or LISTSERV.NET. LISTSERV commands go in the body of the message, not in the Subject: header. They are case-insensitive, that is, SUB, Sub, and sub are all the same LISTSERV command. You can also abbreviate any LISTSERV command as long as it does not become so short it could be confused with another LISTSERV command. For example, SUB is really short for SUBSCRIBE.

Here are some examples of the most common LISTSERV commands. The examples use a nonexistent list named LISTNAME, and a user who also does not exist (although she may be on one of the Majordomo lists we've already used as examples). We present the commands in complete examples of the mail message you would send to LISTSERV, followed in each case by a description of the command.

help

```
To: LISTSERV@LISTSERV.NET

help
```

Tell LISTSERV to mail back a helpful message listing its commonly used commands. The returned message also includes the version number for the responding LISTSERV.

subscribe

```
To: LISTSERV@LISTSERV.NET

SUB LISTNAME Jane R. User
```

You must supply both the name of the list and your own real name (not your address). This real name information is not optional: you must supply it. LISTSERV uses the address for you it finds in the `From:` header of your message. Actually, since LISTSERV version 1.8a of December 1993, LISTSERV will also look in the `From:` header for your real name if you do not supply it with the `SUB` command. However, it is safer to go ahead and supply your real name with the `SUB` command.

post

```
To: LISTNAME@LISTSERV.NET
Subject: strange list

This is a strange list.  I've read the
information about it, and postings in it,
but I still can't figure out what it's for.
```

To post to the list, send mail to the actual list address, not to LISTSERV.

unsubscribe

```
To: LISTSERV@LISTSERV.NET

UNSUB LISTNAME
```

To unsubscribe, you do not need to supply your name. LISTSERV checks the `From:` header of your message and removes the mail address it finds there from the distribution list.

info

```
To: LISTSERV@LISTSERV.NET

INFO LISTNAME
```

Return a description of the list. If the list owner hasn't supplied an info message, LISTSERV returns the list header, which usually contains a short description of the list.

list

```
To: LISTSERV@LISTSERV.NET

List
```

Get a description of all lists served by this LISTSERV. You can subscribe to any LISTSERV list by sending mail to any LISTSERV, but each LISTSERV actually only serves some, not all, LISTSERV lists.

```
To: LISTSERV@LISTSERV.NET

LIST GLOBAL
```

Get a description of every list served by all LISTSERVs. You may need a bit of disk space to hold the answer to this command.

```
To: LISTSERV@LISTSERV.NET

LIST GLOBAL /XYZ
```

List every list on all LISTSERVs that has the string XYZ in its name or address.

review

```
To: LISTSERV@LISTSERV.NET

REView listname
```

Review a list, that is, get the names and addresses of its subscribers. If a list is private, only its subscribers can review it.

stats

```
To: LISTSERV@LISTSERV.NET

STats listname
```

Review list statistics.

query

```
To: LISTSERV@LISTSERV.NET

Query listname
```

Query personal distribution options, such as whether LISTSERV will send you a copy of a message you post to the list.

set

```
To: LISTSERV@LISTSERV.NET

SET listname options
```

Set personal distribution options. To find out what options you can set, send a `query` command first.

To unsubscribe from a LISTSERV list, you must send a message from the same machine you used to subscribe, or at least from a machine that will produce an identical address in the `From:` header of your request. If you have moved to a different machine (perhaps that's why you want to unsubscribe), you can send mail to the list owner and ask for manual unsubscription. The owner of a LISTSERV list is usually named in the response to a `review` command.

Exploders

Big mailing lists tend to have subscribers in many geographical locations and on many different networks. Often it is convenient to have the main list feed several subsidiary lists in certain countries or on certain networks. Such a subsidiary list is called an *exploder*. If a list has exploders on several different networks, such as the Internet and BITNET, you should subscribe to the list through the exploder on your network.

Unfortunately, this means a single list can involve *both* Internet and BITNET conventions for subscriptions. For example, info-nets@think.com is redistributed on BITNET as INFONETS. So, if you want to subscribe to info-nets and you are on the Internet (or UUCP, or FidoNet, or almost any other network or conferencing system in the Matrix), you should use the Internet convention and send mail to info-nets-request@think.com. But if you're on BITNET, you should use the BITNET convention and send mail to LISTSERV@BITNIC (or LISTSERV@UGA, or one of the other LISTSERV hosts). As a BITNET user you could subscribe to the exploder at think.com using the Internet convention, but that would destroy the advantage of having an exploder on BITNET for this list.

Yet, regardless of how you subscribe, you should always post messages to the list by sending mail to info-nets@think.com, not to INFONETS@BITNIC.BITNET. This is because mail to the BITNET posting address will only reach BITNET subscribers, while mail to the Internet address will reach everyone on the list.

Other lists might be set up with the reverse convention. It depends on the list; usually such details will be spelled out in an introductory message when you join the list. Both Majordomo and LISTSERV permit you to retrieve that message at any time; Major-domo recognizes the `info` command for this, and LISTSERV recognizes the `REVIEW` command.

If you previously subscribed to a private list from an address different from the one you are currently using, you may have a difficult time getting off the list, since you will probably need to send mail to the owner of the list. As we have mentioned, you can usually find out who owns a LISTSERV list by sending a LISTSERV a REVIEW command for that list. But in this case LISTSERV will not believe you are a subscriber to the list, since you are posting from an address not found in the list, and so LISTSERV will not let you review the list. One thing to try might be to send a message to POSTMAST@LISTHOST, where LISTHOST is the name of the posting host for the list, and asking for the name of the list owner. The simplest way, however, is to send mail to LISTNAME-REQUEST@LISTHOST since LISTSERV does support the -request convention.

Which Convention is Best?

We provide a summary of common Majordomo and LISTSERV commands in Table 9.3, so that you can choose the appropriate command for the list.

Internet users and BITNET users each say their convention is best, just as Americans and British say hood or bonnet for the part of a car that covers the engine. There's no accounting for taste, but online you will find yourself participating in the national customs of many different networks. If you drive on the right when you should drive on the left, you may not get where you want to go. BITNET is small and shrinking, but LISTSERVs are used by many people on other networks, including the Internet. Internet lists are also used far beyond the Internet. Neither the Internet nor the BITNET convention is more "normal" than the other; most preferences are based on familiarity.

However, LISTSERV long provided capabilities not available on the Internet, starting with automatic subscription request capabilities, and continuing through retrieval of messages from mailing list archives. It is possible to simulate many of the features of LISTSERV through ad hoc use of other Internet facilities. For example, you can retrieve archives via info-servers or anonymous FTP. However, some basic features, such as automatic subscription and unsubscription, have not been available by any other means. There are now several packages that implement parts of LISTSERV on UNIX, for use with TCP/IP. But none of them are complete, and

Majordomo	LISTSERV
To: majordomo@zilker.net help	To: listserv@listserv.net help
To: majordomo@zilker.net subscribe interesting	To: listserv@listserv.net sub listname Joe R. User
To: majordomo@zilker.net unsubscribe interesting	To: listserv@listserv.net unsub listname
To: majordomo@zilker.net info interesting	To: listserv@listserv.net info interesting
To: majordomo@zilker.net which	To: listserv@listserv.net query *
To: majordomo@zilker.net lists	To: listserv@listserv.net list
	To: listserv@listserv.net list global
To: majordomo@zilker.net who interesting	To: listserv@listserv.net review listname
	To: listserv@listserv.net stats listname
	To: listserv@listserv.net set listname options

To: majordomo@zilker.net
end

Table 9.3 Mailing List Commands

there is no widespread network of LISTSERVs on the Internet. The most widespread package of this type appears to be Majordomo, which we have already described.

Majordomo's basic functions are similar to LISTSERV's, but the two programs differ in many ways. For example, there is a network of communicating LISTSERVs, but there is no network of Majordomos. To subscribe to a list that is run by Majordomo, you must know the exact domain name for that particular Majordomo, not for some other Majordomo.

When you post a message to an Internet mailing list, the list typically sends the message to everyone on the list, including you. Some people are surprised when they see their own message come back from a mailing list after they post it. Most Internet mailing lists do this; it's just normal procedure, not an error. Why should the mailing list software make a point of eliminating that one address from that particular mailing? Also, it may not even be possible for the software to do so, since you may be subscribed to the list from a different address than the one from which you are posting the message. Getting a copy of your own message also gives you confirmation that the message went out to the list. Most people like this feature.

LISTSERV, on the other hand, normally does not return a copy of the message to the poster. This seems to confuse new users who wonder if their posting went anywhere. Evidently you can't please everybody.... LISTSERV can look at a BITNET configuration table to equate BITNET hostnames such as UGA with their domain equivalents, like UGA.UGA.EDU. This makes it easy for LISTSERV to eliminate the copy of a message destined for the original poster. It is also possible to configure LISTSERV to send the message anyway, by using the SET command we have already mentioned.

The distinctions between Internet lists and BITNET lists have become very blurred, not only because the vast majority of subscribers to BITNET lists are not BITNET users. We have already mentioned that most BITNET lists now have -request subscription addresses and many Internet lists use majordomo@domain subscription addresses. Most importantly, not all LISTSERVs run on BITNET anymore. For example, LISTSERV@RICEVM1.RICE.EDU is the address of a LISTSERV that is not on BITNET at all, and does not use the BITNET NJE protocols anymore. Instead, RICEVM1.RICE.EDU is on the Internet, but it does run a real LISTSERV, not an imitation. Most LISTSERVS do still run on IBM mainframes, but even that is changing, since there is now a version of LISTSERV that runs on VMS and UNIX systems. However, there is still a clear concept of a LISTSERV list, or a Majordomo list.

If someone has given you the BITNET hostname of a LISTSERV or other BITNET host, and you want to find the Internet domain for

```
Return-Path: <@UGA.CC.UGA.EDU:LISTSERV@UGA.CC.UGA.EDU>
Received: from uga.cc.uga.edu by akasha.tic.com (5.65/akasha.m4.1.16
    id AA02449; Sun, 1 May 94 23:45:44 -0500
Message-Id: <9405020445.AA02449@akasha.tic.com>
Received: from UGA.CC.UGA.EDU by uga.cc.uga.edu (IBM VM SMTP V2R2)
    with BSMTP id 6818; Mon, 02 May 94 00:46:58 EDT
Received: from UGA.CC.UGA.EDU (NJE origin LISTSERV@UGA)
    by UGA.CC.UGA.EDU (LMail V1.1d/1.7f) with BSMTP id 3266;
    Mon, 2 May 1994 00:46:52 -0400
Date:          Mon, 2 May 1994 00:46:52 -0400
From: BITNET list server at UGA (1.7f) <LISTSERV@uga.cc.uga.edu>
Subject:       Output of your job "jsq"
To: jsq@TIC.COM


> show alias uga
UGA is also known as UGA.CC.UGA.EDU and UGA.UGA.EDU.

Summary of resource utilization
-------------------------------
 CPU time:        0.041 sec          Device I/O:      7
 Overhead CPU:    0.005 sec          Paging I/O:      0
 CPU model:       9021               DASD model:   3380
```

Figure 9.4 Domain Names for BITNET Hosts

that host, you can ask any LISTSERV by sending mail like this:

To: listserv@uga.uga.edu

show alias uga

You will get a response like that shown in Figure 9.4.

Note that in both the Internet and BITNET styles of mailing lists, a request for subscription or unsubscription goes in the *body* of the message, not in the `Subject:` header. However, at least for the traditional Internet manual subscription method through a -**request** address, and sometimes for other methods, it is polite to include a `Subject:` header describing what you want, as in:

```
To: interesting-request@zilker.net
Subject: subscribe to interesting@zilker.net

Please subscribe me to interesting@zilker.net.
```

Remember that if you want to join or leave a list, send mail to the subscription address, not to the posting address.

When a Message Bounces

We've already discussed errors and bounce messages in Chapter 8. An error message can originate from any MTA anywhere a copy of a message for a mailing list goes. Just as a copy of a newsletter may be returned from a distant post office, bounce messages usually originate at a machine close to a final destination address, not at the machine that distributes the list. It would be good if the machine producing the bounce message knew to send errors to the mailing list owner. Unfortunately, since mail through the Matrix often goes to places that do not understand RFC822 and other conventions for redirecting error messages, this does not always happen. Sometimes errors get sent to the original sender of the message, rather than to the list owner.

Learn to recognize the most common types of bounce messages, such as `Unknown user` and `Unknown host` so that you can distinguish them from warnings. Warnings usually have `warning` in the `Subject:` header or body or include a key word like `Deferred` in the body.

Also remember that if one copy of your message bounces, this does not mean that all the other copies bounced, any more than one copy of a paper newsletter being returned by one post office means that none of the copies were delivered.

It is useful to complain about bounces to the list owner. If you do so, include a copy of the bounce message. You may not be able to interpret the error messages it contains, but the list owner probably can. Without it, there's not much the list owner can do. Clues to mail errors are often contained in the path used to distribute mail, and this path is recorded in the bounce message, in the `Received` headers of the included original message. Many errors are caused by transient glitches like address cache lookup misses, machines being turned off overnight, dialup links that are incorrectly configured, etc. The bounce message often contains enough detail for the list owner to determine whether a problem is likely to recur, what its source is, and whether it's even a problem at all. If the list owner can't tell, sometimes a postmaster can, but usually only using information in the bounce message. So send the bounce message along with any complaint or query about a bounced message.

Managing a List

You may want to run your own mailing list. Given a list maintenance program such as LISTSERV or Majordomo, you can do this with minimal trouble, and without having to know much more technical material than is required for just using a list. Here we show how to manage a list using Majordomo.

First, get your system administrator to set up a list for you. Suppose you call it **yourlist**. You will be the list owner of **yourlist**. It can be either open or closed If the list is open, anyone can subscribe to it by using the Majordomo `subscribe` command we have already discussed. If the list is closed, subscription requests are forwarded to you, the list owner, for approval. You also get each subscription request for an address that doesn't match the `From:` line of the request message.

Your list will be public unless you tell the system administrator to make it private, so that nonsubscribers cannot retrieve information about it. Actually, Majordomo version 1.90 introduces a configuration file that the list owner can retrieve, modify, and mail back to Majordomo without the intervention of a system administrator. Control over the public or private nature of the list is included in the configuration file parameters.

Someone who wants to subscribe to the list, for example Jack Flash, with an address of jack@tic.com, sends a subscription request to the Majordomo address for the list domain:

```
Return-Path: <jack@tic.com>
Received: by oak.zilker.net (5.65/oak.m4.1.16)
    id AA12836; Mon, 2 May 94 17:59:05 -0500
From: Jack Flash <jack@tic.com>
To: majordomo@zilker.net

subscribe yourlist
```

Figure 9.5 A Subscription Request as Majordomo Sees It

```
Return-Path: <majordomo-owner@zilker.net>
Received: by oak.zilker.net (5.65/oak.m4.1.16)
    id AA12836; Mon, 2 May 94 17:59:05 -0500
Date: Mon, 2 May 94 17:59:05 -0500
Message-Id: <9405022259.AA12836@oak.zilker.net>
To: jack@tic.com
From: majordomo@zilker.net
Subject: Majordomo results
Reply-To: majordomo@zilker.net

--

>>>> subscribe yourlist
Your request to majordomo@zilker.net:

    subscribe yourlist jack@zilker.net
```

has been forwarded to the owner of the "yourlist" list for
approval. This could be for any of several reasons:

    You might have asked to subscribe to a "closed" list,
    where all new additions must be approved by the list owner.

    You might have asked to subscribe or unsubscribe an address
    other than the one that appears in the headers of your
    mail message.

When the list owner approves your request, you will be notified.

If you have any questions about the policy of the list owner,
please contact "yourlist-approval@zilker.net".

Thanks!

majordomo@zilker.net

Figure 9.6 Majordomo Subscription Acknowledgement

```
To: majordomo@zilker.net

subscribe yourlist
```

Once it arrives at the Majordomo for the list, it looks like Figure 9.5,
and Majordomo sends Jack a response that looks like Figure 9.6
when he sees it. The important part of Figure 9.5 is the From:
header, which is what Majordomo uses to know who to subscribe,
and who to send a message like Figure 9.6. If Jack didn't supply a
From: header, his mail system did it for him.

Meanwhile, if the list is closed or the From: in Jack's message
doesn't match the subscription address he gave, Majordomo sends

```
Return-Path: <majordomo-owner@zilker.net>
Received: by oak.zilker.net (5.65/oak.m4.1.16)
    id AA12837; Mon, 2 May 94 17:59:05 -0500
Date: Mon, 2 May 94 17:59:05 -0500
Message-Id: <9405022259.AA12837@oak.zilker.net>
To: yourlist-approval@zilker.net
From: majordomo@zilker.net
Subject: APPROVE yourlist
Reply-To: majordomo@zilker.net


--

jack@zilker.net requests that you approve the following:

    subscribe yourlist jack@tic.com

If you approve, please send a message such as the following
back to majordomo@zilker.net (with the appropriate PASSWORD
filled in, of course):

    approve PASSWORD subscribe yourlist jack@tic.com

If you disapprove, do nothing.

Thanks!

majordomo@zilker.net
```

Figure 9.7 Majordomo Subscription Request

you a message like the one shown in Figure 9.7. That message
spells out what you need to do to subscribe Jack to the list, if you
choose to do so. That is, you need to send a message like this:

```
To: majordomo@zilker.net

approve shazaam subscribe yourlist jack@tic.com
```

The word `shazaam` in this example is a password for yourlist,
which your system administrator assigned when the list was set up.
You can change the list password yourself, and you should; we'll
discuss how later.

Once you approve Jack's subscription request, Jack will get a
message like the one in Figure 9.8. Meanwhile, you will get one like
the one in Figure 9.9.

```
Return-Path: <majordomo-owner@zilker.net>
Date: Mon, 2 May 94 18:13:45 -0500
Message-Id: <9405022313.AA12966@oak.zilker.net>
To: jack@tic.com
From: majordomo@zilker.net
Subject: Welcome to yourlist
Reply-To: majordomo@zilker.net


--

Welcome to the yourlist mailing list!

If you ever want to remove yourself from this mailing list,
send the following command in email to "majordomo@zilker.net":

     unsubscribe yourlist jack@tic.com

Here's the general information for the list you've subscribed to,
in case you don't already have it:

A discussion list about a very interesting topic.
```

Figure 9.8 Majordomo Welcome Message

If the list was open or Jack's `From:` line address matched his subscription request address, Majordomo would have sent him a response like Figure 9.8 immediately, and it would have sent you one like Figure 9.10 at the same time.

If you want to change the password for **yourlist**, you can send a message to Majordomo like this:

```
To: majordomo@zilker.net
```

```
Return-Path: <majordomo-owner@zilker.net>
Date: Mon, 2 May 94 18:13:46 -0500
Message-Id: <9405022313.AA12970@oak.zilker.net>
To: yourlist-approval
From: majordomo@zilker.net
Subject: SUBSCRIBE yourlist
Reply-To: majordomo@zilker.net


--

>>> approve shazaam subscribe yourlist jack@tic.com
succeeded
```

Figure 9.9 Majordomo Approval Acknowledgement

```
Return-Path: <majordomo-owner@zilker.net>
Received: by oak.zilker.net (5.65/oak.m4.1.16)
    id AA12970; Mon, 2 May 94 18:13:46 -0500
Date: Mon, 2 May 94 18:13:46 -0500
Message-Id: <9405022313.AA12970@oak.zilker.net>
To: yourlist-approval
From: majordomo@zilker.net
Subject: SUBSCRIBE yourlist
Reply-To: majordomo@zilker.net

--

jack@tic.com has been added to yourlist.
No action is required on your part.
```

Figure 9.10 Majordomo Subscription Notification

```
passwd yourlist shazaam frobozz
```

Actually, you should pick a better password than that, even though the password in use is kept in clear text in a file and is passed across the network in clear text, and is thus not particularly secure. Don't use the name of your child, spouse, or pet as your password. Don't use the name of the list as a password. Try using the first letters of a verse from your favorite song, for example. At least be sure to use a *different* password than any you use for your login accounts.

```
Return-Path: <majordomo-owner@zilker.net>
Received: by oak.zilker.net (5.65/oak.m4.1.16)
    id AA13034; Mon, 2 May 94 18:20:20 -0500
Date: Mon, 2 May 94 18:20:20 -0500
Message-Id: <9405022320.AA13034@oak.zilker.net>
To: you@zilker.net
From: majordomo@zilker.net
Subject: Majordomo results
Reply-To: majordomo@zilker.net

--

>>>> passwd mailbook mightbe couldbe
Password changed.
```

Figure 9.11 Majordomo Password Change Acknowledgement

Assuming you gave the correct current password for the list, you receive an acknowledgment from Majordomo that the password has been changed, as shown in Figure 9.11.

Majordomo version 1.90 introduces a password for the configuration file. To change it you would first get the configuration file from Majordomo with this command:

```
To: majordomo@zilker.net

config yourlist shazamm
```

Then you would edit the configuration file and mail it back in a message like this:

```
To: majordomo@zilker.net

newconfig yourlist shazamm
[contents of configuration file go here]
EOF
```

The details differ from the older style Majordomo list password, but the same cautions apply for how to pick a password.

In the welcome message Majordomo sent to Jack, shown in Figure 9.12, this line at the end:

```
Return-Path: <majordomo-owner@zilker.net>
Received: by oak.zilker.net (5.65/oak.m4.1.16)
    id AA13166; Mon, 2 May 94 18:33:03 -0500
Date: Mon, 2 May 94 18:33:03 -0500
Message-Id: <9405022333.AA13166@oak.zilker.net>
To: you@zilker.net
From: majordomo@zilker.net
Subject: Majordomo results
Reply-To: majordomo@zilker.net

--

>>>> newinfo yourlist frobozz
New info for list yourlist accepted.
>>>> info yourlist

This list is for postings of real interesting stuff.

[Last updated Mon May  2 18:33:03 1994]
```

Figure 9.12 Majordomo New Information File Acknowledgement

```
A discussion list about a very interesting topic.
```

is the contents of the **info** file for the list. That file isn't very informative, so you may want to update it. You can do that by sending a message like this:

```
To: majordomo@zilker.net
```

```
newinfo yourlist frobozz
```

```
This list is for postings of real interesting stuff.
EOF
info list
```

You have to use the new password because you just changed it. The actual information for the **info** file follows the `newinfo` command line, and continues until the end of the message, or until a line that contains only the *End Of File (EOF)* terminator. The `EOF` marker prevents your signature from appearing in the **info** file unless you want it to. In this example, the `EOF` terminator appears, with another Majordomo command after the `EOF`:

```
info list
```

That command causes Majordomo to send the contents of the **info** file. So this one message will make Majordomo update the **info** file and then return its contents to you, as shown in Figure 9.12.

Summary

You now know how to use mailing lists, and even how to run one. You can use or even run a list from anywhere in the Matrix, using a Majordomo or LISTSERV anywhere in the Matrix. Now that you know the mechanics, let's discuss potential uses.

10

Uses of Mailing Lists

The best way to learn good uses of mailing lists is to use them. However, lists are often hard for new users to understand, because they look much like several traditional media, and are a little like each of them, yet at the same time have their own capabilities and etiquette. The fastest way to explain the unfamiliar is often to compare it to something familiar, so we start this chapter with analogies and examples.

Paper Newsletters

The simplest analogy for a mailing list is a paper newsletter. The names of these media make them sound completely different. You might think a mailing list is just a list of addresses, and a paper newsletter is just a piece of paper. But that's not true any more than a fire truck is just a truck. The important thing about a fire truck is that it is used to put out fires. It usually does that by delivering water. People are usually involved, too.

Similarities

A mailing list has associated content, namely the mail messages that are delivered through it. A paper newsletter has an associated distribution list. So an electronic mailing list and a paper newsletter each use a relatively fixed list of subscribers, and distribute messages to that list. People are also usually involved in the distribution.

As we discussed in Chapter 9, *Mailing List Basics*, most online lists are autoposted, but autoposting is practically impossible for a print medium. A paper newsletter also requires an editor. A mailing list may be moderated, and a moderator is much like a newsletter editor. So lets compare moderated moderated lists to paper newsletters. The differences between moderated lists and newsletters are more numerous than are the similarities.

Submissions

Even a moderated list normally includes far more material from outside writers than most newsletters include, and more than any newspaper does. A list is actually more like a newspaper consisting entirely of letters to the editor.

Submissions to a paper newsletter are almost always sent to a special address for the editor. Submissions for a moderated mailing list is ordinarily sent to an address that looks no different than the posting address for any other list, as shown in Figure 10.1. You can't tell whether or not a list is moderated by looking at the submission address. In fact, a list may shift back and forth from being

```
To: mailbook@tic.com
Subject: found a typo

On page 123 there is a typo in the figure;
it doesn't match the text.
```
Figure 10.1 A moderated list

moderated to being autoposted several times in its lifetime, or even several times in a day. This kind of flexibility is not practical for paper newsletters.

Distribution

To distribute a paper newsletter, someone must

- print it

- duplicate it

- staple it or stuff it in an envelope

- apply postage to it

- put it where the Post Office will pick it up

To distribute a message to an online mailing list, all you have to do is

- send the message to the appropriate distribution alias

Unless a moderator has to look at it first, software takes care of all the rest: no paper, no postage, no copying, no carrying. Even if the list is moderated, you don't need to do anything unless the moderator rejects your message; then you can rewrite it and resubmit it.

There are costs associated with distributing an online mailing list, but they are not usually of the same kind as for paper. Instead of applying a specific amount of postage to each copy according to the distance of its destination, most costs are usually absorbed in the price of the underlying external connection to the rest of the Matrix.

A paper mailing list usually has fixed distribution dates, such as once a month. An online mailing list can do that, too, or distribute each message as soon as it comes in.

Format

Material in a paper newsletter must be made to fit on printed pages. A message in an online list doesn't have to have page breaks at all.

Paper newsletters often have quite long articles. List readers generally prefer each message to be relatively short.

Online Newsletters

One use of a mailing list is to carry an *online newsletter,* which is a document compiled by an editorial process similar to that of a paper newsletter. For information about one example, send mail like this:

```
To: mids@tic.com
Subject: any subject will do.

Doesn't matter what the text of the message is.
```

An online newsletter tends to be like a paper newsletter in many ways, with more or less fixed distribution dates, a usual size per issue, and some sort of editing. But this is only one of many uses of mailing lists. Most online mailing lists do not carry newsletters.

A common kind of online newsletter is called a digest. A *digest* has a moderator who collects submissions to a mailing list until there are enough to fill a digest issue. The digest as sent is simply those submissions plus separators between them, and some front and back matter. An example of a digest is shown in Figure 10.2, shortened to fit on a page.

Some distributions of online newsletters are formatted with the intention of having subscribers print them. We call such a newsletter an *online paper newsletter.* Any online newsletter, like any online message, can be printed. But these online paper newsletters are designed to be read on paper, not online. For them, computer

```
From: mn-dist
Subject: Matrix News V4 N4 April 1994; ASCII Digest format
Matrix News              April 1994            Volume 4 Number 4
This is the ASCII online distribution of Matrix News, the monthly
newsletter of Matrix Information and Directory Services, Inc.
[more general description]
--------------------------------------------------------------------
From: mids@tic.com (Matrix, Inc.)
Subject: In This Issue
In This Issue
[list of contents]
------------------------------
From: mids@tic.com (Matrix, Inc.)
Subject: masthead
Contact Information
Matrix Information and Directory Services, Inc.
mids@tic.com
[addresses and such]
------------------------------
End of Matrix News V4 N4 April 1994; ASCII Digest format
***********************************************************
```

Figure 10.2 A Digest

networks are only used for distribution, not for reading.

If the newsletter is plain text, this seems rather counterproductive, since it is easier to find information of interest online than on paper. Newsletters with graphics, or long newsletters, may also seem better on paper, since online they take a lot of bandwidth, CPU time, and disk space. Even in those cases, online distribution still has advantages over paper distribution, such as speed and ease of worldwide distribution.

Face to Face Meetings

Suppose that instead of holding meetings you could communicate with the meeting participants online and not have to gather in the same room at the same time. Mailing lists can at least reduce the need for meetings, although they cannot completely replace most kinds of meetings.

Lack of Visual Cues

In a face to face meeting, you can see what everyone is doing. In a mailing list, you only get the words of one person at a time. You don't see the meeting chair leaning back and staring at the ceiling in boredom, or the two people in the corner whispering, or the lawyer suddenly shuffling notes. On the other hand, you aren't distracted by all that, either. Not to mention you can participate in a mailing list from your house before getting dressed to go to the office.

Before and After a Meeting

Reaching a decision in a mailing list is notoriously difficult, although it is possible, as we discuss in Chapter 11, *Mailing List Etiquette*. However, mailing lists are very useful for discussing real issues before and after face to face meetings. We often forget the advantages of mailing lists, such as:

- it is very easy to ask for clarification, either on the list or privately

- everyone can speak at once and be heard

- everyone does not have to be available at the same time

- participants can be geographically distributed

- the time frame can extend as long as necessary

- people can take time to think and research before responding

In addition, information received by email can make more of an impression than exactly the same words spoken in a meeting, since the mail message arrives asynchronously in the addressees' mailboxes. Such a message may stand out more than words spoken among many others on the same subject in a meeting.

Telephone

One of the first signs of a new mail user is when they say "why don't you just pick up the telephone and call?" The telephone is sometimes more appropriate than mail. But when you get used to mail, you'll use the telephone a lot less.

Asynchronicity

You don't have to get other people on the telephone at the same time. No more hours, days, or weeks wasted trying to make contact. No more *telephone tag*.

You don't have to answer mail the minute it comes in, the way you have to answer a ringing telephone. If everyone used mail for routing communications, we'd all have a lot fewer interruptions.

If you want to communicate with people in Austin, Osaka, and Kiev, you can do so through a mailing list. You are unlikely to get them all on the telephone at the same time very often, because of the differences in time zones.

If you are Scottish and you want to discuss a project with people who are Japanese and German, you will usually manage a lot better through a list than on the telephone, since most people can write a foreign language better than they can handle it verbally in real time.

Asking and answering questions takes longer in electronic mail than on the telephone, even if you have a fast network connection. The real delay is not so much in delivery of mail messages, as in waiting for the other person to read and reply. But that time is an advantage. On a list, everyone can take time to think, if they wish. In informal contexts, this can give you time to think of a witty rejoinder. In serious contexts, time to think can let you frame a more focused and meaningful message. Instead of saying "um" and rephrasing while talking, you can redraft your message until it says what you want it to say and then send it. Your message may thus be less likely to be ignored, and more likely to say what you mean.

Aural Cues

In a meeting or on the telephone, you hear the tone of voice and pacing of the person speaking. In a mailing list, you don't. Many people consider the loss of this information to be distressing. But since you don't get distracting visual or auditory cues through a mailing list, you have to pay more attention to the words on the screen, and so does the other person.

With a receptionist, an answering machine, or voice mail, people can leave voice messages that can convey subtle inflections of the spoken word. In practice, most people use their telephone voice in these situations, and keep the message as brief as possible, but the potential is there.

You can set up a mailing list that sends an automatic response of general information back to anyone who sends mail to it; this is called an *autoresponder*. Such a list may be set up so that it also sends a copy of that person's message to several people who can deal with any further interactions that are needed.

```
To: info@zilker.net
Subject: broken PPP

My dial script isn't working correctly; here's what happens....
```

The person thus gets an immediate response, plus later followup, if necessary.

An autoresponder is rather like voice mail, or having a receptionist. But it's a rare receptionist who records technical words correctly after hearing over the telephone. Answering machines and voice mail are not much better, since there are still problems of volume, foreign accents, running out of tape, or getting into the wrong voice mail menu. A autoresponding mailing list can return much more information immediately, and can distribute the person's message automatically to several people, any one of whom can respond if appropriate.

Large Groups

Mailing lists that include more than 1,000 people are common. Try a telephone conference call with 1,000 people and see how well it goes. Many people will try to talk at once, many others won't hear, and chaos will result. In addition, a single speaker can hog the line while other people want to speak.

On a mailing list, everyone who wants to can post at once, and everyone can read everything at any time. Anyone can ignore any message without waiting for the speaker to finish, and nobody can keep others from posting by simply continuing to post. Power games with throat clearing or jumping in first don't work well on lists, so people who would not get a chance to be heard in a telephone conference call have more of a chance on a list.

In an ideal world, perhaps the quick of tongue and assertive of personality might yield a bit on a list to the coherent of expression and the reasonable. In practice, this doesn't always happen, yet it definitely is easier for more people to post and be read on a list than to be heard on a telephone conference call.

Also, a mailing list is usually a recorded medium. Even if the list owner has not set up an archive, it is a safe assumption that someone is saving every message. This realization can lead to less dissembling, and certainly can make it easier for you to tell later what somebody really said. With a list, whoever has the task of secretary for the meeting has a complete transcript of all the messages, with no need for transcribing; condensation is still needed, of course.

Fax

Some press and public relations organizations fax reports or press releases to large numbers of recipients. This usually requires a bank of fax machines, each with its own telephone line, and numerous retries. The same information could be sent through a mailing list over whatever existing network link you have, with no extra equipment, and no special arrangements for retries. Also, you won't have to pay long distance telephone tolls for every distant recipient, since most of the long distances involved are covered by common backbone networks and you pay directly only for your local link.

If the information being sent is primarily text, sending it by electronic mail will take about a quarter of the bandwidth of sending a fax image. If the mailed version goes over a link of the same speed as the 14,400 bps (bits per second) of a typical fax modem, each copy will take a quarter of the time. Of course, since many network connections are faster than that, the electronic version will probably go out faster, anyway. And since big mailing lists can be set up to use exploders that remail the message to more recipients from a remote site, not every mailed copy has to go through the local link anyway.

An even bigger win with mail is that the recipient can use the text immediately in articles or forwards. With fax, the information received is a raster image, and anything to be reused has to be typed or scanned in again. Even if the information being sent includes images, using a page description language such as PostScript will save even more bandwidth, and the result can be previewed on almost any hardware and software platform that includes a bitmapped screen, or can be printed on most modern printers.

If you start communications with electronic mail, there is no need to switch from fax to mail later. For example, if you send a notice of a new product to a list, an interested party can respond to you with a request for a price quotation and you can send back the quote, all in a few mail interactions, much more conveniently and faster than handling the paper involved with traditional fax.

Convenience isn't everything. Electronic mail is not only user-friendly, it is environment-friendly. Save some trees by not using fax or paper newsletters. Sun Microsystems once won an environmental award for moving an in-house newsletter into a mailing list. Political campaigns, public relations outfits, and news agencies could consider doing the same with at least some of their faxes. For that matter, newspapers constitute the largest single component of most public waste disposal sites. With more information online, fewer newspapers are probably needed.

Television

You may wonder why we bother to compare mostly-text mailing lists with mostly-visual television. Both are addictive, in their way. If you don't believe this is true of mailing lists, wait until you are reading your mail and decide to continue doing so instead of eating dinner, sleeping, going out with friends, etc. Just a few keystrokes bring you the conversation of the world.

Although lists are still mostly text, that is actually one of their major advantages. With the telephone and television of the twentieth century, few people write letters anymore. Electronic mail is a strong incentive to learn the art of letter writing. Once you try it, you may be amazed to find that words can communicate much of what visuals can. Not only that, words can also communicate things that are difficult for visuals to convey. It's not accidental that great movie directors are few, and that the contents of a novel must be compressed and simplified to fit in a movie. Conveying simple emotions such as anger or amusement is easier with pictures and sounds than with words. But conveying subtle emotions such as belated recognition, or philosophical or political concepts such as democratic federalism, or technical material, or extended historical or personal narratives, or anything in great detail, is more readily done in words.

The most obvious advantage of lists over television is that television is one-way and lists are two-way. Some television shows permit some viewers to call a special telephone number and perhaps even appear on the air, but only a few people can take advantage of such limited input. With a mailing list, anyone with something to say can contribute. Much has been written recently about interactive television. Most of the examples have boiled down to movies on demand or home shopping. These are no doubt fine services, but they facilitate viewers watching movies and consumers buying goods from distributors, not people communicating with people.

Finally, the number of television channels available in an area is limited, as is the number of hours in the day for broadcast over each one. Mailing lists are not so severely limited in the number of topics that can be discussed or the specialized forums that can be supported. Television networks often promote homogenization. Computer networks generally promote diversity.

Communicating through Lists

In addition to the technical advantages and disadvantages of mailing lists, there are some social advantages and disadvantages to this medium of communication.

Problems of Mailing Lists

Mailing lists have some disadvantages. We address ways of dealing with most of them in Chapter 11, *Mailing List Etiquette*.

Lack of visual and auditory cues often leads to misunderstandings. However, any kind of communication often leads to misunderstandings, especially when the people using it are unfamiliar with it. Experienced mail users learn how to avoid most common kinds of misunderstandings, using techniques similar to those we describe in Chapter 11. Besides, as we have already discussed, lack of extraneous cues can lead to increased focus on content, not personalities, power plays, and distractions.

The most famous problem with mailing lists is *flaming,* which is nasty, overly emotional, verbose, or just plain inappropriate messages. Flaming usually results from misunderstandings, although some people just like to do it. Anti-commercial flames, such as the one in Figure 10.3, are among the more popular ones.

```
From: I. Rate <irate@typical.edu>
To: roots-l@vm1.nodak.edu
Subject: Re: genealogical publisher

While I think this list should be for all types of information
about genealogy, it is totally inappropriate for commercial
publishers to hawk their wares here!  We're all amateurs and
we don't want nasty capitalists making money off of us, especially
not in this pristine forum!  Those of you who are doing it,
you KNOW who you ARE!  And who do you think you are, anyway?
Just GO AWAY!
```

Figure 10.3 A Flame

```
To: I. Rate <irate@typical.edu>
From: So Sensible <sense@bigco.com>
To: roots-l@vm1.nodak.edu
Subject: Re: genealogical publisher

>While I think this list should be for all types of information
>about genealogy, it is totally inappropriate for commercial
>publishers to hawk their wares here!

Well, actually, the publisher was responding to a specific
request for information, with relevant material.  IMHO that
was a good thing to do.

>  We're all amateurs and
>we don't want nasty capitalists making money off of us, especially
>not in this pristine forum!  Those of you who are doing it,
>you KNOW who you ARE!  And who do you think you are, anyway?
>Just GO AWAY!

Now now.  Let's all calm down.

Please send further flames to /dev/null.
```
Figure 10.4 A Reply to a Flame

This kind of flame is particularly amusing because it almost always provokes a slew of counterpostings defending the right of commercial companies to respond to questions in public lists, similar to the example in Figure 10.4. These in turn often lead to more of the original type of flame.

The line

```
Please send further flames to /dev/null.
```

is an example of *flame retardant,* which is words intended to prevent further flames. Sometimes that works, but often not. The odd acronym *IMHO (in my humble opinion)* (which we have already discussed in Chapter 5, *The Basics*) is popular in some lists as a kind of generic flame retardant. While it may be of some use in lists where people are particularly apt to suspect others of arrogance, it can also, ironically, produce an effect of pompousness if used in a list where it is not common. The invitation to calm down was probably also intended as flame retardant, but would almost certainly produce the opposite effect, as in "who are you, posting from a commercial domain, to tell me to calm down?"

With a little luck or lack of prudence, one flame like the one in Figure 10.4 can produce a veritable *flame fest* or *flame war*, which is an escalating series of flames going on for some appreciable amount of time, such as hours or days, or for a really good one, weeks.

The examples in Figure 10.3 and Figure 10.4 involve a real mailing list, roots-l@vm1.nodak.edu, where we have seen such flames recently. Flames are by no means unique to that list; you'll see them most anywhere. We hasten to add that we constructed the example messages from scratch and they are not real postings from real persons (no doubt we'll get flamed for them anyway :-).

Flaming is one of the first things people new to lists notice, because similar messages are filtered out of most traditional media, such as letters to the editor and television news. However, anyone who has been to a political rally or a football game has seen equivalent behavior. Just as in those situations, some lists permit or even encourage flaming. Most lists discourage it. Most list users learn not to do it, at least not very often. Eventually it becomes more amusing than irritating. The best response to a flame is sometimes no response. Sometimes a good response is to send a simple factual reply, ignoring any personal insults or other irrelevant material.

Advantages of Mailing Lists

This whole book is about the advantages of mail and lists, so we won't go into a lot of detail here. Suffice it to say here that lists can handle discussions among large or small groups of people across time zones, languages, networks, and software.

What Lists Can Replace

Mail and lists are useful for many purposes, but will not completely replace many traditional media. However, mail and lists can completely replace a few media.

Memos

Mail and lists can replace paper memoranda completely. Why send slips of paper to inform people about routine events? Instead, just send a mail message, either to a specific person or to a mailing list that reaches everyone who needs the information. Some memoranda do include graphics which are somewhat more difficult to distribute online, but most are just plain text, and modern mail systems are moving towards being able to support graphics, voice, and text. We discuss this further in Chapter 14, *MIME: Multipurpose Internet Mail Extensions*.

Electronic mail was originally modeled after paper memoranda, so it is not surprising that it seems so similar. Even these two media are quite different, however. In a paper memorandum, anyone mentioned in a `Cc:` header is usually expected to listen and not to respond. In an online message, however, particularly one to a mailing list, anyone named in a `Cc:` header is practically *expected* to respond. This difference can be shocking to an administrator who sends out a new policy electronically and discovers the employees talking back! However, lists can be distributed so that responses do not go to the list itself. Instead, responses may be sent to an alias that reaches someone who has the task of dealing with them. Lists can even be distributed so that responses are difficult, if not impossible, though this is very seldom done, since it is a waste of feedback.

Telephone Messages

If your receptionist is taking a message on a paper pad and sticking it in a box for you to pick up, you can, instead, have it typed into a mail message and sent to you. With earphones to free the hands and a keyboard readily available, typing the message takes no longer than hand writing it. If the receptionist can't type it right then, you can have it typed in later, and you can then receive it on the road without having to call up your office just for telephone messages. If the message is general, ask the receptionist to send it to a general list, such as **support**.

Notes to Yourself

If you're online anyway, why scribble on pieces of paper? Mail notes to yourself, or to an alias that writes into a file.

Summary

Mailing lists can completely replace a few media, such as paper memoranda. Lists have some advantages over several other media in certain circumstances, but they do not completely replace all those others.

Mailing lists are not a replacement for face to face meetings, any more than the telephone is. Mail and lists don't replace the telephone or paper mail, either. All these and other media complement each other. If you need a decision from one person quickly, the telephone may be your best bet. If you want to send a large document such as a project proposal or a book draft, paper mail (or a courier service) may be best. But for extended discussions, mailing lists have advantages, such as reaching people without requiring them to all be in the same place or even at the same time. If you want to communicate with more than one person about a certain topic over a long period of time, a mailing list can be very useful.

11

Mailing List Etiquette

To use a mailing list to best effect, you need to know how pick the right list, post messages that will be read, and avoid offending other list participants.

The first rule is that there are no hard and fast rules. The people, topics, and situations involved in a given mailing list at a given time vary greatly, and you must use your own judgement. Don't depend too much on *common sense,* however, until you have some experience with lists, or the kind of superficial similarities with other media that we discussed in Chapter 10, *Uses of Mailing Lists* may mislead you into inappropriate reactions.

Things to Do	Things to Avoid
Remember the person	Mailing lists are different
Emulate experienced users	People look different online
Read first	Each list is different from every other list
Label your message	People have different styles
Identify yourself	People act differently at different times
Be brief	Don't believe everything you read
Use paragraphs	Don't use the `Caps Lock` key
Edit your text	Don't write in all lowercase
Check spellings	Don't use very long lines
Assume anyone may read your message	Don't use very short lines
Respect privacy	Be careful with character sets
Quote enough for context	Don't quote the headers
Quote only enough for context	Don't quote the whole message
Retain attribution	Avoid misattribution
Summarize where appropriate	Avoid rebutting every point
Use smileys if you like them	Be careful with humor
Use stage directions if you like them	Be careful with sarcasm
Say what you mean	Don't digress too much
Pick appropriate styles	Don't mix styles
Pick an appropriate list	Don't crosspost
Subscribe or unsubscribe correctly	Don't mail unsubscribes to the list
Write for your audience	Don't move discussions
Look before you leap	Don't respond in anger
Post new ideas	Don't monopolize the list
Remember you could be wrong	Don't try to convince everyone
Encourage when appropriate	Discourage when necessary

Table 11.1 Dos and Don'ts

You may rely more on *common courtesy,* although you need to be aware that in lists you are dealing not only with new media but also with people in many disciplines, countries, and religions with their own traditions. Parts of the online world are like your back yard. Other parts are like the whole world, and it's often hard to tell the difference. Don't worry though; nobody else knows all the answers, either.

You wouldn't try to play baseball with a football; you wouldn't sing falsetto in a barbershop quartet; you wouldn't serve oregano pesto. If you did, nobody would play, sing, or eat with you. But if you learn a few simple rules appropriate to the group you're trying to join, you can fit in.

Many of the conventions of etiquette that have grown up around electronic mailing lists serve the very simple purpose of saving everybody involved time and effort. If you ignore these conventions, your messages will require other people to devote more time and effort to read them and to respond to them. Many people simply won't take that time. So if you want to get the best use out of electronic mailing lists, and if you want to be received into the electronic communities they support, it will be well worth your while to learn the basic conventions of those lists and communities. Most of those conventions are really not that hard to learn, and they will save you time and effort, too.

Here are some guidelines that are useful much of the time. They are summarized in Table 11.1.

Ground Rules

Let's look at some things to do, and then at some things to avoid.

Things to Do

When posting a message, try to remember to do these things. Most of these points are related to the culture of mailing lists.

Remember the person.   Electronic mail is written and read by people. In one sense mail is just dots on a screen, but it's a screen read by a person. Write messages you think people would want to read.

Emulate experienced users.   You might be able to learn to play a piano by tinkering with the keys long enough. You will learn faster by finding someone who knows how to play, and even faster by taking lessons. Sending mail to a mailing list is simpler than playing the piano. It is, however, at least as difficult as talking on the telephone, and that is something that people have to learn to do:

- Speak into the mouthpiece.

- Say hello.

- Identify yourself.

- State your business.

- Listen to the receiver.

- Don't shout.

- Don't whisper.

- Don't talk at the same time.

- Don't leave the other person on hold.

- Don't hang up until the other person is also ready.

- Say goodbye.

- Don't bang the phone down.

The telephone is so familiar to you that you forget it has all those rules. Mail and lists are new to you, so you may not yet know they have rules. They do.

Read first.   Read the introductory message for the list before posting anything to the list. If there's a FAQ for the list, read that, too. Read some postings by others in the list, as well.

Label your message.   Use an appropriate `Subject:` header. If your mail program can't handle `Subject:` headers, get one that can. If you're starting a new subject, compose a new `Subject:` header. If you're responding to an ongoing thread of conversation, let your mail program use the same `Subject:` header, adding a prefix `Re:` to the subject text if necessary. Messages without subjects are time-consuming to interpret (you have to actually read the message to decide if it's relevant), difficult to follow in conversations, and difficult to file.

Identify yourself.   Many mail systems automatically put your real name in the `From:` header of your message. Some let you supply your own `From:` message. That may be enough for many messages. But sometimes people want to know your organization or title, or even your telephone number, fax number, or postal address. Make up a signature block that contains as much contact information as you want to give out, and append it to most messages you send to mailing lists. We've already discussed how to do this, in Chapter 5, *The Basics*. Keep it short; nobody wants to read a full-page signature block. You may want more than one signature for use in different lists, depending on whether you want to be known for your job, hobby, professional association, or some other quality.

Be brief.   Many people depend on mail for their jobs and personal lives. Those who get 100 messages a day are unlikely to read more than a single screen per message before deciding if the message is interesting. Some people write long mail messages in an effort to avoid being misunderstood, but verbosity is likely to produce the opposite effect: people will skim the message and pick whatever point first catches their attention. A mail message isn't a paper letter, and doesn't have to be a page long. One line may be enough; two pages is often too much.

Use paragraphs.   If you can't be bothered to break your stream of consciousness into coherent fragments, many people will not be bothered to read it. Separate paragraphs with blank lines, not indentations, to ease to quoting a single paragraph in a reply.

Edit your text.   If you change your mind in the middle of a message or notice a misspelling, go back and fix it. Don't just add more text like "(xyzzy should have been phlugh)." You may think that looks chatty, but most readers will see it as careless and a waste of their time. Try to use reasonably correct punctuation. If your mail program doesn't let you edit a message or if you can't figure out how to use its editor, get help or get new software.

Check spellings.   A spell checker won't catch everything, but it will save you some incoming flames.

Assume anyone may read your message.   Mailing lists are usually archived at the list distribution site and often elsewhere. Such archives are often made available to the public, or at least to other list members. A typo in an address or a network problem may cause your message to be sent to the administrator of your system, or of another system. Don't assume that anything you say is hidden or will ever be forgotten. If you don't want your boss, teacher, colleague, spouse, parent, or child to read it, consider whether you really want to post it.

Respect privacy.   If someone sends mail to your personal address, assume it is a personal mail message unless it is clearly labelled otherwise. Keep personal mail private unless the sender gives you permission to make it public. Don't forward a personal mail message to a mailing list without permission unless you have a very good reason for doing so, such as documenting a threat.

Things to Avoid

Here are some general points to watch out for. Most of these points are closely related to the technology of mailing lists.

Mailing lists are different.   Using a mailing list is not like using other forms of communication: not paper mail or memoranda, not telephone or two-way radio, not business meetings or sporting events. If you get a message from an online list and wait a week to respond to it, as you might with a paper newsletter, you will be last in line to get what you want. If you answer a message from a list with halting phrases and sloppy grammar as you might in a telephone conversation, you risk being considered inexperienced or just plain inept. If you assume your presence will be noted even if you don't say anything, as it would be at a business meeting, you will find yourself either ignored or chastised for not speaking up.

People look different online.   Even if you are communicating with people you already know well, you will see them differently through a list, and they will see you differently. Don't waste your time trying to imagine the vocal inflections and timing you would hear on a telephone. There is no subtext. The words in the message *are* the message. They may include indications of facial expressions or feelings, or they may not. Don't assume you can reconstruct something that is not there. If you don't understand, ask. Don't accuse, either; if you do, you'll probably just add to a flame war or start a new one. Ask, with an interrogative sentence and a question mark.

Each list is different from every other list. People involved in a business discussion will not appreciate random bits of poetry and ad hominem attacks, regardless of how well such things may be accepted on recreational lists.

People have different styles. The Matrix is not television, and not everyone communicates like a news anchor or a sitcom actor. Becoming offended at someone simply because they don't write like you do is the mark of a naive newcomer. Naivete may be refreshing, but it isn't attractive for long. Practice tolerance and exercise your sense of humor. However, there are inappropriate styles for most contexts, and some styles that are inappropriate almost everywhere in the Matrix.

People act differently at different times. Sometimes people answer their mail immediately and you can have what appears to be a relatively realtime conversation. At other times, this same person may not answer a mail message for several hours or even days. One of the biggest advantages of electronic mail is that it is asynchronous; the participants do not have to all act at the same time. Don't fall into the trap of expecting someone to answer mail the same way every time. Don't think that because someone sends you mail on a weekend you must respond the same day. Don't feel that you have to respond to every mail message as soon as you receive it. But don't wait forever to answer your mail, either.

Don't believe everything you read. Jokers abound on the net, and mail was not designed to be authenticated, private, or secure. Some people have been known to send messages with fake addresses. We recently saw a mail message with the following sender address:

```
From: jeanp2@vatican.org (The Pope)
```

While it is not at all inconceivable that the Pope would send mail in an age when president@whitehouse.gov is a real working address, vatican.org is not a real domain, and the message was a forgery. If it looks too good to be true, it may be. Check it out.

Don't use the Caps Lock **key.** Many people simply won't read messages that are written in all uppercase letters, since they're ugly and hard to read. Strings of capitals inside a message are very rarely useful, because they will be read as SHOUTING! And shouting is seldom the best way to get your point across. Experienced mail users almost never send such messages, since not using the Caps Lock key is extremely easy. Many readers will therefore assume that anyone who does leave that key on has made no effort to write a legible message, nor possibly even to learn basic mail conventions. For that reason many mail readers will just delete such messages. So you need to learn not to put such signs in your mail.

Don't write in all lowercase. Some old-timers still write messages in all lowercase characters because they are apparently offended by the shift key. You probably can't get away with it.

Don't use very long lines. Many mail readers cannot handle lines longer than 80 characters, so keep yours shorter than that. If you are using a system such as a Macintosh that believes in paragraphs without line breaks, output your message with line breaks.

Don't use very short lines. When told not to use long lines, some people react by making every line 20 characters long. This is not necessary, and is hard to read. Lines about 60 to 70 characters long are best.

Be careful with character sets. If you don't know for sure that another character set will be readable by the recipient's system, stick to US ASCII.

Context

Now that we've discussed some general principles, let's get into more details. Because mail messages often arrive in people's mailboxes at various times of the day and night and interspersed with messages on other topics, it is important to include clues to context in your messages.

The main ways of supplying context in a mail message are through the headers, such as the `Subject:` header, by quoting (including) parts of a message when replying to it, and by providing clues to your own state of mind in your message. We've discussed some of this in Chapter 5, *The Basics*, but here is some more detail.

Contextual Headers

Subject: Every message should have a `Subject:` header. If you are posting a new message, not in response to another one, you must enter a subject. If your message is in response to another message, for example with this header,

```
Subject: another interesting message
```

normally your message's `Subject:` header should be the same as that of the previous message, except with `Re:` prepended, as in:

```
Subject: Re: another interesting message
```

Your mail program should do this for you; if it doesn't, consider using another mail program. If you are responding to a message but changing the topic, remember to edit the `Subject:` header instead of using the one supplied by your mail program.

From: Your mail program should insert a `From:` line for you, and this line will provide the recipient with some minimal context. Don't expect the recipient to know what you are writing about just because they can see it is you who is writing it, however. Busy correspondents can easily forgot what someone was saying after 100 intervening mail messages from other people. Also use an apropriate `Subject:` header and selected quoted text in the body of the message.

To: The `To:` header tells all recipients of a message who is the primary addressee of the message. The message is quite likely in response to a previous message from that person. Some list management software unfortunately puts the list address in the `To:` header. Worse, some list software makes each copy of a message to a list different, setting the `To:` header to the address of the single recipient of that copy of the message. Fortunately, it's easy to tell when list software is doing this (the `To:` header that you see is always the same for every message you receive from the list).

Cc: The address of a mailing list is often in the `Cc:` line of messages distributed to the list. When you see such a message, this tells you not only which list you are dealing with, but also that the message was probably a direct response to someone specific, who is named in the `To:` header.

In-Reply-To: Some mail programs automatically insert an `In-Reply-To:` header when you reply to a message, recording in it information from the `From:`, `Date:`, and `Message-ID:` headers of the message you are responding to. Some mail programs can use this information to find the previous message. The human reader can also glean some information from it, such as how old the previous message was.

Quoting

Most mail readers make it very easy to quote all or part of a message when you respond to it. This capability can be very useful in preserving context.

Don't quote the headers.   Sometimes it is useful to quote the information from the `From:` header of a previous message so that it will not get lost if somebody else quotes your message. But there is no point in quoting the `Subject:` header in the body of your message, since it is already quoted in the `Subject:` header of your message. There is certainly no point in quoting `Received:`

headers unless you are forwarding a bounce message or otherwise attempting to debug a mail problem.

Don't quote the whole message.   If you want to be considered new and naive, quote a whole page long mail message from someone else and then just say "I agree." Of course, many people won't read past the first half page of quoting anyway, so perhaps the `Caps Lock` key is more useful for labeling yourself as clueless.

Quote enough for context.   Don't post a message with no context and consisting only of "I agree." Such a message can be even more effective at making you appear clueless than a huge quote, since more people will read the whole thing.

Quote only enough for context.   Do include enough quoted context from the previous message so that anyone reading your message can tell what is going on. While you're composing a message, note what parts of the quoted previous message are not relevant to your reply, and delete them.

Do retain attribution.   That is, make sure the reader can tell whom you're quoting. Do this either by quoting the `From:` and `Date:` line from the other person's message, or by creating an attribution line for the person. Pine and some other mail programs will do this for you.

Don't misattribute.   It's easy to file off one too many attribution headers and end up attributing a quotation to the wrong person. Be careful about that.

Summarize where appropriate.   If you would have to quote a page or several paragraphs of a message to get at the point, it might be better to just summarize your understanding of the point in your own words, or, even better, make your point with enough underlying context in your own words that nobody has to refer to the other person's message.

Avoid rebutting every point.

It's easy to indulge in the notorious *point-by-point rebuttal,* by quoting every single point of a someone's message and appending a rebuttal to each one. This can produce a very long message, and many people will not read it. Phrasing your own position in your own words can work better.

Contextual Cues

Many people like to indicate their state of mind in their messages.

Use smileys if you like them.   Many people take mail messages too seriously, so the *smiley face* was invented to show the writer wasn't overly serious. The simplest smiley face looks like this :-) and is easiest to see if you look at it sideways. Hundreds of variations exist, intended to show all sorts of facial inflections and states of mind; we have discussed some of them in Chapter 5, *The Basics*. However, all most people are going to see, regardless of the variation, is that it's a smiley face. Also, some people use a smiley face to indicate they want to be seen as literally smiling. This is different from the traditional use, but then, irony is not a mass-market item.

Or perhaps stage directions.   Some people insert comments like `*grin*` to indicate what they are supposedly doing when they are writing, similarly to the way stage directions are given in plays.

Be careful with humor or sarcasm.   If you use it in any large list, some people just won't get it, and most likely somebody will be offended, no matter how many smileys and stage directions you use. Some people will interpret *any* sarcasm as mean spirited. As a Steve Martin character said in a movie: "sarcasm; we don't get that here. I was the last practitioner, but I got tired of blank stares." The irony- and humor-impaired are legion. You can use humor or sarcasm if you want to, just be aware of the drawbacks.

Say what you mean.   It is also possible to write prose that simply says what it means; good writing still has its uses. If you want to convey that you are amused, you can just write "that's amusing." If you are offended by something, you can say "I'm offended by that."

```
From: P. Jamas <p-jamas@catwalk.com>
To: derivatives@bigco.com
Subject: bond futures

I've found the recent introduction of buy and sell options
for municipal bond futures to be quite useful in leveraging
my portfolio.

P. Jamas
Vice President for Silly Walks
Furlick Dept.
Hairball Extractors, Inc.
Catwalk, MD
```

Figure 11.1 A Mismatched Message

Novelists and short story writers have spent generations developing other mechanisms for indicating context.

Stick to the point. Or you can decide to get to the point, assuming the reader wants to read what you have to say, not the rest of your mind. Some people will interpret such an approach as humorless, but others will interpret smileys and stage directions as silly and a waste of time. If you have several unrelated topics to address, post several different messages.

Avoid digressions. If you have several unrelated things to say, consider posting several messages. Bits are cheap, and attention isn't.

Pick appropriate styles. Find a style of writing that is comfortable for you and use it. You don't have to limit yourself to one style, either. You may choose to be frivolous in a list about pets, but serious in a list about financial investments.

Don't mix styles. Do make whatever style you are using agree with the signature you are using in the same message. Suppose you send a message like that in Figure 11.1. It's conceivable you may not be taken seriously.

Mailing Lists as Places

Mailing lists are places where people gather to discuss relatively well defined topics. This metaphor of a list as a meeting room or a coffee house is useful, but the people who inhabit the room really determine the particular personality of each mailing list.

Using a Place

If you need to attend a board meeting, you go to the board room. If you want coffee and amicable discussion, you go to a coffee house. You don't normally hold a board meeting in a coffee house. You want to pick an appropriate place online, too. Once you choose a list, you will need to learn its particular rules.

Pick an appropriate list.   If you drop into a discussion about gun control and start discussing religion, you're probably not going to be very welcome. Mailing lists are like rooms, but most of them are not like living rooms where any subject can be discussed. Most lists are like meeting rooms at a convention where only certain posted subjects are discussed.

Subscribe or unsubscribe correctly.   There is always a related but different alias for joining or leaving the list. See Chapter 10 for the usual conventions for subscribing and unsubscribing.

Don't mail unsubscribes to the list.   Don't send a request to subscribe or unsubscribe to the list itself.

Write for your audience.   Use language, references, and subjects the readers of this list will understand. If it's international, don't use obscure slang. If it's a chat list, don't use bibliographic references. If it's academic, act collegial. If you use jargon, use jargon appropriate to the subject and the readers. If you use terms your readers won't understand, define them in your message. Be aware that certain topics are objectionable to some people: politics, religion, sex, and history are usually pretty sure-fire flame-starters.

Look before you leap.   You can't know your audience until you observe it. Read the list for a while before posting to it. When participating in a thread of conversation, read what others have said before jumping in.

Don't respond in anger.   Misunderstandings are common, and it's easier to fire off a mail message in anger than to write a paper letter or dial a telephone. You also probably wouldn't call somebody up at midnight just to say "you jerk!" but saying that online is all too easy, no matter what time of day or night. If you write a message in anger, reread it and think about it. Maybe even put it aside until tomorrow and then read it again. However, if you are still angry, don't pretend not to be; say so.

Post new ideas.   Repeating what three people have already said is usually not useful. Post new information, or information from a new point of view.

Don't monopolize the list.   Give others a chance to respond.

Remember you could be wrong.   No matter how important your job, employer, profession, or yourself, by your estimation or anybody else's, you could be wrong. Don't try to force your views down everyone else's throat.

You can't convince everyone.   Even if you're right, and have a mandate of the electorate plus a physical law to prove it, people will disagree. Assume you can't convince everyone and move on.

Encourage when appropriate.   If you see someone posting useful, entertaining, or otherwise appropriate information to the list, tell them so, and perhaps post a followup, as well.

Discourage when necessary.   Sometimes suffering a fool only encourages the fool and wastes everybody's time. Point out errors of fact without taking the bait of personal attacks. Try sending a personal mail message, but only a few times, and only if argument in the list doesn't work. Record everything both you and the other person send to each other, as a precaution against convenient memory lapses or fabrications on the part of the other person. Try asking the opinion of the other subscribers. For a moderated list, you may want to ask the moderator to take action.

Between Places

You will probably participate in several mailing lists at once. This raises questions about what to post where, and how to do so.

Don't crosspost. You may think your message is important, witty, entertaining, and really necessary for everyone on every list to read, but everybody else is unlikely to think so. Remember that anyone subscribed to more than one of the lists you crosspost to will see your message more than once. Pick the right list in the first place and you will reach those who have expressed their interest in the topic by subscribing to that list.

Don't move discussions. Taking a discussion from one list to another is usually not prudent. The problems of such a practice are manifold:

• Confusion. People on the new list don't know what's going on.

• Suppression of future postings. People won't post to a list if they think somebody is likely to suddenly quote them elsewhere in mid-discussion, before any conclusion has been reached.

• Disruption of business. Inviting lots of other people into a discussion automatically makes it harder, and adds to the confusion.

• Insulting the original poster. Did they not know where they wanted to post in the first place?

There are appropriate ways to move a discussion if it's needed:

1. Post a note to the original list that announces a plan to move it and that asks for objections by a certain date.

2. Post a *new* note on the other list, with *no* text from other posters in the previous discussion, (you can quote your own messages, if you like) but including enough summary of the topic that people on the new list will have some idea what's going on.

Lists and Other Media

Not every discussion or message is appropriate to a mailing list. Often you will want to have a detailed discussion with someone in personal mail messages. If you want a quick response or a minimal kind of privacy, or if you just want to hear the other person's voice, a telephone call may be appropriate. Sometimes the only solution is to fly there and discuss it in person.

Reaching Decisions

Reaching a decision in a mailing list is notoriously hard, whether about pizza toppings or financial expenditures. However, it is possible. Here are some guidelines that may make it easier.

- Propose a solution. Describe it briefly. If detail is needed, make it available, but provide a brief summary.

- Set a deadline for a decision. Make it at least a week away.

- Make clear your solution is the default if there are no objections.

- If a certain number of objections or yes votes are necessary, spell out how many are required and what will count as yes or no.

Running a Mailing List

If you decide to run your own mailing list, here are some basic points to ponder; they're listed in Table 11.2.

Normal Operations

Here are some basics.

Let subscribers volunteer.   Don't put somebody on a mailing list without asking them first.

Normal Operations	Moderation Etiquette
Let subscribers volunteer	Charter the moderator
Provide information about the list	Accept promptly
Automate as much as possible	Annotate discretely
Be timely	Reject politely
Keep the list usable	No one is a censor
Everyone is responsible	No one is in charge

Table 11.2 Running a Mailing List

Provide information about the list.   Tell the subscribers the topic of the list, any necessary background information or prerequisites, and any rules. Send similar information to each new subscriber, and post it to the list periodically. If you advertise a list to people other than its subscribers, give the subscription address, such as list-request@bigco.com, not the list owner's address, such as joe@bigco.com. If a list is successful, it may well outlive its original owner. Many list owners choose to handle mail about the list separately from personal mail, anyway.

Automate as much as possible.   If you have access to Majordomo or LISTSERV, you'll save yourself a lot of trouble by using it, since it can automate many functions, such as subscribing and unsubscribing.

Be timely.   If you can't or do not choose to automate subscriptions and unsubscriptions, try to handle them in a day or so. Waiting a week is considered impolite.

Moderation Etiquette

A moderated list has some additional considerations.

Charter the moderator.   Provide clear, written, and public instructions for the moderator's tasks. Have the moderator post this charter to the list periodically. Include the other points in this section in the moderator's charter.

Accept promptly.   The moderator should accept and post submissions quickly, in hours or days, not weeks.

Annotate discretely.   Most list readers are more interested in what subscribers have to say than in what the moderator has to say. Keep any annotations by the moderator to a minimum.

Reject politely.   If the moderator has to reject a message, it should be done politely. The rejection message should suggest changes that would make the submission acceptable. If a submission is completely off the topic of the list, the rejection message should suggest a more appropriate place to post it.

Problems and Politics

Nothing works perfectly; certainly not mailing lists. Personal mail mostly falls under idiosyncratic personal conventions. Moderated mailing lists (and moderated newsgroups) have appointed overseers. Centralized conferencing systems may have benevolent dictators. Unmoderated mailing lists (and unmoderated newsgroups) are usually anarchies.

No one is a censor.   Even on a moderated list, the moderator is typically charged with keeping posters to the topic of the list, and with minimizing redundancy, not with censoring content. Etiquette is enforced by the participants. A single person complaining about the conduct of a participant means only that one person doesn't like the conduct of another person. Many participants complaining about the conduct of a participant may cause a change. The person may cease to post, post differently, or even be removed from the list. Such complaints can be delivered in private mail to the other person, or in the list itself. If that doesn't work, try the list owner, but don't necessarily expect action from that direction.

No one is in charge.   Decisions are made by consensus. A single person making cogent arguments can alter or break the consensus. The group can decide to go ahead even in the face of objections by a minority, but that is difficult. Experience counts, as does a reputation of conduct developed on the list. Participants may hold positions or have records outside the list that affect deliberations on the list. But no one has final authority on the list itself.

Everyone is responsible.   A moderator can facilitate useful functioning of a mailing list, and the list owner has the final responsibility. But every subscriber is responsible for keeping the list running. A few people who insist on posting inappropriate messages can drive many other users off a list. Misuse it and you may lose it.

Keep the list usable.   Even an unmoderated list still has a list owner, who has a responsibility to keep the list usable. This responsibility can extend to removing abusive, dishonest, or overly verbose subscribers. There's often no good way to do this, but sometimes it is necessary. If you start a list, eventually you will probably need to do this.

Such anarchic consensus may seem strange to those accustomed to the direct democracy of a political referendum, or the representative democracy of a city, county, or state government, or a federal republic like the United States or Germany, or even the benevolent dictatorship of a centralized conferencing system. Yet it can and often does work. For example, the protocol specifications and much of the organizational structure of the world's largest computer network, the Internet, were worked out largely on just such lists.

Summary

Lists are almost never used as an exclusive method of communication. Local groups often use the telephone, and that is also often the channel for sounding out basic opinions between two distant groups. Some groups use interactive video teleconferencing. Many use FTP to exchange files of various sizes. Many use fax. Some use the paper postal service. Most use periodic face-to-face meetings. All these media have problems, as well as particular do's and don'ts, and mailing lists have them, too. But for ongoing discussions among all of a geographically and occupationally distributed group, mailing lists are hard to beat.

12

Finding Things

By this point in the book, you already know how to send mail to communicate with people throughout the Matrix. In this chapter we show you how to use mail to find and retrieve information of all kinds by mail, using services such as LISTSERV, Majordomo, FTP, archie, WAIS, and Gopher. LISTSERV and Majordomo you will recognize from Chapter 9, *Mailing List Basics* as mailing list management servers; they can also be used to retrieve files related to lists they manage. The other services you may have heard of as Internet services; we mentioned some of them in Chapter 4, *The Networks*. You don't need an actual connection to the Internet to use them. If the network you use has a mail connection with the Internet so that you can send mail to the Internet and get mail back, however indirectly, you can use these services by mail. All the examples in this chapter use the Internet or BITNET, but you can use the recommended commands from anywhere in the Matrix.

You can use most of these services from your usual mail interface on your computer, regardless of whether it is a Macintosh, or is running DOS, Windows, UNIX, or some other operating system. Many of the services described in this chapter are actually provided by servers running on VMS, UNIX, or CMS. You don't have to run any of those operating systems. In many cases, you don't even have to know what operating system the server is running. For example, many Gopher servers use MacOS, and others use UNIX or VMS, and you will never know which is running which unless you go to some trouble to find out. As long as each Gopher server you use responds correctly to the Gopher protocol, there's no reason you should care. That's the beauty of network protocols. As long as both the client (your end) and the server (the other end) speak the same protocol (such as the Gopher protocol) correctly, it does not matter what kind of hardware, operating system, or application program is being used on each end.

When you use an Internet service by mail, you are not actually using the Internet protocol for that service directly. Instead, you are sending mail to a client program on a computer that is on the Internet and that uses the protocol for you. It's somewhat like sending a letter to Copenhagen to ask a friend to look up tourist information for you. If you were there yourself, you could go to the local tourist bureau in person and ask. If you decide you want to go look at a cathedral yourself, you will have to go to Denmark, just as if you want direct interactive access to the most of the services we describe in this chapter, you will have to get an Internet connection. If you want to do that, see Appendix A, *Places to Connect* for an overview of the kinds of connections you can get, and for more detail, see *The Internet Connection* (Addison-Wesley, 1994). Fortunately, communicating between different computer networks is easier than travelling to another country. Computer networks supply various forms of information, and you can transfer most of that information through electronic mail, just more slowly than through a direct

Internet connection. In this chapter we explain how to get all sorts of information from the Internet by mail.

You can use the tools you have to retrieve information by mail: the same mail program and network communication software you already use to communicate with people by mail. Of course, if you retrieve a GIF file, you will need software to display that file as a picture. If you don't already have a software tool to display GIF files, you will need to get one. We recommend some software sources in Appendix B, *Software*. Some of these sources are on the networks themselves; you may be able to retrieve much of the software you need by mail across the net. You may need other software tools for other file types you encounter. But this is an aspect of the format of the information you retrieve, not of how you retrieve it. To retrieve information by mail, all you need is mail software.

You've already learned how to use mail to expand the utility of your computer into communications with people throughout the world. In this chapter we show you how to use mail for *resource discovery*, that is, finding sources of information (such as weather reports) or services (such as mailing lists). We also show you how to use mail for *information retrieval*, that is, retrieving information once you have found its source. And we show you how to send information by mail to other people, so that in addition to being a consumer of information, you can participate in *resource sharing*, that is, exchanging information. This chapter shows how to use your mail software to add resource discovery, information retrieval, and resource sharing to communications. As a result, you will be able to use electronic mail as a more effective tool of collaboration.

Using Mail to Transfer Files

If you know how, you can use electronic mail to send any type of file. In Chapter 5, *The Basics*, we discussed how to use a mail program to include an ASCII text file in a mail message. The most common mail format is RFC-822, which uses seven bit US-ASCII characters. Many files are in binary data formats that require all eight bits per byte; for example pictures in GIF or TIFF format.

Other files use more combinations of seven bits than are permitted by US-ASCII; many languages other than English require such combinations. You can't transfer a file like that through many mail systems without first encoding it somehow into US-ASCII. Other mail formats and mail systems have similar constraints,

Fortunately, there are ways to mail non-ASCII files. Here's how to do it if you have a UNIX system. Most of these methods also work on DOS, Macintosh, or other systems, with appropriate software tools. Many mail systems have many of these tools built into them. You may need to obtain software for some of them; see Appendix A, *Places to Connect*. Of course, much interesting information you will want to retrieve by mail is in plain ASCII. But you will eventually want to retreive or send non-ASCII files.

Encoding a GIF File

Let's say you are trying to append a GIF file to a mail message. A GIF file consists of binary data, not ASCII text. In an ASCII file, each byte of data represents a printable character, such as a letter of the alphabet or an ampersand, or a control function, such as carriage return. A GIF file, however, is a binary file. A byte of data in a GIF file does not represent a character. Instead, it is part of an image, such as a photograph of Lake Travis, a diagram of a toaster oven, or a picture of your spouse. Also, because GIF files are binary, there are no line breaks in the file, so a program that expects ASCII text can get very confused if it tries to read a binary file. When you use an appropriate program to display a GIF file, you see the picture it encodes. But if you try to look at a GIF file with a program that expects ASCII text, you will see meaningless patterns of characters, and you probably won't see many of the bytes of the file at all, because their numeric values don't happen to correspond to printable ASCII characters. Even if you could enclose a GIF file directly in a mail message without any encoding, it is unlikely that the mail transport system could handle it, since the transport system expects lines of ASCII characters.

As a result of this limitation, many ad hoc methods have been developed for including binary data in mail messages. Several of

```
begin 644 world.gif
M1TE&.#========AX@,$ \(         #^_/[____\ +\ O____P ____P     "P      X@,$
M P #_EBZW/XPRRw...
```

Figure 12.1 uuencode

the more popular methods encode the binary data as ASCII characters divided into lines, so it looks like text to mail systems. A popular method used on UNIX systems (and also available for many other systems) is called **uuencode**. Before you include a GIF file as a part of a mail message, you first run the file through the uuencode utility. This utility creates a file which contains nothing but printable ASCII characters. Figure 12.1 shows the format of such a file. The file looks like gibberish, but is really a careful encoding of a binary file into ASCII characters. The first line of the file contains information which will be needed by the **uudecode** utility that decodes the file back into its binary format.

After you've run the GIF file through the uuencode utility, you can include it in a mail message, since the encoded GIF file is now just plain ASCII text. You also need to include some annotation telling the receiver what the encoded file is and how to decode it. Figure 12.2 shows such a message that was created with the Pine mailer. The Pine `Read File` command was used to explicitly include the encoded GIF file. The message is then sent as plain ASCII text.

Although this method does work, there are some problems with it. One problem is that the recipient must manually decode the message by using the instructions you included in the message text.

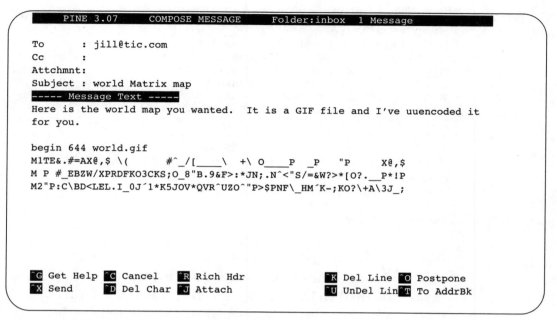

Figure 12.2 A Message with a uuencoded file

Another, more serious problem is that the recipient may not have the uudecode facility available and therefor will be unable to decode the file. But, probably the biggest problem with this method is that there is no standard way to include non-textual data into a mail message. Maybe I have uuencode, but you have btoa.

The good thing about this method is that the non-textual data is transported as ASCII text, which means current mail transport systems can handle this kind of data encoding.

Common Utilities for Sending Binary Files

There are several common ways of encoding, grouping, and compressing files so you can mail them. Implementations of all these programs are available over the Matrix for free.

Here are the three pairs of programs most commonly used to send and receive binary files through ASCII mailers.

The most commonly used pair is uuencode and uudecode.

uuencode   Converts binary data into ASCII text.

uudecode   Converts ASCII back into binary data.

The btoa and atob pair is also widely used. Why use them instead of uuencode and uudecode? Because they are widely distributed as part of certain common software packages, and some people just like them better. A lot of networking is determined by personal taste.

btoa   Converts binary data into ASCII text.

atob   converts ASCII text back into binary data.

The tarmail and untarmail pair is also sometimes used. This pair's advantage is that it handles multiple files. It uses the UNIX tar utility to package files that have been encoded with btoa.

tarmail   Uses tar and btoa to prepare files for mailing.

untarmail   Uses atob and tar to extract files.

Sending More than One File at Once

If you want to send several ASCII files at once, and you're using a UNIX system, consider the *shar* utility, which makes bundles of files that can be extracted with nothing but a UNIX shell.

```
#!/bin/sh                         # Use the Bourne shell.
for f in $*                       # Loop on all files named...
do                                # Echo filename on extraction.
        echo "echo $f
cat >$f <<´shar.$f.$$´"
        cat $f                    # Put file in archive.
        echo "shar.$f.$$"         # Mark end of file.
done                              # ...end of loop.
echo "exit"                       # Avoid junk after archive.
```

Figure 12.3 Using shar

The source code for a usable version of the shar utility is shown in Figure 12.3. That's the whole program; there's no need for more. It's written in Bourne shell, which is a simple programming language that every UNIX system supports. To use this shar command, take for example a file named **fox**:

```
The quick brown fox
jumped over the lazy packet.
```

and a file named **rabbit**:

```
The rabbit was quicker, and
sent many packets.
```

To produce a shar file, type these UNIX commands:

```
shar fox rabbit > /tmp/wildlife.shar
```

The system creates the shar file:

```
echo fox
cat >fox <<´shar.fox.28306´
The quick brown fox
jumped over the lazy packet.
shar.fox.28306
cat >rabbit <<´shar.rabbit.28306´
The rabbit was quicker, and
sent many packets.
shar.rabbit.28306
exit
```

You can mail this shar file to someone else, or put it on a floppy, or otherwise transport it however seems appropriate. To extract the shar file, type these UNIX commands:

```
cd appropriate_directory
sh /tmp/wildlife.shar
```

Reducing the Size of Files for Transport

Programs such as shar, uuencode, and btoa, which bundle files or convert files from binary to ASCII can produce large files. Many mailers limit the size of the messages they will carry. Some mail links are expensive. Therefore, reducing the size of a mail message is useful.

compress   Uses the Lempel-Ziv algorithm to compress text files to about half of their original size.

uncompress Can uncompress files produced by compress.

gzip   Uses a variant of the Lempel-Ziv algorithm to get somewhat better compression than the compress utility gets.

gunzip   Can uncompress files that were compressed with either compress or gzip.

Compress and gzip produce binary output that must be converted to ASCII (with a program such as uuencode) before you mail it. Here is an example of using shar, compress, and uuencode to mail a file:

```
shar * | compress -c | uuencode src.shar.Z \
   | mailx -s src.shar.Z you@bigu.edu
```

This is a UNIX *pipeline,* with shar producing output that is read by compress, which produces output that is read by uuencode, which produces output which is read by a mail program, **mailx**. If you're familiar with UNIX, there's no mystery here. If you use DOS, you can also write pipeline commands like this, although DOS doesn't really run all the programs at once. Here's what each part of this particular pipeline does:

- `shar *`
  The asterisk (*) causes the shell to list all the files in the current directory, which shar then bundles together.

- `compress -c`
  Compress the bundled files; the `-c` option merely causes compress to pass the compressed data through the pipeline rather than trying to write it on a file.

- uuencode src.shar.Z
  Encode the compressed data into ASCII. The src.shar.Z argument is prepended to the encoded data so uudecode will later know what filename to use after decoding the data.

- mailx -s src.shar.Z you@bigu.edu
  This common UNIX mail command mails the encoded compressed bundled files to **you@bigu.edu** and the -s src.shar.Z option includes

      Subject: src.shar.Z

  in the message so the recipient will know what sort of file it is. The recipient can tell it's a uuencoded file by looking at beginning of the message, which has the line

      begin src.shar.Z

  The Subject: header is therefore redundant. However, the reader will see the contents of the Subject: header before seeing the body of the message, and can use that information to decide what to do with the message. The capital Z filename extension is the usual marker for a compressed file. The shar extension indicates a shar file inside the compressed file.

When the mail message arrives at the other end, the recipient can save it in a file, such as **src.uu**. The recipient can then enter these commands to decode, uncompress, and extract it:

```
uudecode src.uu
uncompress src.shar.Z
sh src.shar
```

Anonymous FTP by Mail

You can retrieve any of terabytes (thousands of billions of bytes) of information from thousands of file repositories across the world by using anonymous FTP by mail. *Anonymous FTP* is a method for using the *File Transfer Protocol (FTP)* to retrieve files that people and organizations have made available on the Internet. It may not be the friendliest way to retrieve information, but is still the most widespread.

With FTP in general you must have a local personal login account on the FTP server computer. But with anonymous FTP, you don't need your own account. Instead, you log in as the user **anonymous**. You can get files from anonymous FTP by mail. By this we don't mean that you make anonymous FTP send you mail; FTP doesn't send mail. You send mail to a specialized server that uses anonymous FTP *for* you and then that specialized server mails the results to you. FTP doesn't send you any mail; the specialized server does. This process is illustrated in Figure 12.4.

Digital Equipment Corporation (Digital) graciously makes available to the Matrix a server called *FTPmail* that accepts anonymous FTP commands by mail and mails the result back to the sender. For the most current details on how FTPmail works, send the word `help` in the body of a mail message, like this:

```
To: FTPmail@decwrl.dec.com

help
```

The FTPmail server accepts many other commands, most of which are FTP commands, plus some additional commands for format settings. The one you're most interested in is `get`, which causes a file to be retrieved and mailed to you. All other commands merely set the stage for one or more get commands. The FTPmail server does

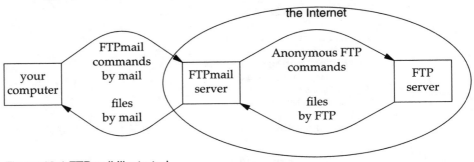

Figure 12.4 FTPmail Illustrated

not allow you to send files to an FTP server, and therefore does not support the FTP `put` command.

Figure 12.5 shows an example of a typical message to FTPmail. This message will cause FTPmail to connect to zilker.net with anonymous FTP, set ASCII mode, change directories to **pub/zip**, set the reply address to you@bigu.edu, and arrange for results to be compressed and uuencoded. Two commands in the example actually cause results to be sent to you@bigu.edu:

- `dir`
  All the files in the current directory on the anonymous FTP server are listed. The current directory is **pub/zip**, because a previous command in the same message set it to that.

- `get README`
  This command causes the file **README** to be retrieved and mailed.

Presumably this file contains some kind of information about the other files in that directory, since that is the convention for **README** files on FTP servers. **README** files are typically plain ASCII, so you should be able to read one with any text editor or word processor. Note that if the anonymous FTP server is running UNIX, the filename really is **README**, not **readme**, since UNIX filenames preserve case; uppercase and lowercase are not equivalent. Most anonymous FTP servers do in fact run UNIX, so you should assume case matters.

```
To: ftpmail@decwrl.dec.com

connect zilker.net
ascii
chdir pub/zip
reply you@bigu.edu
compress
uuencode
dir
get README
quit
```

Figure 12.5 FTPmail Example

Both the directory listing and the **README** file are compressed
and uuencoded before mailing. Of course, in this case, both those
items are ASCII to start with, so the compressing and uuencoding is
unnecessary.

FTPmail FTP Setup Commands

Here is a list of the FTP commands FTPmail accepts by mail and
uses to set the stage for a file transfer.

`connect domain`

Usually, you supply a domain argument, such as zilker.net, to the
`connect` command, and FTPmail uses FTP to connect to that host.
If you supply no domain argument, FTPmail will connect to **gate-
keeper.dec.com**. Usually, you do not need to supply a username or
a password, since FTPmail will use the anonymous FTP conventions of login **anonymous**, password **guest** by default. You can,
however, append a username and a password to the `connect` command.

`ascii`

Set FTP ASCII mode, so that line terminators will be transferred
properly for ASCII files. This is usually redundant, since ASCII is
the default mode for FTP servers.

`binary`

Set FTP binary mode, for compressed, tar, or other binary files. If
you are going to retrieve such a file, you must set binary mode. If
you do not set binary mode, FTP will try to transfer the binary file
in ASCII mode, and the result will be unusable.

`chdir directory`

Change to the specified directory. Only one `chdir` command is
allowed per session, that is, per mail message sent to FTPmail. If
there is a `chdir` command in the mail message, it is performed by
FTPmail before any `ls`, `dir`, or `get` commands, so that any

directory listings or file retrievals are performed from the directory indicated by the `chdir` command. After all, there wouldn't be much point in changing to a new directory afterwards.

FTPmail Mail Setup Commands

The FTPmail server needs to know where to send files you request, and in what format to send them.

```
reply you@bigu.edu
```

Since your mail message may arrive at the FTPmail server after traveling through many other systems or networks, the address in the `From:` header (if there even is such a header in the message), may not work for return mail. So it is prudent to include an FTP-mail `reply` command with a domain address for yourself. If there is no `reply` command, FTPmail will attempt to send to the address in the `From:` header.

```
compress
```

This command causes a file to be compressed with the compress program before sending. Because files found on anonymous FTP servers are often large, and network bandwidth is often not as large as we would like, compressing files before sending is usually a good idea.

```
uuencode
```

Most mail systems in the Matrix expect seven bit ASCII in eight bit bytes, with lines no longer than 80 characters. Many files available on anonymous FTP servers are in non-ASCII formats. Even if they are ASCII to start with, once you compress a file, it is not ASCII. So, for mailing, you will want convert a binary or compressed file back to ASCII, but without uncompressing it and making it big again. The `uuencode` command causes FTPmail to use the uuencode program (after compressing, but before sending), to convert a file into ASCII acceptable for mailing through most known mail systems.

`btoa`

Some people prefer their binary files converted to ASCII with the btoa program, and the `btoa` command will do this.

`chunksize 10240`

This FTPmail command splits each file into chunks of the specified size in bytes before mailing. If no size is specified, the default is 64000 bytes. Many mail messages have limits on the size of messages they will transfer, so this command may be necessary to get mail through a network between the FTPmail program and you. If you try to retrieve a large file from FTPmail and it never arrives, probably it's too big to get through some network, so try a smaller chunksize. You will need to put the pieces back together on your end somehow. If you are using a UNIX system, the standard *cat* command may be sufficient.

FTPmail File Transfer Commands

In your mail message to the FTPmail server, you first set the stage with some of the commands described in the previous sections. Then you can put in the message commands that actually cause FTPmail to retrieve files by FTP and send them to you.

`ls filename`

Make a brief directory listing and mail it, so that you will know what files are available in a directory on the anonymous FTP server. The format is similar to the UNIX command of the same name. If you supply no filename, the current directory is assumed. You can set the current directory with a `chdir` command.

`dir filename`

Make a long directory listing and mail it. Just like the FTPmail `ls` command, except the result has more detail for each file listed, in a format more like the DOS `dir` command.

```
index keyword
```

Search for the keyword in the FTP server's index, if it has one, and return the results of the search.

```
get filename
```

Tell the FTPmail server to retrieve the named file from the anonymous FTP server and then mail it to you. The FTPmail server will accept up to 10 `get` commands in a single mail message. If you want to include more than one, just put them all in, each on a separate line. That way you can use one mail message to tell FTPmail to send you more than one file. You could also send FTPmail several messages, each with a single `get` command, but then you would have to repeat all the setup information in each message.

```
quit
```

Ignore the rest of the mail message. This command is useful in case your mail program automatically appends a signature to your mail messages. The `quit` command will prevent FTPmail from trying to interpret your signature as commands.

Popular Anonymous FTP Archives

The FTPmail host itself, gatekeeper.dec.com, is a popular anonymous FTP archive, so for many files FTPmail doesn't have to look very far. Many other anonymous FTP servers are mentioned in Appendix B, *Software*.

archie: an FTP Index

The *archie* service looks up a word in an index of thousands of anonymous FTP servers, and produces a list of every file that contains that keyword on each server. In this section, we show you how to use archie by mail. Unlike anonymous FTP, archie has mail service built into it, so you don't have to send mail to a different specialized server; you send archie commands directly by mail to an archie server. If you are on the Internet, you can also query archie by a variety of other methods, but you can query archie by mail from anywhere in the Matrix. Once you have used archie to find a file, you can use anonymous FTP to retrieve that file. As we discussed in the previous section, you can use FTPmail to get from an anonymous FTP server by sending mail from anywhere in the Matrix. So the combination of archie by mail and FTPmail lets you find and retrieve files from anywhere in the Matrix.

For the most current details on how to use archie, send a message like this:

```
To: archie@archie.unl.edu
Subject: help
```

Most archie commands go in the body of the message, but the archie mail server treats the `Subject:` header as part of the body.

For problems with archie, write to archie-admin@sura.net.

An archie Example

Here is a typical mail message to archie:

```
To: archie@archie.unl.edu

path you@bigu.edu
prog compress
quit

Y. Self
Big State U.
you@bigu.edu
```

This message tells archie to send replies to you@bigu.edu, to search for the keyword compress and to mail the results, and to ignore everything in the message after the word `quit`, including the signature at the end of the message. We explain each archie command in detail in the next subsection. Part of the result of this message is shown in Figure 12.6. It includes a listing for every anonymous FTP server where archie found the keyword. For each server, archie supplies the hostname, time of last update, directory name, and filename, with permissions, size in bytes, and date. This information isn't sorted in any particular order, but you can pick an appropriate FTP server by choosing the one in your country or state, or the one with the file with the most recent date.

```
Return-Path: <archie-errors@crcnis2.unl.edu>
Received: from crcnis2.unl.edu by cc.bigu.edu (5.65/cc.m4.1.16)
    id AA17899; Tue, 3 May 94 04:42:05 -0500
Received: by crcnis2.unl.edu (4.1/SMI-4.1)
    id AA21361; Tue, 3 May 94 04:42:02 CDT
Message-Id: <9405030942.AA21361@crcnis2.unl.edu>
To: <you@bigu.edu>
From: (Archie Server) archie-errors@crcnis2.unl.edu
Reply-To: (Archie Server) archie-errors@crcnis2.unl.edu
Date: Tue, 3 May 94 9:41 GMT
Subject: archie [prog compress] part 1 of 1


>> path <you@bigu.edu>

>> prog compress
# Search type: exact.
Host agate.berkeley.edu     (128.32.155.1)
Last updated 10:54 29 Apr 1994

    Location: /bin
       FILE     -rwxr-xr-x   106496 bytes   00:00 15 Jun 1993   compress

    Location: /usr/ucb
       FILE     -rwxr-xr-x   32768 bytes   01:00  9 Nov 1992   compress


Host tesla.ee.cornell.edu     (128.84.253.11)
Last updated 10:53 29 Apr 1994

    Location: /bin
       FILE     ---x--x--x   17408 bytes   01:00  9 Jan 1992   compress

    Location: /usr/ucb
       FILE     ---x--x--x   17408 bytes   01:00  9 Jan 1992   compress
    .
    .
    .

>> quit
```

Figure 12.6 Results of an archie Search

archie Commands

Here is a list of the commands archie accepts by mail.

`help`

A help message.

`prog what`

What to search for. You can supply more than one argument if you want to search for more than one thing at a time. Searches are case sensitive, that is, uppercase and lowercase letters are not the same thing. Even though the command name is `prog`, you can search for anything, not just programs.

`site which`

Tell archie to return its entire list of the contents of the named site, as of the last time archie polled that anonymous FTP server.

`compress`

Have archie compress and uuencode any files before mailing them.

`path you@bigco.com`

Send results back to you at the address you specify instead of the address in the `From:` line.

`quit`

Ignore anything that appears in the message after this command. This is so that archie does not attempt to interpret anything else in the message as a command. If your mail program usually appends a signature line for you, this command will keep archie from trying to interpret your signature as archie commands.

WAIS: a Document Index

WAIS (Wide Area Information Servers) is an information service that provides hundreds of databases containing a wide variety of information, all searchable by keywords. Here is how to use WAIS by mail, and an example of using it to find a mailing list of interest to you.

How to Use WAIS

WAISmail commands go in the body of the mail message, after the headers. To query a WAIS database by mail, send a message like this to the *WAISmail* server:

```
To: waismail@quake.think.com

search lists people
```

This example searches the WAIS database named `lists` for mailing lists about people.

Query WAIS weather by Mail

To query WAISmail about `weather` Austin, Texas, use this command:

```
To: waismail@quake.think.com

search weather austin
```

The response will be like that in Figure 12.7.

Since only one document matched, it's easy to pick one to retrieve. We tell WAISmail we want that message by sending this message:

```
To: WAISmail@quake.think.com
Cc: jsq@tic.com (John Quarterman)
Subject: Re: Your WAIS Request:
In-Reply-To: Your message of "Wed, 20 Jan 93 16:11:59 PST."
            <9301210011.AA12010@quake.think.com>
From: jsq@tic.com

DocID: 0 1865 /proj/wais/db/weather/Austin-TX.txt:
/proj/wais/wais-sources/weather@quake.think.com:210%TEXT
```

WAISmail responds with the message shown in Figure 12.8. If you
send several WAISmail requests, responses to them may come back
in a different order, due to network routing. You can tell them apart
by looking at the DocID, which is included at the beginning of each
response.

Summary of WAISmail commands

Here is a summary of WAISmail commands:

```
help
```

Gets a help message.

```
search database keywords
```

Search a WAIS database for a set of keywords. The database argument is a WAIS database name. If you don't know the name of a
database, any name will do, because if WAISmail doesn't recognize
the database you name, it will return a list of valid database names.
The keywords are what you want to search for; any words will do.
Only one `search` command is permitted per message. The search
returns a document identifier, called a DOCID, in a mail message
back to you.

```
retrieve DOCID
```

You can take a DOCID out of the response to a WAISmail search
and send it back to WAISmail in a `retrieve` command to get the
actual item WAISmail found. You can put many `retrieve` commands in a single message. If you do, be sure to put a blank line
between each pair of `retrieve` commands so WAISmail can tell
them apart.

```
Date: Wed, 20 Jan 93 16:11:59 PST
Message-Id: <9301210011.AA12010@quake.think.com>
From: WAISmail@quake.think.com
To: jsq@tic.com (John Quarterman)
Subject: Your WAIS Request:

Searching: weather
Keywords: austin

Result # 1 Score:1000 lines: 52 bytes: 1865 Date:930120 Type: TEXT
Headline: Austin-TX.txt
DocID: 0 1865 /proj/wais/db/weather/Austin-TX.txt:
/proj/wais/wais-sources/weather@quake.think.com:210%TEXT
```

Figure 12.7 WAISmail Search Response

```
Date: Wed, 20 Jan 93 16:22:51 PST
Message-Id: <9301210022.AA12180@quake.think.com>
From: WAISmail@quake.think.com
To: jsq@tic.com
Subject: Your WAIS Request:  Re: Your WAIS Request:

Retrieving: "0 1865 /proj/wais/db/weather/Austin-TX.txt:
/proj/wais/wais-sources/weather@quake.think.com:210%TEXT"
```

```
AUSTIN METROPOLITAN FORECAST
NATIONAL WEATHER SERVICE AUSTIN TX
1120 AM CST WED JAN 20 1993

  THIS AFTERNOON...MOSTLY SUNNY AND MILD. HIGH IN THE LOW 60S.
NORTHWEST WIND 5 TO 15 MPH.

  TONIGHT...PARTLY CLOUDY AND COOLER WITH FOG FORMING TOWARDS MORNING
AND A LOW NEAR 40 WITH A NORTH WIND 5 TO 10 MPH.
  THURSDAY...MORNING FOG BECOMING SUNNY AND WARMER IN THE AFTERNOON WITH
A HIGH IN THE UPPER 60S AND A NORTHWEST WIND 10 MPH.

  EXTENDED FORECAST.
  FRIDAY AND SATURDAY...A FAIR SKY WITH LOWS NEAR 40 AND HIGHS IN THE 60S.
  SUNDAY...PARTLY CLOUDY AND COLDER.  LOW 30S  HIGH 50S.
WITHROW

[etc]
```

Figure 12.8 WAISmail Retrieve Response

Here are some tricks that can make your WAISmail searches simpler and more powerful.

`DOCID`

If you send just a DOCID to WAISmail, it treats that the same as if you sent:

```
retrieve DOCID
like DOCID
```

You can use the `like` command to tell WAISmail to look for documents like the one specified by a DOCID. The `like` command must go in the same message as a `search` command, and must go before the `search` command. The document specified by DOCID and the database in the `search` command must be on same WAIS server. You can put multiple `like` commands in a single message, but be sure to separate them with blank lines.

`maxres 5`

You can use the `maxres` command to limit the number of results WAISmail will return in a single message. Sometimes WAIS will find a large number of matches, but since WAIS reports the most likely matches first, you're probably only interested in the first few. The default value for this maximum is 10, so if a WAIS search finds more than 10 matches, the rest are not returned to you by mail unless you reset the `maxres` parameter.

Gopher: Menus for Many Services

As we have seen, the Internet and the Matrix provide much information and through many different services, such as FTP, archie, WAIS, and others. Remembering which service to use to find a particular piece of information and how to use it can be a problem. One solution to this problem is the Internet Gopher, which uses menus to list information selections. Each menu item can, when selected, lead to another menu or to a file or other piece of information. The idea is similar to the kinds of menus you see in a Macintosh or MS-Windows interface, where any menu item can be a directory (file folder) or a file.

Gopher menus are different in three ways from Macintosh or Windows menus.

1. Gopher menus can look exactly like any other menus on a Macintosh or Windows system, if you have a Gopher client program running on your computer, and an Internet connection for it to use. But Gopher menus may also look like something else on some other system, since Gopher uses a network protocol that can be accessed by many different client programs. In other words, Gopher can be a Macintosh or MS-Windows application, but it is not just a Macintosh or MS-Windows application, since it retrieves information across a network from some other computer, and someone else can retrieve the same information by using a completely different interface. One Gopher interface may be a *Graphical User Interface (GUI)* that expects a mouse to point and click; another interface may use ASCII menus and key letters as commands; and another interface may use plain ASCII mail messages, as we will describe in this section.

2. Any item in any Gopher menu may be anywhere in the Internet. This is because each Gopher menu item is actually a pointer to a piece of information in a specific server computer, and the server can be different for each item. In other words, when you move around in Gopher menus, you are probably retrieving information not from just one single computer, rather from a variety of computers all over the Internet.

3. Any item in a Gopher menu may actually be accessed by some other protocol. If you are using Gopher through the Internet, Gopher can even use TELNET to establish an interactive connection to a remote server such a for a library catalog. You can't use that facility without an Internet connection, but you can use Gopher items that retrieve files by FTP or that search WAIS databases even if you are sending Gopher commands by electronic mail.

So Gopher uses menus to let you select items of information from servers all over the Internet, and it retrieves that information for you by a variety of methods. Gopher is thus a general purpose menu-oriented information front end for Internet services. That is, it sits in front of many Internet services and provides you with a menu interface to them.

You can now use Gopher by mail from anywhere in the Matrix by sending messages to any of several *GopherMail* servers. Table 12.1 is a list of GopherMail servers, compiled by Glee Willis.

For usage instructions, send a message like this:

```
To: GopherMail@domain
Subject: help
```

Note that, unlike most of the other mail servers we've been looking at, this one wants its `help` command in the `Subject:` header. To get a top level Gopher menu from a GopherMail server, send a message with nothing at all in the `Subject:` or body. Once you get the menu, put an *X* before each item you want, and send that reply back to the server, as in the example in Figure 12.9. You'll get a message back for each item you marked. If you didn't mark any items, you'll get one message for each item in the menu.

When the server sends you another menu, you can mark it up and send it back, too. When you send a marked-up menu back, you can edit some lines that limit the size of messages the server will send back to you. Other items you get back may be ordinary files;

gophermail@eunet.cz
gophermail@calvin.edu
gopher@ucmp1.berkeley.edu
gopher@ftp.technion.ac.il
gopher@solaris.ims.ac.jp
gopher@nig.ac.jp
gopher@nips.ac.jp
gopher@join.ad.jp
gomail@ncc.go.jp
gopher@earn.net
gopher@dsv.su.se

Table 12.1 GopherMail servers

```
To: GopherMail Server   <gopher@dsv.su.se>
From: jsq@tic.com
Subject: Re: Phone Books and E-Mail addresses

Mail this file back to gopher with an X before the menu items
that you want.  If you don't mark any items, gopher will send
all of them.


    1.   Netfind <TEL> (Not supported)
X   2.   Phone Books European Universities/
    3.   Phone Books--Other Institutions (Notre Dame)/
    4.   Phone books US Universities (Minnesota)/
    5.   World Country & Area Telephone Codes Index (Not USA or CANAD
         <?> (Send keywords in Subject:)
    6.   World Telephone Code Information/
    7.   x.500(Michigan type, Umea)/
```

Figure 12.9 Marked GopherMail Menu

there's no point in marking those up and sending them back.

You can use GopherMail to search the same servers (WAIS, WHOIS, X.500, etc.) that you can access via regular Gopher. Just follow the menus.

LISTSERV

Probably the most sophisticated server for returning information by mail is *LISTSERV*. LISTSERV was developed on BITNET, but is widely used from other networks. As we've already seen in Chapter 9, *Mailing List Basics*, the basic function of LISTSERV is to subscribe people to mailing lists. But LISTSERV also keeps archives of those lists, and permits users to search for and retrieve files from them.

To get a list of LISTSERV commands, send a message like this:

```
To: listserv@uga.cc.uga.edu

help
```

Many other computers support LISTSERVs, but all of them expect LISTSERV commands to go to the alias listserv. Any LISTSERV commands go in the body of the message, not in the `Subject:` header (BITNET did not traditionally have `Subject:` headers).

LISTSERV File Commands

LISTSERV has several basic commands for finding and retrieving files. These examples use a LISTSERV at one particular BITNET node, but any LISTSERV will do.

```
To: LISTSERV@zilker.net

info interesting
```

Retrieve the general introductory information for the list named **interesting**. We've already discussed this command in Chapter 9.

```
To: listserv@listserv.net

INDex filelist
```

A *filelist* is what LISTSERV calls a directory. If you don't know the name of any filelist, leave it off, and the LISTSERV will send you a list of the filelists it knows. Then use the `index` command again with the name of a specific filelist. As we discussed in Chapter 9, *Mailing List Basics*, the capital letters `IND` indicate that that's all of the word `index` you need to type for LISTSERV to understand which command you mean. You don't have to type them in all caps, either; you can give LISTSERV commands in any combination of uppercase and lowercase.

```
To: listserv@listserv.net

GET filename filetype
```

Once you've seen the contents of a filelist, you can pick a filename from it and retrieve that file with the `get` command. The filetype argument is a filename extension and serial number used to distinguish among several files of the same basic name. You may have to provide both filename and filetype with the `get` command. The `index` command will list some files that you cannot retrieve. These are marked in the message you get in response to the `index` command. If you try to get such a file, you will instead get a message saying you are not authorized to retrieve it.

```
To: listserv@listserv.net

INFO infofile
```

This command retrieves a file from a collection that has been put together by LISTSERV administrators for general information. If you don't know the name of any infofile, leave it off, and the LISTSERV will send you a list of them.

```
To: listserv@listserv.net

INFO REFCARD
```

This command will get you a complete list of all LISTSERV commands.

Imitations of LISTSERV

LISTSERV has proven very popular, but until recently it only ran on IBM mainframes. However, many partial imitations of it have been written and deployed on UNIX and other systems on the Internet and elsewhere. None of these imitations implement the actual LISTSERV command set, none of them implement all LISTSERV features, and none of them is integrated into the LISTSERV information distribution network.

However, some of these other programs are quite popular in themselves. Of them, Majordomo is probably the most widely used. And LISTSERV itself is now available on multiple platforms.

Majordomo

A common mailing lists manager with file retrieval capability is *Majordomo*. If you know a list such as booklist@tic.com is handled with Majordomo, you can find related information by sending mail to Majordomo at the same domain, as in majordomo@tic.com. We've discussed Majordomo's commands for handling lists in

Chapter 9, *Mailing List Basics*. To get a list of Majordomo commands, send a message like this:

```
To: majordomo@tic.com

help
```

Majordomo File Commands

Majordomo has a several major file retrieval commands. These examples use the Majordomo at one particular domain; as we discussed in Chapter 9, each Majordomo handles certain lists, and you must use the right Majordomo for the list. The examples use an example list named interesting.

```
To: majordomo@zilker.net

index interesting
```

Return an index of files related to a list. This Majordomo `index` command has a different function than the LISTSERV `index` command, since it provides a list of files directly related to a particular mailing list.

```
To: majordomo@zilker.net

get interesting filename
```

Get a file related to a list. The Majordomo `get` command is different from the LISTSERV `get` command, since it retrieves only files directly related to a mailing list, not more general files.

```
To: majordomo@zilker.net

info interesting
```

Retrieve the general introductory information for the list. We've already discussed this command in Chapter 9.

Summary

You've seen in this chapter a wide range of methods and services for finding things through electronic mail, and retrieving things you want. Let's see how to find people, too.

13

Finding People

To send mail, you need an address. To find someone's address, you often need to find that person. This chapter is about ways of finding a person's address, or the actual person.

The simplest way to get someone's address is by looking at one of their mail messages. If someone sends you a private mail message or posts a message to a mailing list you subscribe to, you can see what the other person's address is by looking at the `From:` header, or at the person's signature at the end of the message. In many cases, you can simply tell your mail program to reply to the message, and the program will automatically send the reply to the correct address, without you having to do anything specific.

If you do not have a message from the person you seek, you may have other information about that person, such as a telephone number or a business card. If you can simply call the person up on the telephone and ask for a network address, do so. If you don't know their telephone number, but you do know their organization name and location, telephone directory assistance for their city or organization can often locate them quickly.

Whenever possible, ask the person you want to reach, or an information service whose job it is to locate that person. Only if that does not work, try asking other people. Start with someone close to you, such as a coworker who would be likely to have met the person or exchanged mail with them.

A query to an appropriate mailing list will often get you the name and address of a person you seek. However, you want to avoid sending such requests to lists unless you are sure the other people on the list have some interest in helping you find the person you seek. In this chapter, we describe some of the basic services, techniques, and strategies you can use to find people in the Matrix.

WHOIS: a Directory

One of the simplest places to look for people is in the *WHOIS* directory. This directory lists mostly system and network administrators, but those are often the people for you are looking for, so it's a good place to look first.

```
To: service@rs.internic.net
Subject: whois perot
```

Most WHOIS responses are self-explanatory. For more details on their format, send a message like this:

```
To: service@rs.internic.net
Subject: help
```

The InterNIC WHOIS server is one of the more central servers, since InterNIC is tasked with providing information for a large segment of the Internet, but many other organizations also run WHOIS servers. Whenever, in your search for a person, you ask a network's *NIC (Network Information Center)* for information, you may find it useful to ask if that NIC has a WHOIS server, so that you can query it.

Other Sources of Information

Many kinds of sources provide information about people on the various networks in the Matrix. Many information servers are located on the Internet, and were originally designed for interactive use across the Internet. If you do not have Internet access, but you do have mail, you can still access all the services listed in this chapter and in the previous chapter. For example, various directories with user information are available as WAIS databases; for example, the databases named **usenet** and **uumap**. Still more information servers, such as the X.500 directory, are available through Gopher by mail, as we have discussed.

A few Internet information services, such as *KIS (Knowbot Information Services)* and *netfind,* apparently do not have mail interfaces. However, there are enough others that do.

General Strategies for Finding People

Let's be more specific about how you can go about finding a person in the Matrix. Suppose you are looking for Jane Doe at Bigco, Inc. Try these things first:

- Ask Jane.

- Ask a directory service.
  Find a computer, database, or service that knows.

- Ask a user service.
  Find an organization whose purpose is to catalog and give out such information.

We provide hints about finding each of these information sources. When looking for such information, prefer sources that are:

- local to the person you are trying to find

- local to you

- general dedicated-information services and organizations

The basic idea here is to find the other person with the least inconvenience to anyone else. Sources such as these are also usually the fastest way to find someone.

What to Look for

Don't look only for an electronic mail address for the person you seek. Other information may be easier to find first, and will probably lead you to a mail address.

First, look for specific information about the person, such as an electronic mail address, a telephone number, a fax number, or a postal address. If you can't find any information about the person, maybe you can find one of their colleagues.

Also look for information about the person's organization, such as its name, location, electronic mail address, telephone number, fax number, or postal address. You may find the name or other information about a coworker, secretary, manager, or other affiliate of the person at the person's organization. Don't forget that a person's employer is usually not the only organization they're affiliated with. Consider clubs, churches, and of course, electronic mailing lists.

You may also be able to discover information about a network host somehow affiliated with the person, perhaps because it is widely used for sending mail by other people at the person's organization.

Network White Pages

Here we sketch a general strategy for searching various network information services to find a specific person. This is similar to looking in the white pages of a printed telephone directory, and in fact that is one of the steps suggested in this strategy. Don't worry about following the steps in order. Skip ahead or do steps in another order if it seems appropriate. This strategy is simply intended to give you some ideas on how to start.

Start Nearby

- Ask the user.
  You may have to translate the address the user supplies. For example, the user may only know the local hostname, and you will then have to deduce a domain name for the user's organization. (WHOIS is useful for this.) Or the user may supply a name in DECNET format when you need to use Internet DNS domain format. We have discussed translating such formats in Chapter 7, *Mail Addressing and Routing*. If you can't get an actual electronic mail address, remember to get details of the person's organization or location. Ask for someone there who would be likely to know more, such as the local network administrator.

- Look in your notes.
  You may have a copy of the person's business card, or some other record of how to reach them. Check for any address of anyone else at their company; the address format might be obvious. For example, if Joe Blow at Bigco has an address jblow@bigco.com, it's a good bet that jdoe@bigco.com will work for Jane Doe.

- Check for aliases on your host or in your network.
  Somebody else may have cached an address for the person, and you may be able to find the organization, at least. How to do this depends on your local setup. On most UNIX systems, global aliases are kept in a simple format in a text file named **/etc/aliases** or **/usr/lib/aliases**.

Here's another method for finding mail addresses; one which only works on IP networks. If you have TELNET, and you know which host on your network handles your mail, you can try connecting to the main mail server on port 25, which is the *Simple Mail Transfer Protocol (SMTP)* port. Suppose you want to see if there is an alias for jdoe on your mail server. You could ask your SMTP server, like this:

```
telnet mail.yourco.com 25
SMTP server ....
VRFY jdoe
```

Network Information Services

- Ask general network information services,
  such as WHOIS, X.500, KIS, and netfind.

- Ask network-specific directories,
  such as the UUCP map, FidoNet map, and BITNET GATES. All of these are available as WAIS databases, which means you can use WAIS or Gopher to search them, as we discussed in Chapter 12, *Finding Things*.

- Ask at the user's end.
  Many organizations run local WHOIS and finger servers.

Sources Close to the User

- postmaster@their.dom.
  Every Internet host is supposed to support a **postmaster** alias that reaches someone responsible for mail functions there. Actually, about 12 percent of Internet domains do not support this alias, so it's unpredictable whether a message you send to a postmaster will really reach anyone, but it's worth a try. Don't send mail to **postmaster** as the first thing you try, however; these people do have other jobs to do. Also, many postmasters will forward your request to the person you're trying to reach, rather than responding directly to you. Many BITNET hosts support a similar address named **postmast**. If you know the target host is a UNIX

machine, it may be worth trying to send mail to root@their.dom, since mail for that user is usually read by system administrators.

- Telephone information.
  Call telephone directory assistance for the person's city, organization, or department. Don't forget printed telephone books. Your local library probably has a wide selection.

- Their colleagues.
  Ask the person's colleagues. Try to pick someone who has some other reason to talk to you, such as someone who is attending the same conference, who works in similar specialties, or who participates in the same mailing lists.

- Your colleagues.
  Ask around your own department for someone who knows the person or the person's organization.

User Services   Many networks and other organizations support groups whose purpose is to supply information to network users. Such an organization is often called a *NIC (Network Information Center).* Try asking a NIC.

- Your NIC.
  You are connected to the Matrix through some network. It may be in your company or university, or it may be a commercial or noncommercial network provider. It probably has a NIC, and that NIC should have an interest in helping you find the answer to your questions. Get your NIC's electronic mail address and telephone number and keep them handy. If you don't know how to reach your NIC, ask whoever set up your network connection.

- NIC of NICs.
  Some NICs try to act as referral services for other NICs. The best known such NIC is probably InterNIC. Try sending mail to postmaster@internic.net.

- Network NICs.
  Many individual UUCP or IP providers have their own NICs for

their specific networks. If you can determine that the person you want to reach is accessible through a certain network, ask the NIC for that network.

- Their NIC.
  If you can determine that the person communicates with the Matrix through a certain organization, network provider, or conferencing system, ask the NIC for that outfit. It's their job to provide information about their own users. Usually postmaster@domain will work, once you find the domain for that NIC.

- info-nets@think.com
  This is a mailing list that reaches people who are interested in unusual questions about networks. Don't try it first, because you can find most people more quickly by other means. The people answering questions are volunteers. They don't verify information, so use what you find out with a grain of salt. However, they are all over the world, and often they can find out things that most NICs don't know.

Other Sources   Find something the user published or in which they are mentioned. This usually involves asking a library service or a library.

- Your library services.
  Your organization probably has a library, and if it doesn't, your city, county, or local college or university probably does.

- General library services.
  Many libraries have made their catalogs available over the networks. You can get to many of them by using Gopher or WAIS.

- Library information.
  Don't be shy about calling up your local library or going there and asking for help. Librarians like to discover information; it's their job and their vocation.

- Their library.
If you've found out enough about the person to know their city or employer, try the library there.

Summary

A good strategy to find a user's address should have these aspects:

- Speed.

- Least effort on your part.

- Minimal effort on the user's part.

- Use of automated services when possible.

- Asking people when necessary.

- Least effort to people not directly involved.

14

MIME: Multipurpose Internet Mail Extensions

MIME (Multipurpose Internet Mail Extensions) lets you add graphics, complicated text, and even sound to your email messages. As originally designed, the basic Internet mail system was meant to carry only text messages. And simple ASCII text at that. While simple text is often an adequate communications medium, you will find that the ability to add graphics to your email messages is a nice bonus. Let's first see how MIME gets around the original text-only limitation of the basic Internet mail system; then we will discuss how to use MIME with the Pine mailer.

How MIME Works

As we discussed in Chapter 6, a mail message consists of a header and a body. You can use only characters from the 127-character ASCII set in the header and body. Also, both the header and the body must consist of text lines with a maximum length of 1,000 characters, and each line must be terminated by the CR LF characters.

MIME is a standard way of encoding non-text data into mail messages without some of the limitations of the more ad hoc methods we discussed in Chapter 12. MIME extends the mail message from consisting of only a header and a body, to a header followed by several body parts. Each body part can represent simple ASCII text or, perhaps, a graphical image. All the body parts are carefully encoded into standard ASCII characters before the message is transported, so the ASCII-based transport system will work without error. However, unlike the uuencode method, MIME encoding methods use easily implemented standards, so a mailer that is MIME compliant can decode a message sent from any other MIME-compliant mailer. Let's look at an example MIME message to see how this works.

In Figure 14.1 we see a message which uses the MIME protocol to send the GIF graphic we used in the uuencode example in Chapter 12. MIME sends the graphic file as ASCII text included in a mail message. In the example, the sender has added a couple of special header lines to the header to indicate that the enclosed message is MIME encoded. The first line is the `Mime-Version:` header that tells the receiving mail program which version of MIME was used to encode the message. In this case, Version 1.0 of MIME is used.

The `Content-Type:` line tells the receiving mail program how to tell when one MIME body part starts and another ends. In this case, a unique string of ASCII characters is used to separate one body part from another. The `multippart/mixed` keyword signals that there are several body parts in the message. The `boundary` keyword tells what string is used to separate each body part. Note that the string is a unique value which does not appear in any other line of the message.

```
To: smoot@tic.com
Subject: MIME example
Mime-Version: 1.0
Content-Type: multipart/mixed; boundary="----- =_aaaaaaaaaa0"
Date: Tue, 14 Sep 93 15:34:20 -0500
From: jack@tic.com

------- =_aaaaaaaaaa0
Content-Type: text/plain; charset="us-ascii"

This is an example of a MIME message.

------- =_aaaaaaaaaa0
Content-Type: image/gif; name="logo.gif"
Content-Transfer-Encoding: base64

R01GODdh4gMEA8IAAAAAAD+/P7////8AAL8Av////wAA/wAAACwAAAAA4gME
AwAD/li63P4wykmrvTjrzbv/YCiOZGmeaKqubOu+cCzPdG3feK7vfO//wKBw
```

Figure 14.1 MIME Example

In the example, the message has two parts. Within each part, another `Content-Type:` tells the mail program how to interpret each part of the message.

The first body part is simply plain ASCII text. This part is interpreted just like an ordinary text message.

The second body part is the ASCII-encoded GIF file. The `Content-Type;` indicates this fact by the keyword `image/gif.` In addition, another MIME header, `Content-Transfer-Encoding:` says how this body part has been encoded for transport. In this case the binary GIF file is encoded using the MIME standard `base64` encoding scheme. Without going into details about the `base64` encoding, suffice it to say it takes the original binary GIF file and converts it into printable ASCII for mail transport. The important thing about `base64` encoding is that it is a standard encoding method that all MIME-compliant mailers must understand and implement.

Each of the body parts is separated from the special headers by a blank line, just as in a regular mail message. The mail transport system treats the entire message as a single mail message. It does not know or care about the special MIME headers. They are considered to be just another line in the body of the message.

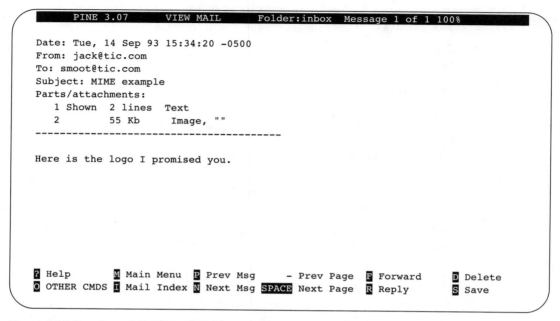

Figure 14.2 Reading a MIME Mail Message

MIME and Pine

Let's see how this message is interpreted when it is received by a MIME-capable mail program like Pine. In Figure 14.2 we see the message displayed in the Pine mailer. In Figure 14.3 we show the GIF file as it is displayed in a separate window on a bit-mapped display. In this case a display device (say, a UNIX workstation with a bitmapped display running the X Window System) capable of showing a GIF image is used. The textual part of the mail message is shown in the standard Pine terminal window. A second window is opened in which a GIF interpreter is run on the second part of the message (after the mail program has decoded it).

Pine also shows how many parts the message contains and what each part is. Note that Pine (and other MIME-capable mailers) always know how to interpret the various MIME headers and know the parts of each message body. If you are not using a device that can display a particular MIME body type, Pine does the next

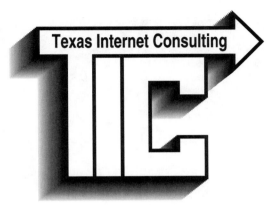

Figure 14.3 Example GIF Image

best thing--it complains that it cannot display the body part and asks you if you want to save it to a file.

MIME messages are not just restricted to two body parts. Messages can contain many body parts with varying contents. You can include as many as you want.

It is relatively easy to send a message that has been encoded with MIME. Mail programs that understand MIME let you type a mail message and also include other non-textual body parts within the message. The usual assumption is that the non-text part of the message is contained in a single file. Let's see how Pine does this.

In Figure 14.4, we see the Pine COMPOSE MESSAGE screen with a text message. The text part of the message is entered in the normal way. In Pine, the Attchmnt: header line lets you enclose a file as a MIME body part. In this example, two attachments are included. Each of them will be converted to base64 representation and included in the message with the proper MIME headers.

You may wonder what happens when a non-MIME mailer receives a MIME message. The non-MIME mail program simply displays the body of the message as ASCII text. Since the entire body of the message is ASCII this does no harm. The special MIME headers and body parts are all displayed as text. A message recipient who is familiar with MIME can then manually decode the various parts of the message.

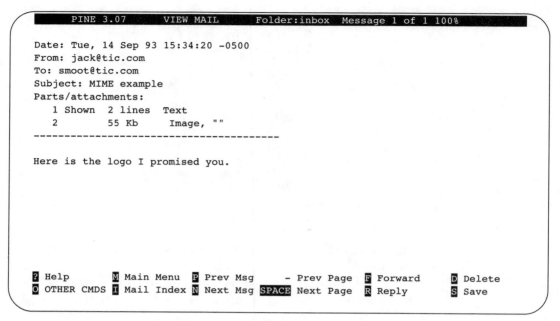

Figure 14.4 Reading a MIME Mail Message

MIME is very useful because it enables you to send information which is not just text. It also enables you to send text in character sets other than ASCII, which is useful because ASCII doesn't have enough characters to support languages other than English and Hawaiian. ASCII also doesn't support type styles such as italic and boldface, but MIME does, through its *richtext* format.

Of course, you must have a computer display capable of interpreting and displaying the information encoded in a MIME message. A MIME mailer does not normally contain the capabilities to display a MIME body part itself. Instead, it calls on other programs to do the chore of actually displaying the body part correctly. This gives MIME a certain amount of flexibility in configuration. It also means that you must understand how to configure your own computer to take advantage of the full MIME capabilities.

Summary

MIME is not everywhere yet, but it is rapidly becoming the standard for sending email messages which contain more than just text. In addition to the graphical possibilities we showed in this chapter, MIME can also carry sound and moving images. With MIME you can extend plain ASCII to multimedia by mail.

Appendix A

Places to Connect

You can send and receive electronic mail in more different ways than for any other computer network service, mostly because more different kinds of systems carry mail than any other service. In this chapter we describe methods of connecting to some of the most prominent of these systems, and we include details of how to contact them.

We already described general types of systems in Chapter 4, *The Networks*. We also described many specific networks in some detail in that chapter, and we will not repeat all that discussion here. Here we say some more about what you need to know about each type if you want to connect to it. We start with the least expensive kind of network connection, which is generally to a distributed mail network such as UUCP, FidoNet, or WWIVnet. We continue with commercial mail networks, such as ATT Mail, SprintMail, EasyLink, and MCI Mail. Then there are commercial conferencing systems, such as Prodigy, CompuServe, GEnie, AOL, NIFTY-Serve, Delphi, BIX, PC-lan, ASCII-net, People, and Asahi-net.

Finally, there are the several levels of connectivity to the Internet, from packaged dialup software to login hosts and freenets to dialup IP with PPP or SLIP to dedicated IP links. We didn't discuss these methods of connecting to the Internet in detail in Chapter 4, so we'll say more about them in this appendix.

Hardware and Software

In this appendix we describe the kinds of hardware and software you will need; we discussed this question in general in Chapter 3, *Common Questions*. In most of the cases we describe, you will need a modem, to convert the digital signals computers produce to analog sounds that can be carried over ordinary telephone connections.

If you're using mail through a commercial conferencing system or an Internet login host, you probably won't need any extra software, although such systems often supply additional software that can ease your use of their services.

If you're setting up a UUCP or IP link to your computer, you will need local software. If you're using a commercial connectivity provider, you can usually get the software you need from that provider. If you want to get your own software yourself, see Appendix B, *Software*.

Your Organization's LAN

If your company, university, agency, or other organization has a LAN with external mail connectivity, your easiest mail solution may be be to connect to that LAN. You will need to contact your organization's network administrator. LANs vary so much that it is difficult to say anything more specific.

In most cases, you will need a hardware device to connect your computer to the LAN; a common example is an Ethernet transceiver. Even in the case of Ethernet, you will need to get the administrator to tell you which kind of Ethernet (10BaseT, thinnet, thicknet, IEEE 802.3, etc.).

The kind of software you will need also depends on the type of LAN. Even if it is an Ethernet, the computers connected to it may be using, for example, Novell Netware, AppleTalk, or IP. You will need software on your computer that handles the appropriate one of those protocols. In addition, your network administrator will need to assign you an address for the appropriate protocol, such as 192.189.132.33 for an IP address. You will need to pick a mnemonic name for your computer, such as diamond, and the network administrator will need to fit it into the general naming scheme for your organization, for example as diamond.bigco.com.

You will also need a mail interface, and there may be several that work with your LAN's combination of network hardware and protocol software.

Fortunately, the administrator of your LAN will probably have a recommended set of hardware and software for your computer hardware (IBM PC clone, Macintosh, or other) and software (DOS, MS-Windows, Mac-OS, UNIX, or other) platform. You should be able to get what you need from your network administrator.

Even if you have a mail connection through your organization's LAN, sometimes organizational limitations on use of the internal LAN can make separate external personal mail access attractive.

Mail Networks

Some networks are intended primarily for carrying mail. Such networks include FidoNet, WWIVnet, and UUCP, plus a variety of commercial mail networks.

FidoNet and WWIVnet

FidoNet and WWIVnet are mostly BBS networks. The simplest way to connect to one of them is to find a local node, dial it up, and log in on that BBS. You can probably find a local BBS list by asking around your area. You can also run the FidoNet or WWIVnet software yourself and connect your machine directly to one of those networks. In that case, you need to get a copy of the node list for that network and look for a nearby node. FidoNet and WWIVnet are essentially DOS networks.

UUCP

Most people think of UUCP as a UNIX network, and most computers on the UUCP network may run UNIX. However, there are several UUCP implementations for DOS, and many DOS computers on the UUCP network.

Traditionally, the way you connect to UUCP is to find someone who already has a connection and ask that person if you can set up a link to their system. This is very convenient financially because the only direct monetary cost is for telephone calls. If you can find a UUCP feed within your local telephone dialing area and your telephone company does not charge for the time you use, you will pay essentially nothing. Even if your feed is long distance, the only obvious charge is the long distance telephone bill. This is also convenient administratively, because you probably won't have to ask your management to approve new dedicated funds.

Likely people to ask for a UUCP link would be at the local university, at a customer or vendor company, at a local organization in your city, or someone you know from college or previous work.

Commercial UUCP Providers

In areas such as Silicon Valley the number of people wanting UUCP connections is too large for traditional free connections to work well. Few organizations want to support huge numbers of UUCP connections, so the number of hops from one machine to another becomes large. In addition, UUCP is not always the most robust of protocols, so it is good to deal with a UUCP provider with personnel dedicated to keeping your UUCP feed working. Vendors who supply UUCP feeds for a fee have sprung up to address these needs. Well known large UUCP vendors include UUNET, PSINet, CERFNET, and EUnet. Many other companies and networks provide UUCP service for a fee. Look for a more local provider in the list at the end of this appendix, or check around your area. See also *The Internet Connection* (Addison-Wesley, 1994).

Nixpubs

Many small systems running UNIX and providing mail service by UUCP exist; such a system may be called a *public access UNIX system (nixpub).* Dialing up one of these and logging in gives you access to the UUCP network in the same way that dialing up a FidoNet BBS and logging in can give you access to FidoNet. One advantage is that nixpubs generally support domain addresses, such as mailbook@tic.com, so you don't have to learn FidoNet or WWIVnet addressing.

Some nixpubs charge nothing, and others charge fees. If you don't want to run UUCP yourself, dialing up a nixpub and logging in there may be easier. It may also be cheaper, since the nixpub would then be carrying the cost of any necessary long distance UUCP (or USENET) feed, and sharing that cost among all its users. There is a nixpub list, but it is copyrighted and republication is prohibited, so we do not list its contents in this book. However, you can get it by sending a message like this:

```
To: mail-server@bts.com

get PUB nixpub.short
```

USENET

Remember USENET isn't really a network; it's just a news service. If you want to get USENET news, you should check with the providers you are contacting about mail service, and pick one that also provides USENET news. There is also an additional for-pay

USENET news service, called ClariNet. ClariNet provides stock market quotations, several press wire services, and many other services that are not found on the rest of USENET. If you want to read ClariNet news, ask potential providers if they have it.

> *ClariNet*
> info@clarinet.com
> +1-408-296-0366
> 4880 Stevens Creek Blvd. #206
> San Jose, CA 95129-1034
> U.S.A.

Commercial Mail Networks

UUCP, FidoNet, and WWIVnet are essentially volunteer networks, and nixpubs are often also staffed by volunteers. If you want to buy mail access from a commercial organization, and thus presumably obtain commercial support for mail service, try one of the commercial mail networks.

> *ATT Mail* +1-800-631-8097
>
> *EasyLink* +1-800-631-8097
>
> *MCI Mail* +1-800-888-0800
>
> *SprintMail* +1-800-877-4020

Commercial Conferencing Systems

If you want mail plus other specialized database and conferencing services, you may want to try one of the centralized commercial conferencing systems, such as Prodigy, CompuServe, GEnie, AOL, NIFTY-Serve, Delphi, BIX, PC-VAN, ASCII-net, People, and Asahi-net.

> *AOL* +1-800-827-6364

ASCII-net +81-044-989-9432

Asahi-net +81-03-3666-2881

BIX +1-800-695-4882

CompuServe +1-800-848-8990

Delphi +1-617-491-3342

e-World +1-408-974-4778

GEnie +1-800-638-9636

NIFTY-Serve +81-03-5471-4900

Nikkei Mix +81-3-5210-8188

PC-VAN +81-0120-00-9805

People +81-03-5563-4150

Prodigy +1-800-776-3449

Internet Connectivity

If you want to use interactive Internet services such as remote login (TELNET) or hypertext (WWW), you will need an Internet connection. Here we provide a list of the major methods of connecting to the Internet. For a more complete list of systems that provide commercial Internet access, see *The Internet Connection* (Addison-Wesley, 1994).

Packaged Dialup Software and Services

WorldLink (see PSINet)

Sprint (see SprintMail)

Internet Login Hosts

Perhaps a hundred different providers worldwide now will let you log in on a computer they run that has Internet connectivity. Most of them charge for access, but some do not.

Freenets

Some people object to charging users for Internet access. Some of these people provide Internet login hosts that provide services of the same sort as other login hosts, but with little or no charge for those services. Costs are instead supported by volunteer labor and by grants, often from local, state, or federal goverments, or from telephone companies. Such a login host is called a *freenet*. Many of these freenets have banded together in a loose organization called the *National Public Telecomputing Network (NPTN)*.

> *National Public Telecomputing Network (NPTN).*
> +1-216-368-2733
> PO Box 1987
> Cleveland, OH 44106
> U.S.A.

Dialup IP

Many local providers supply dialup IP connections in addition to login host access.

Direct IP

Many local providers supply direct IP connections in addition to dialup IP and login host access. However, if you cannot find a local provider, or if you prefer a larger scale operator, you may want to approach one of the national or international scale Internet providers. These include, but are not necessarily limited to, the several dozen *Commercial Internet Exchange (CIX)* members. For several regions of the world there are coordinating bodies that can direct you to nearby IP providers.

Commercial Internet Exchange (CIX)
CIX secretariat
+1-303-482-2150
info@cix.org
3110 Fairview Park Drive, Ste. 590
Falls Church, VA 22042
U.S.A.

InterNIC
+1-703-742-4777
hostmaster@internic.net
505 Huntmar Park Dr.
Herndon, VA 22070
U.S.A.

RIPE (Reseaux IP Européens)
+31-20-592-5065
ncc@ripe.net
c/o NIKHEF-H
Kruislaan 409
NL-1098 SJ Amsterdam
The Netherlands

JPNIC (Japan Network Information Center)
+81-03-5684-7256
office-contacts@nic.ad.jp
c/o Computer Centre, University of Tokyo
2-11-16, Yayoi
Bunkyo-ku, Tokyo 113
Japan

APNIC (Asia-Pacific Network Information Center).
+81-03-3812-2111
nakayama@nic.ad.jp
c/o Computer Center, University of Tokyo
2-11-16, Yayoi
Bunkyo-ku, Tokyo 113
Japan

Providers by Name

Here is a list of network connectivity providers by name. To find a provider near you, you may first want to look in the list of providers by telephone area code in the next section.

For each provider in the list, we give a line like this:

Zilker Internet Park   +1-512-206-3850   X   —   X   —   —

under these fields:

> Provider   Telephone   Type

The fields in each line are:

Provider   The name of the providing company or the network it supplies. In this example, *Zilker Internet Park.*

Telephone   A voice contact telephone number for the provider (or a modem number if we couldn't find a voice number). In this example, +1-512-206-3850. The +1 in this example is not the digit 1 you usually need to dial in the U.S. to call a long distance number. It is the telephone country code for the United States, Canada, and many Caribbean countries. Someone calling one of these countries from some other country would use that country code. To call another country from the United States, you would typically dial 011, then the telephone country code, for example 33 for France, then the rest of the telephone number. Since you'll usually be calling a provider within your country, you won't usually need to dial the telephone country code at all.

Type   One or more of:

Host   for Internet login host; you can dial up this kind of system, log in, and use most Internet services

Freenet   for Freenet; you can dial up this kind of system, log in, and use a specialized menu system that typically provides use of some Internet services

Dial. IP   for dialup IP; you can use an implementation of TCP/IP on your computer to dial up this kind of system and put your computer on the Internet

Dir. IP   for direct (continuous) IP; like dialup IP, except with a dedicated connection

CIX   for CIX member

This table lists more than 350 Matrix connectivity providers, ranging from the most basic mail access to various ranges of Internet access. More network service providers appear daily, so you may find one that we didn't list. If you do, please drop a note to mailbook@tic.com and tell us about it.

Provider	Telephone	Login Host	Free-net	Dial. IP	Dir. IP	CIX
404 Free-Net	+1-404-892-0943	—	X	—	—	—
a2i communications	+1-408-293-8078	X	—	X	X	X
AARnet	+61-6-249-3385	—	—	—	X	—
Able Tech	+1-408-441-6000	—	—	X	X	X
Acadiana Free-Net	+1-318-837-9374	—	X	—	—	—
Actcom	+972-4-676114	—	—	—	X	—
Actrix	+64-4-389-5478	X	—	—	—	—
agora.rdrop.com	+1-503-452-0960	X	—	X	—	—
Akron Regional Free-Net	+1-216-972-6352	—	X	—	—	—
Alachua Free-Net	+1-904-372-8401	—	X	—	—	—
Almont Expression	+1-313-798-8171	—	X	—	—	—
The Aloha Free-Net Project	+1-808-533-3969	—	X	—	—	—
AlphaNet	+1-414-821-0334	—	—	X	X	X

Provider	Telephone	Type				
		Login Host	Free-net	Dial. IP	Dir. IP	CIX
Alternet	+1-703-204-8000	—	—	X	X	X
Ameritech Extended Classroom	+1-517-774-3975	—	X	—	—	—
AnchorNet	+1-907-261-2891	—	X	—	—	—
ANS CO+RE Services	+1-800-456-8267	—	—	X	X	X
Apex Global Info Systems	+1-313-278-0300	—	—	X	X	X
Ashton Communications	+1-619-424-5362	—	—	X	X	X
Aurora.Net	+1-415-327-3001	—	—	X	X	X
Austin Free-Net	+1-512-288-5691	—	X	—	—	—
AzTeC Computing	+1-602-965-5985	—	X	—	—	—
BARRNet	+1-415-725-1790	—	—	X	X	X
Baton Rouge Free-Net	+1-504-346-0707	—	X	—	—	—
BCnet	+1-604-822-3932	—	—	—	X	—
Berbee Information Networks	+1-608-233-2228	—	—	X	X	X
Big Country Free-Net	+1-915-674-6964	—	X	—	—	—
Big Sky Telegraph	+1-406-683-7338	—	X	—	—	—
BlackBox	+1-713-480-2684	X	—	X	—	—
Blue Ridge Free-Net	+1-703-981-1424	—	X	—	—	—
Blue Sky Free-Net Of Manitoba	+1-204-945-1413	—	X	—	—	—
BOLNET	+591-2-359585	—	—	—	X	—
Buffalo Free-Net	+1-716-877-8800x451	—	X	—	—	—
CA*net	+1-416-978-1255	—	—	X	X	X
Calgary Free-Net	+1-403-264-9535	—	X	—	—	—
California Online Resources for Education	+1-800-272-8743	—	X	—	—	—
cam.org	+1-514-923-2102	X	—	X	—	—
Canton Regional Free-Net	+1-216-499-9600	—	X	—	—	—
Cape Breton Free-Net	+1-902-862-6432	—	X	—	—	—
Cape Girardeau Free-Net	+1-314-334-9322	—	X	—	—	—
Capital Region Information Service	+1-518-442-3728	—	X	—	—	—
Capitol City Free-Net	+1-517-321-4972	—	X	—	—	—
CARNet	+38-41-629-963	—	—	—	X	—
CCC	+54-1-783-0729	—	—	—	X	—
CedarNet	+1-319-273-6282	—	X	—	—	—
CentNet	+1-617-868-1198	—	—	X	X	X

Provider	Telephone	Type				
		Login Host	Free-net	Dial. IP	Dir. IP	CIX
Central Virginia's Free-Net	+1-804-828-6650	—	X	—	—	—
CERFnet	+1-800-876-CERF	X	—	X	X	X
Charlotte's Web	+1-704-358-5245	—	X	—	—	—
Chebucto Free-Net	+1-902-425-2061	—	X	—	—	—
Chester County Free-Net	+1-215-430-6621	—	X	—	—	—
Chippewa Valley Free-Net	+1-715-836-3715	—	X	—	—	—
CIAO! Free-Net	+1-604-368-2233	—	X	—	—	—
CICnet	+1-313-998-6102	—	—	—	X	—
Clark County Free-Net	+1-206-696-6846	—	X	—	—	—
class	+1-800-488-4559	X	—	—	—	—
Cleveland Free-Net	+1-216-368-3888	—	X	—	—	—
Colorado SuperNet	+1-303-273-3471	X	—	X	X	—
Columbia Online Information Network (COIN)	+1-314-884-7000	—	X	—	—	—
Commonwealth Telephone Company	+1-717-675-1121	—	—	X	X	X
Community News Service	+1-719-592-1240	X	—	X	—	—
Community Service Network	+1-410-822-4132	—	X	—	—	—
CONACYT	+52-5-327-7400	—	—	—	X	—
CONCERT-CONNECT	+1-919-248-1999	X	—	X	X	—
ConnectedNet	+1-206-820-6639	—	—	X	X	X
CPBI	+1-203-278-5310	—	X	—	—	—
CR Labs Dialup Internet Access	+1-415-381-2800	X	—	X	X	—
CRACIN	+1-809-759-6891	—	—	—	X	—
crash.cts.com	+1-619-593-9597	X	—	X	X	—
CRnet	+506-341013	—	—	—	X	—
CSC	+358-0-4572239	X	—	X	—	—
CSUnet	+1-310-985-9661	—	—	X	X	—
The Cyberspace Station	+1-619-634-1376	X	—	X	—	—
Cyberstore Systems	+1-604-526-0607	—	—	X	X	X
Danbury Area Free-Net	+1-203-797-4512	—	X	—	—	—
Databank	+1-913-842-6699	—	—	X	X	X
DataNet	+358-31-243-2242	—	—	—	X	—
Dataserve	+972-3-6474448	X	—	X	X	—
Davis Community Network	+1-916-752-7764	—	X	—	—	—

Provider	Telephone	Type				
		Login Host	Free-net	Dial. IP	Dir. IP	CIX
Dayton Free-Net	+1-513-873-4035	—	X	—	—	—
DCI	+886-2-3443010	—	—	X	X	X
DELPHI	+1-800-544-4005	X	—	—	—	—
Demon Internet	+44-81-349-0063	X	—	X	X	X
Denver Free-Net	+1-303-270-4865	—	X	—	—	—
DKnet	+45-39-17-99-00	X	—	X	X	—
DMConnection	+1-508-568-1618	X	—	X	—	—
Durham Free-Net	+1-905-668-3390	—	X	—	—	—
Eastmanet	+1-204-753-2311	—	X	—	—	—
EBONE	+31-20-639-1131	—	—	—	X	—
ECUANET	+593-2-433-006	X	—	X	X	—
Edmonton Free-Net	+1-403-423-2331	—	X	—	—	—
ElectriCiti	+1-619-338-9000	—	—	X	X	X
EMI Communications	+1-518-458-1102	—	—	X	X	X
EUnet Deutschland	+49-231-972-2222	—	—	—	X	—
EUnet GB	+44-227-475497	X	—	X	X	—
EUnet	+31-20-592-5109	X	—	X	X	X
Express Access	+1-800-969-9090	X	—	X	X	—
Fairfield Free-Net	+1-515-472-7494	—	X	—	—	—
FairNet	+1-907-474-5089	—	X	—	—	—
Fapesp/CNPq	+55-011-869-1041	—	—	—	X	—
Finland Free-Net	+358-0-451-4007	—	X	—	—	—
Forsyth County Free-Net	+1-919-727-2597	—	X	—	—	—
Free State Free-Net	+1-410-313-9259	—	X	—	—	—
Free-Net Bayreuth	+921-553134	—	X	—	—	—
Free-Net du Montreal Metropolitain	+1-514-278-9173	—	X	—	—	—
Free-Net Erlangen-Nuernburg	+49-9131-85-4735	—	X	—	—	—
Fujitsu	+1-614-457-8600	—	—	X	X	X
Garrett Communiversity Central	+1-301-387-3035	—	X	—	—	—
Genesee Free-Net	+1-810-762-3309	—	X	—	—	—
Global Enterprise Services/JvNCNet	+1-609-897-7310	—	—	X	X	X
Goldnet	+972-3-543-3777	X	—	X	X	—
Goya-EUnet Spain	+34-1-413-48-56	—	—	X	X	—
Grand Rapids Free-Net	+1-616-459-6273	—	X	—	—	—
The Granite State Oracle	+1-508-442-0279	—	X	—	—	—
Great Lakes Free-Net	+1-616-961-4166	—	X	—	—	—

Provider	Telephone	Type				
		Login Host	Free-net	Dial. IP	Dir. IP	CIX
Great Plains Free-Net	+1-306-584-9615	—	X	—	—	—
Greater Columbus Free-Net	+1-614-292-4132	—	X	—	—	—
Greater Detroit Free-Net	+1-313-825-5293	—	X	—	—	—
Greater Knoxville Community Network	+1-615-974-2908	—	X	—	—	—
Greater New Orleans Free-Net	+1-504-286-7187	—	X	—	—	—
Greater Pulaski County Free-Net	+1-501-666-2222	—	X	—	—	—
grebyn	+1-703-281-2194	X	—	X	—	—
GreenCo-NET	+1-803-223-8431	—	X	—	—	—
Greenet	+1-803-242-5000	—	X	—	—	—
Halcyon	+1-206-455-3505	X	—	X	X	—
Heartland Free-Net	+1-309-677-2544	—	X	—	—	—
HoloNet	+1-510-704-0160	X	—	X	X	X
Hong Kong Supernet	+852-358-7924	X	—	X	X	X
HookupNet	+1-519-747-4110	—	—	X	X	X
Houston Civnet	+1-713-869-0521	—	X	—	—	—
Huron Valley Free-Net	+1-313-662-8374	—	X	—	—	—
The IDS World Network	+1-408-884-7856	X	—	X	—	—
IEunet	+353-1-6719361	—	—	X	X	—
IIJ	+81-3-3580-3781	—	—	X	X	X
Illuminati Online	+1-512-447-7866	X	—	—	—	—
InfoRISC	+506-53-45-02	—	—	X	X	X
InfoTek	+27-21-419-2690	—	—	X	X	X
Inland Northwest Community Network	+1-509-359-6567	—	X	—	—	—
INS Info Services	+1-515-830-0110	—	—	X	X	X
InterAccess	+81-3-5478-7601	X	—	—	X	X
InterCon	+1-703-709-9890	—	—	X	X	X
Intercon	+593-2-528-716	—	—	—	X	—
The Internet Solution	+27	—	—	X	X	X
Internetworks	+1-503-642-7074	—	—	X	X	X
Iowa Knowledge Exchange	+1-515-242-3556	—	X	—	—	—
Jackson Area Free-Net	+1-901-425-2640	—	X	—	—	—
JvNCNet	+1-800-35-TIGER	X	—	X	X	X
Kav Manche	+972-3-290466	—	—	—	X	—
KC Free-Net	+1-816-340-4228	—	X	—	—	—
Kitsap Free-Net	+1-206-377-7601	—	X	—	—	—

Provider	Telephone	Login Host	Free-net	Dial. IP	Dir. IP	CIX
Korea Telecom	+82-42	—	—	X	X	X
Lamoille Net	+1-802-888-2606	—	X	—	—	—
Learning Village Cleveland	+1-216-247-5800	—	X	—	—	—
Lehigh Valley Free-Net	+1-610-758-4998	—	X	—	—	—
Lima Free-Net	+1-419-226-1218	—	X	—	—	—
Lorain County Free-Net	+1-800-227-7113x2451	—	X	—	—	—
Los Angeles Free-Net	+1-818-954-0080	—	X	—	—	—
Los Nettos	+1-310-822-1511	—	—	—	X	—
LYNX	+1-809-295-8777	—	—	X	X	X
Maine Free-Net	+1-207-287-6615	—	X	—	—	—
Maine.net	+1-207-657-5078	—	—	X	X	X
Maui Free-Net	+1-808-572-0510	—	X	—	—	—
MBnet	+1-204-474-9590	X	—	X	X	—
MCNet	+1-407-221-1410	—	X	—	—	—
MCSNet	+1-312-248-UNIX	X	—	X	X	X
Medborgarnas Datanat	+46-11-150000	—	X	—	—	—
Medina County Free-Net	+1-216-725-1000	—	X	—	—	—
Melbourne Free-Net	+61-3-652-0656	—	X	—	—	—
Meridian Area Free-Net	+1-601-482-2000	—	X	—	—	—
MEXnet	+52-83-582000	—	—	—	X	—
Miami Free-Net	+1-305-357-7318	—	X	—	—	—
Michiana Free-Net Society	+1-219-282-1574	—	X	—	—	—
MichNet	+1-313-764-9430	X	—	X	X	—
MIDnet	+1-402-472-8971	—	—	X	X	—
MidNet	+1-803-777-4825	—	X	—	—	—
MindVOX	+1-212-989-2418	X	—	—	—	—
Mobile Free-Net	+1-205-344-7243	—	X	—	—	—
MRnet	+1-612-342-2570	—	—	X	X	—
Msen	+1-313-998-4562	X	—	X	X	—
MV Communications	+1-603-429-2233	—	—	X	X	X
Naples Free-Net	+1-800-466-8017	—	X	—	—	—
National Capital Free-Net	+1-613-788-2600x3701	—	X	—	—	—
NB*net	+1-506-453-4573	—	—	—	X	—
NEARnet	+1-617-873-8730	—	—	X	X	X
Netcom	+1-408-554-UNIX	X	—	X	X	X
netILLINOIS	+1-708-467-7655	—	—	—	X	—
netmbx	+49-30-8555350	X	—	X	X	—
NevadaNet	+1-702-895-4580	—	—	—	X	—
New Mexico Free-Net	+1-505-277-8148	—	X	—	—	—

Provider	Telephone	Type				
		Login Host	Free-net	Dial. IP	Dir. IP	CIX
Niagara Free-Net	+1-416-688-5550	—	X	—	—	—
Nordic Carriers	+358-400-625	—	—	X	X	X
North Shore Free-Net	+1-705-848-5106	—	X	—	—	—
North Texas Free-Net	+1-214-320-8915	—	X	—	—	—
Northern California Regional Computing Network	+1-916-891-1211	—	X	—	—	—
Northfield Free-Net	+1-507-645-9301	—	X	—	—	—
Northwest Nexus	+1-206-455-3505	X	—	X	—	—
NorthWestNet	+1-206-562-3000	—	—	X	X	X
NSTN	+1-902-468-NSTN	—	—	—	X	—
NYSERnet	+1-315-453-2912	—	—	X	X	—
Nyx	+1-303-871-3324	X	—	—	—	—
OARnet	+1-614-292-8100	X	—	X	X	—
Ocean State Free-Net	+1-401-277-2726	—	X	—	—	—
Oklahoma Public Information Network	+1-405-947-8868	—	X	—	—	—
oldcolo	+1-719-632-4848	X	—	X	—	—
Olympic Public Electronic Network (OPEN)	+1-206-417-9302	—	X	—	—	—
Omaha Free-Net	+1-402-554-2516	—	X	—	—	—
ONet	+1-416-978-4589	—	—	—	X	—
Orange County Free-Net	+1-714-762-8551	—	X	—	—	—
ORION	+1-417-837-5050	—	X	—	—	—
Orlando Free-Net	+1-407-833-9777	—	X	—	—	—
Owensboro Bluegrass Free-Net	+1-502-686-4530	—	X	—	—	—
Pactok	+61-2-692-0231	X	—	—	X	—
Palm Beach Free-Net	+1-305-357-7318	—	X	—	—	—
PANIX	+1-212-877-4854	X	—	—	—	—
Pegasus Networks	+61-7-257-1111	X	—	—	—	—
Pennyrile Area Free-Net	+1-502-886-2913	—	X	—	—	—
Philadelphia Free-Net	+1-215-688-2694	—	X	—	—	—
Philippine Public Telecomputing Network	+632-931-5314	—	X	—	—	—
Pilot Network Services	+1-510-748-1836	—	—	X	X	X
PIPEX	+44-223-250120	—	—	X	X	X
Pittsburgh Free-Net	+1-412-622-6502	—	X	—	—	—
Ponca City/Pioneer Free-Net	+1-405-767-3461	—	X	—	—	—

Provider	Telephone	Type				
		Login Host	Free-net	Dial. IP	Dir. IP	CIX
The Portal System	+1-408-973-9111	X	—	X	X	X
Prairienet	+1-217-244-3299	—	X	—	—	—
Praxis Free-Net	+1-403-529-2162	—	X	—	—	—
PREPnet	+1-412-268-7870	X	—	X	X	—
Prince George Free-Net	+1-604-562-2131 loc 296	—	X	—	—	—
Proyecto HURACAN	+506-241431	X	—	—	X	—
Proyecto Wamani	+54-1-382-6842	X	—	—	—	—
PSINet	+1-800-82-PSI-82	X	—	X	X	X
Public Telecomputing Network	+1-312-464-5138	—	X	—	—	—
PUC	+56-2-5524703	—	—	—	X	—
Quack	+1-408-249-9630	X	—	—	—	—
RAU	+598-2-41-3901	—	—	—	X	—
Real/Time	+1-512-451-0046	X	—	X	—	—
RECyT	+54-1-312-8917	—	—	—	X	—
Red Cientifica Peruana	+51-14-35-1760	X	—	X	X	—
REDID	+1-809-689-4973	—	—	—	X	—
REUNA	+56-2-274-4537	—	—	X	X	—
Richland Free-Net	+1-419-521-3111-3110	—	X	—	—	—
Rio Grande Free-Net	+1-915-775-6077	—	X	—	—	—
RISQ	+1-514-340-5700	—	—	X	X	—
Rochester Free-Net	+1-716-594-0943	—	X	—	—	—
Sacramento Free-Net	+1-916-484-6789	—	X	—	—	—
San Antonio Free-Net	+1-210-561-9815	—	X	—	—	—
Sandpoint Free-Net	+1-208-263-6105	—	X	—	—	—
Santa Barbara RAIN	+1-805-967-7246	—	X	—	—	—
Santa Fe Metaverse	+1-505-989-7117	—	X	—	—	—
SASK#net	+1-514-340-5700	X	—	—	X	—
Saskatoon Free-Net	+1-306-966-5920	—	X	—	—	—
SEARDEN Free-Net	+1-204-437-2016	—	X	—	—	—
Seattle Community Network	+1-206-865-3424	—	X	—	—	—
SEFLIN Free-Net	+1-305-357-7318	—	X	—	—	—
SENDIT	+1-701-237-8109	—	X	—	—	—
SEORF	+1-614-662-3211	—	X	—	—	—
SesquiNet	+1-713-527-4988	—	—	X	X	—
Shawnee Free-Net	+1-618-549-1139	—	X	—	—	—
Silicon Valley Public Access Link	+1-415-968-2598	—	X	—	—	—
Singapore Telecom	+65-772-65-23	—	—	X	X	X
SLONET	+1-805-544-7328	—	X	—	—	—
SMART	+1-813-951-5502	—	X	—	—	—

Provider	Telephone	Type				
		Login Host	Free-net	Dial. IP	Dir. IP	CIX
SouthCoastComputing	+1-713-917-5000	—	—	X	X	X
Southern Tier Free-Net	+1-607-752-1201	—	X	—	—	—
Sovam Teleport	+1-415-346-4188	—	—	X	X	X
SPIN	+81-3 5561-3333	—	—	X	X	X
SprintLink	+1-703-904-2167	—	—	X	X	X
St. John's Free-Net	+1-709-737-4594	—	X	—	—	—
Sudbury Regional Free-Net	+1-705-675-1151	—	X	—	—	—
SugarLand UNIX	+1-713-438-4964	X	—	—	—	—
Suncoast Free-Net	+1-813-273-3714	—	X	—	—	—
SURAnet	+1-301-982-4600	—	—	X	X	X
SURFnet	+31-30-310290	—	—	—	X	—
SWIF-NET	+1-618-397-0968	—	X	—	—	—
SWIPnet	+46-8-6324040	X	—	X	X	—
SWITCH	+41-1-268-15-15	X	—	X	X	—
Synergy Communications	+1-402-346-4638	—	—	X	X	X
Tallahassee Free-Net	+1-904-644-1796	—	X	—	—	—
Tarrant County Free-Net	+1-817-763-8437	—	X	—	—	—
Telerama BBS	+1-412-481-3505	X	—	X	—	—
Tennessee Valley Free-Net	+1-205-544-3849	—	X	—	—	—
THEnet	+1-512-471-3241	—	—	X	X	X
Thunder Bay Free-Net	+1-807-343-8354	—	X	—	—	—
TICSA	+27-21-4192768	—	—	X	X	X
Toledo Free-Net	+1-419-537-3686	—	X	—	—	—
Toronto Free-Net	+1-416-978-5365	—	X	—	—	—
Tri-Cities Free-Net	+1-509-586-6481	—	X	—	—	—
Triangle Free-Net	+1-919-962-9107	—	X	—	—	—
Tristate Online	+1-513-397-1396	—	X	—	—	—
Tuscaloosa Free-Net	+1-205-348-2398	—	X	—	—	—
TWICS	+81-3-3351-5977	X	—	X	—	—
Twin Cities Free-Net	+1-507-646-3407	—	X	—	—	—
UDC	+56-41-234985	—	—	—	X	—
UK PC User's Group	+44-81-863-6646	X	—	—	—	—
UMASSK12	+1-413-545-1908	—	X	—	—	—
UNdlP	+54-21-35102	—	—	—	X	—
uropax.contrib.de	+49-30-694-6907	X	—	X	—	—
USIT	+1-800-218-USIT	—	—	X	X	X
UTFSM	+56-32-665053	—	—	—	X	—
Vancouver Regional Free-Net	+1-604-665-3579	—	X	—	—	—

Provider	Telephone	Type				
		Login Host	Free-net	Dial. IP	Dir. IP	CIX
VaPEN	+1-804-225-2921	—	X	—	—	—
Venezia Free-Net	+39-41-721900	—	X	—	—	—
VERnet	+1-804-924-0616	—	—	—	X	—
Victoria Free-Net	+1-604-385-4302	—	X	—	—	—
Wariat	+1-216-481-9428	X	—	—	—	—
Wellington Citynet	+64-4-801-3303	—	X	—	X	—
West Texas Free-Net	+1-915-655-7161	—	X	—	—	—
Westnet	+1-303-492-8560	—	—	X	X	X
Wis.com	+1-715-387-1700	—	—	X	X	X
world.net	+1-503-642-7074	—	—	—	X	X
The WORLD	+1-617-739-0202	X	—	—	—	—
Worth County-Sylvester Ga. Free-Net	+1-912-776-8625	—	X	—	—	—
WVNET	+1-304-293-5192	—	—	—	X	—
Wyoming.com	+1-307-777-7218	—	—	X	X	X
Wyvern	+1-804-622-4289	X	—	—	—	—
York Sunbury Community Server	+1-506-453-4566	—	X	—	—	—
Youngstown Free-Net	+1-216-742-3075	—	X	X	—	—
Zilker Internet Park	+1-512-206-3850	X	—	X	X	—

Providers by Area Code

Here is a list of providers by area code. Once you find the name of a provider you wish to contact, you can locate its voice telephone number in the list of providers by name in the previous section. For telephone numbers in the United States and Canada, the table gives the area code and the state or province name. For telephone numbers elsewhere, the table gives the telephone country code and the country name. For all listings the table gives the provider name and the same type codes as in the other table.

Telephone	Place	Provider	Type				
			Login Host	Free-net	Dial. IP	Dir. IP	CIX
+1-203	Connecticut	CPBI	—	X	—	—	—
+1-203	Connecticut	Danbury Area Free-Net	—	X	—	—	—
+1-203	Connecticut	PSINet	X	—	X	X	X
+1-204	Manitoba	Blue Sky Free-Net Of Manitoba	—	X	—	—	—
+1-204	Manitoba	Eastmanet	—	X	—	—	—
+1-204	Manitoba	SEARDEN Free-Net	—	X	—	—	—

Tele-phone	Place	Provider	Type				
			Login Host	Free-net	Dial. IP	Dir. IP	CIX
+1-205	Alabama	Mobile Free-Net	—	X	—	—	—
+1-205	Alabama	Tennessee Valley Free-Net	—	X	—	—	—
+1-205	Alabama	Tuscaloosa Free-Net	—	X	—	—	—
+1-206	Washington	Clark County Free-Net	—	X	—	—	—
+1-206	Washington	ConnectedNet	—	—	X	X	X
+1-206	Washington	Halcyon	X	—	X	X	—
+1-206	Washington	Kitsap Free-Net	—	X	—	—	—
+1-206	Washington	Netcom	X	—	X	X	X
+1-206	Washington	Northwest Nexus	X	—	X	—	—
+1-206	Washington	NorthWestNet	—	—	X	X	X
+1-206	Washington	Olympic Public Electronic Network (OPEN)	—	X	—	—	—
+1-206	Washington	PSINet	X	—	X	X	X
+1-206	Washington	Seattle Community Network	—	X	—	—	—
+1-207	Maine	Maine Free-Net	—	X	—	—	—
+1-207	Maine	Maine.net	—	—	X	X	X
+1-207	Maine	PSINet	X	—	X	X	X
+1-208	Idaho	PSINet	X	—	X	X	X
+1-208	Idaho	Sandpoint Free-Net	—	X	—	—	—
+1-210	Texas	San Antonio Free-Net	—	X	—	—	—
+1-212	New York	MindVOX	X	—	—	—	—
+1-212	New York	PANIX	X	—	—	—	—
+1-212	New York	PSINet	X	—	X	X	X
+1-213	California	PSINet	X	—	X	X	X
+1-214	Texas	Netcom	X	—	X	X	X
+1-214	Texas	North Texas Free-Net	—	X	—	—	—
+1-214	Texas	PSINet	X	—	X	X	X
+1-215	Pennsylvania	Chester County Free-Net	—	X	—	—	—
+1-215	Pennsylvania	Philadelphia Free-Net	—	X	—	—	—
+1-215	Pennsylvania	PSINet	X	—	X	X	X
+1-216	Ohio	Akron Regional Free-Net	—	X	—	—	—
+1-216	Ohio	Canton Regional Free-Net	—	X	—	—	—
+1-216	Ohio	Cleveland Free-Net	—	X	—	—	—
+1-216	Ohio	Learning Village Cleveland	—	X	—	—	—
+1-216	Ohio	Lorain County Free-Net	—	X	—	—	—

Tele- phone	Place	Provider	Login Host	Free- net	Dial. IP	Dir. IP	CIX
+1-216	Ohio	Medina County Free-Net	—	X	—	—	—
+1-216	Ohio	Netcom	X	—	X	X	X
+1-216	Ohio	Wariat	X	—	—	—	—
+1-216	Ohio	Youngstown Free-Net	—	X	X	—	—
+1-217	Illinois	Prairienet	—	X	—	—	—
+1-219	Indiana	Michiana Free-Net Society	—	X	—	—	—
+1-301	D.C.	Express Access	X	—	X	X	—
+1-301	Maryland	Garrett Communiversity Central	—	X	—	—	—
+1-301	Maryland	SURAnet	—	—	X	X	X
+1-303	Colorado	Denver Free-Net	—	X	—	—	—
+1-303	Colorado	Nyx	X	—	—	—	—
+1-303	Colorado	PSINet	X	—	X	X	X
+1-303	Colorado	Westnet	—	—	X	X	X
+1-304	West Virginia	WVNET	—	—	—	X	—
+1-305	Florida	Miami Free-Net	—	X	—	—	—
+1-305	Florida	Palm Beach Free-Net	—	X	—	—	—
+1-305	Florida	PSINet	X	—	X	X	X
+1-305	Florida	SEFLIN Free-Net	—	X	—	—	—
+1-306	Saskatchewan	Great Plains Free-Net	—	X	—	—	—
+1-306	Saskatchewan	Saskatoon Free-Net	—	X	—	—	—
+1-307	Wyoming	Wyoming.com	—	—	X	X	X
+1-309	Illinois	Heartland Free-Net	—	X	—	—	—
+1-310	California	Los Nettos	—	—	—	X	—
+1-310	California	Netcom	X	—	X	X	X
+1-312	Illinois	MCSNet	X	—	X	X	X
+1-312	Illinois	PSINet	X	—	X	X	X
+1-312	Illinois	Public Telecomputing Network	—	X	—	—	—
+1-313		Apex Global Info Systems	—	—	X	X	X
+1-313	Michigan	Almont Expression	—	X	—	—	—
+1-313	Michigan	Greater Detroit Free-Net	—	X	—	—	—
+1-313	Michigan	Huron Valley Free-Net	—	X	—	—	—
+1-313	Michigan	Msen	X	—	X	X	—
+1-313	Michigan	PSINet	X	—	X	X	X
+1-314	Missouri	Cape Girardeau Free-Net	—	X	—	—	—
+1-314	Missouri	Columbia Online Information Network	—	X	—	—	—

Tele- phone	Place	Provider	Type				
			Login Host	Free- net	Dial. IP	Dir. IP	CIX
		(COIN)					
+1-315	New York	NYSERnet	—	—	X	X	—
+1-315	New York	PSINet	X	—	X	X	X
+1-318	Louisiana	Acadiana Free-Net	—	X	—	—	—
+1-319	Iowa	CedarNet	—	X	—	—	—
+1-401	Rhode Island	The IDS World Network	X	—	X	—	—
+1-401	Rhode Island	Ocean State Free-Net	—	X	—	—	—
+1-401	Rhode Island	PSINet	X	—	X	X	X
+1-402	Nebraska	MIDnet	—	—	X	X	—
+1-402	Nebraska	Omaha Free-Net	—	X	—	—	—
+1-402	Nebraska	Synergy Communications	—	—	X	X	X
+1-403	Alberta	Calgary Free-Net	—	X	—	—	—
+1-403	Alberta	Edmonton Free-Net	—	X	—	—	—
+1-403	Alberta	Praxis Free-Net	—	X	—	—	—
+1-404	Georgia	404 Free-Net	—	X	—	—	—
+1-404	Georgia	Netcom	X	—	X	X	X
+1-404	Georgia	PSINet	X	—	X	X	X
+1-405	Oklahoma	Oklahoma Public Information Network	—	X	—	—	—
+1-405	Oklahoma	Ponca City/Pioneer Free-Net	—	X	—	—	—
+1-406	Montana	Big Sky Telegraph	—	X	—	—	—
+1-407	Florida	MCNet	—	X	—	—	—
+1-407	Florida	Orlando Free-Net	—	X	—	—	—
+1-407	Florida	PSINet	X	—	X	X	X
+1-408	California	a2i communications	X	—	X	X	X
+1-408	California	Able Tech	—	—	X	X	X
+1-408	California	class	X	—	—	—	—
+1-408	California	Netcom	X	—	X	X	X
+1-408	California	The Portal System	X	—	X	X	X
+1-408	California	PSINet	X	—	X	X	X
+1-408	California	Quack	X	—	—	—	—
+1-410	Maryland	Community Service Network	—	X	—	—	—
+1-410	Maryland	Express Access	X	—	X	X	—
+1-410	Maryland	Free State Free-Net	—	X	—	—	—
+1-410	Maryland	PSINet	X	—	X	X	X
+1-412	Pennsylvania	Pittsburgh Free-Net	—	X	—	—	—
+1-412	Pennsylvania	PREPnet	X	—	X	X	—
+1-412	Pennsylvania	PSINet	X	—	X	X	X
+1-412	Pennsylvania	Telerama BBS	X	—	X	—	—
+1-413	Massachusetts	UMASSK12	—	X	—	—	—

Tele-phone	Place	Provider	Type				
			Login Host	Free-net	Dial. IP	Dir. IP	CIX
+1-414	Wisconsin	AlphaNet	—	—	X	X	X
+1-415	British Columbia	Aurora.Net	—	—	X	X	X
+1-415	California	BARRNet	—	—	X	X	X
+1-415	California	CR Labs Dialup Internet Access	X	—	X	X	—
+1-415	California	Netcom	X	—	X	X	X
+1-415	California	The Portal System	X	—	X	X	X
+1-415	California	PSINet	X	—	X	X	X
+1-415	California	Silicon Valley Public Access Link	—	X	—	—	—
+1-415	California	Sovam Teleport	—	—	X	X	X
+1-416		CA*net	—	—	X	X	X
+1-416	Ontario	Niagara Free-Net	—	X	—	—	—
+1-416	Ontario	Toronto Free-Net	—	X	—	—	—
+1-417	Missouri	ORION	—	X	—	—	—
+1-419	Ohio	Lima Free-Net	—	X	—	—	—
+1-419	Ohio	Richland Free-Net	—	X	—	—	—
+1-419	Ohio	Toledo Free-Net	—	X	—	—	—
+1-501	Arkansas	Greater Pulaski County Free-Net	—	X	—	—	—
+1-502	Kentucky	Owensboro Bluegrass Free-Net	—	X	—	—	—
+1-502	Kentucky	Pennyrile Area Free-Net	—	X	—	—	—
+1-503	Oregon	agora.rdrop.com	X	—	X	—	—
+1-503	Oregon	Internetworks	—	—	X	X	X
+1-503	Oregon	Netcom	X	—	X	X	X
+1-503	Oregon	PSINet	X	—	X	X	X
+1-504	Louisiana	Baton Rouge Free-Net	—	X	—	—	—
+1-504	Louisiana	Greater New Orleans Free-Net	—	X	—	—	—
+1-505	New Mexico	New Mexico Free-Net	—	X	—	—	—
+1-505	New Mexico	Santa Fe Metaverse	—	X	—	—	—
+1-506	New Brunswick	NB*net	—	—	—	X	—
+1-506	New Brunswick	York Sunbury Community Server	—	X	—	—	—
+1-507	Minnesota	Northfield Free-Net	—	X	—	—	—
+1-507	Minnesota	Twin Cities Free-Net	—	X	—	—	—
+1-508	Massachusetts	DMConnection	X	—	X	—	—
+1-508	Massachusetts	PSINet	X	—	X	X	X
+1-508	Massachusetts	The WORLD	X	—	—	—	—
+1-508	New Hampshire	The Granite State	—	X	—	—	—

Tele-phone	Place	Provider	Type				
			Login Host	Free-net	Dial. IP	Dir. IP	CIX
		Oracle					
+1-509	Washington	Inland Northwest Community Network	—	X	—	—	—
+1-509	Washington	PSINet	X	—	X	X	X
+1-509	Washington	Tri-Cities Free-Net	—	X	—	—	—
+1-510	California	HoloNet	X	—	X	X	X
+1-510	California	Netcom	X	—	X	X	X
+1-510	California	Pilot Network Services	—	—	X	X	X
+1-512	Texas	Austin Free-Net	—	X	—	—	—
+1-512	Texas	Illuminati Online	X	—	—	—	—
+1-512	Texas	PSINet	X	—	X	X	X
+1-512	Texas	Real/Time	X	—	X	—	—
+1-512	Texas	THEnet	—	—	X	X	X
+1-512	Texas	Zilker Internet Park	X	—	X	X	—
+1-513	Ohio	Dayton Free-Net	—	X	—	—	—
+1-513	Ohio	Tristate Online	—	X	—	—	—
+1-514	Quebec	cam.org	X	—	X	—	—
+1-514	Quebec	Free-Net du Montreal Metropolitain	—	X	—	—	—
+1-514	Quebec	RISQ	—	—	X	X	—
+1-514	Quebec	SASK#net	X	—	—	X	—
+1-515	Iowa	Fairfield Free-Net	—	X	—	—	—
+1-515	Iowa	INS Info Services	—	—	X	X	X
+1-515	Iowa	Iowa Knowledge Exchange	—	X	—	—	—
+1-516	New York	PSINet	X	—	X	X	X
+1-517	Michigan	Ameritech Extended Classroom	—	X	—	—	—
+1-517	Michigan	Capitol City Free-Net	—	X	—	—	—
+1-518	New York	Capital Region Information Service	—	X	—	—	—
+1-518	New York	EMI Communications	—	—	X	X	X
+1-518	New York	PSINet	X	—	X	X	X
+1-519	Ontario	HookupNet	—	—	X	X	X
+1-601	Mississippi	Meridian Area Free-Net	—	X	—	—	—
+1-602	Arizona	AzTeC Computing	—	X	—	—	—
+1-602	Arizona	PSINet	X	—	X	X	X
+1-603	New Hampshire	MV Communications	—	—	X	X	X
+1-603	New Hampshire	PSINet	X	—	X	X	X
+1-604	British Columbia	BCnet	—	—	—	X	—
+1-604	British Columbia	CIAO! Free-Net	—	X	—	—	—
+1-604	British Columbia	Prince George Free-Net	—	X	—	—	—

Telephone	Place	Provider	Type				
			Login Host	Free-net	Dial. IP	Dir. IP	CIX
+1-604	British Columbia	Vancouver Regional Free-Net	—	X	—	—	—
+1-604	British Columbia	Victoria Free-Net	—	X	—	—	—
+1-604		Cyberstore Systems	—	—	X	X	X
+1-607	New York	PSINet	X	—	X	X	X
+1-607	New York	Southern Tier Free-Net	—	X	—	—	—
+1-608	Wisconsin	Berbee Information Networks	—	—	X	X	X
+1-609	New Jersey	Global Enterprise Services/JvNCNet	—	—	X	X	X
+1-609	New Jersey	PSINet	X	—	X	X	X
+1-610	Pennsylvania	Lehigh Valley Free-Net	—	X	—	—	—
+1-613	Ontario	National Capital Free-Net	—	X	—	—	—
+1-614	Ohio	Fujitsu	—	—	X	X	X
+1-614	Ohio	Greater Columbus Free-Net	—	X	—	—	—
+1-614	Ohio	PSINet	X	—	X	X	X
+1-614	Ohio	SEORF	—	X	—	—	—
+1-615	Tennessee	Greater Knoxville Community Network	—	X	—	—	—
+1-616	Michigan	Grand Rapids Free-Net	—	X	—	—	—
+1-616	Michigan	Great Lakes Free-Net	—	X	—	—	—
+1-617	Massachusetts	CentNet	—	—	X	X	X
+1-617	Massachusetts	NEARnet	—	—	X	X	X
+1-617	Massachusetts	Netcom	X	—	X	X	X
+1-617	Massachusetts	The WORLD	X	—	—	—	—
+1-618	Illinois	Shawnee Free-Net	—	X	—	—	—
+1-618	Illinois	SWIF-NET	—	X	—	—	—
+1-619	California	Ashton Communications	—	—	X	X	X
+1-619	California	CERFnet	X	—	X	X	X
+1-619	California	crash.cts.com	X	—	X	X	—
+1-619	California	The Cyberspace Station	X	—	X	—	—
+1-619	California	ElectriCiti	—	—	X	X	X
+1-619	California	Netcom	X	—	X	X	X
+1-701	North Dakota	SENDIT	—	X	—	—	—
+1-703	Virginia	Alternet	—	—	X	X	X
+1-703	Virginia	Blue Ridge Free-Net	—	X	—	—	—
+1-703	Virginia	grebyn	X	—	X	—	—
+1-703	Virginia	InterCon	—	—	X	X	X
+1-703	Virginia	Netcom	X	—	X	X	X
+1-703	Virginia	PSINet	X	—	X	X	X

Tele-phone	Place	Provider	Type				
			Login Host	Free-net	Dial. IP	Dir. IP	CIX
+1-703	Virginia	SprintLink	—	—	X	X	X
+1-704	North Carolina	Charlotte's Web	—	X	—	—	—
+1-705	Ontario	North Shore Free-Net	—	X	—	—	—
+1-705	Ontario	Sudbury Regional Free-Net	—	X	—	—	—
+1-708	Illinois	netILLINOIS	—	—	—	X	—
+1-709	Newfoundland	St. John's Free-Net	—	X	—	—	—
+1-713	Texas	BlackBox	X	—	X	—	—
+1-713	Texas	Houston Civnet	—	X	—	—	—
+1-713	Texas	PSINet	X	—	X	X	X
+1-713	Texas	SouthCoastComputing	—	—	X	X	X
+1-713	Texas	SugarLand UNIX	X	—	—	—	—
+1-714	California	Express Access	X	—	X	X	—
+1-714	California	Netcom	X	—	X	X	X
+1-714	California	Orange County Free-Net	—	X	—	—	—
+1-715	Wisconsin	Chippewa Valley Free-Net	—	X	—	—	—
+1-715	Wisconsin	Wis.com	—	—	X	X	X
+1-716	New York	Buffalo Free-Net	—	X	—	—	—
+1-716	New York	PSINet	X	—	X	X	X
+1-716	New York	Rochester Free-Net	—	X	—	—	—
+1-717	Pennsylvania	PSINet	X	—	X	X	X
+1-717	Virginia	Commonwealth Telephone Company	—	—	X	X	X
+1-719	Colorado	Community News Service	X	—	X	—	—
+1-719	Colorado	oldcolo	X	—	X	—	—
+1-800	California	California Online Resources for Education	—	X	—	—	—
+1-800	Florida	Naples Free-Net	—	X	—	—	—
+1-800	Massachusetts	DELPHI	X	—	—	—	—
+1-800	Ohio	Lorain County Free-Net	—	X	—	—	—
+1-800	Tennessee	USIT	—	—	X	X	X
+1-802	Vermont	Lamoille Net	—	X	—	—	—
+1-803	South Carolina	GreenCo-NET	—	X	—	—	—
+1-803	South Carolina	Greenet	—	X	—	—	—
+1-803	South Carolina	MidNet	—	X	—	—	—
+1-804	Virginia	Central Virginia's Free-Net	—	X	—	—	—
+1-804	Virginia	PSINet	X	—	X	X	X
+1-804	Virginia	VaPEN	—	X	—	—	—
+1-804	Virginia	VERnet	—	—	—	X	—

Tele-phone	Place	Provider	Type				
			Login Host	Free-net	Dial. IP	Dir. IP	CIX
+1-804	Virginia	Wyvern	X	—	—	—	—
+1-805	California	Santa Barbara RAIN	—	X	—	—	—
+1-805	California	SLONET	—	X	—	—	—
+1-807	Ontario	Thunder Bay Free-Net	—	X	—	—	—
+1-808	Hawaii	The Aloha Free-Net Project	—	X	—	—	—
+1-808	Hawaii	Maui Free-Net	—	X	—	—	—
+1-809	Bermuda	LYNX	—	—	X	X	X
+1-809	Dominican Rep.	REDID	—	—	—	X	—
+1-809	Puerto Rico	CRACIN	—	—	—	X	—
+1-810	Michigan	Genesee Free-Net	—	X	—	—	—
+1-813	Florida	PSINet	X	—	X	X	X
+1-813	Florida	SMART	—	X	—	—	—
+1-813	Florida	Suncoast Free-Net	—	X	—	—	—
+1-816	Missouri	KC Free-Net	—	X	—	—	—
+1-817	Texas	Tarrant County Free-Net	—	X	—	—	—
+1-818	California	Los Angeles Free-Net	—	X	—	—	—
+1-901	Tennessee	Jackson Area Free-Net	—	X	—	—	—
+1-902	Nova Scotia	Cape Breton Free-Net	—	X	—	—	—
+1-902	Nova Scotia	Chebucto Free-Net	—	X	—	—	—
+1-902	Nova Scotia	NSTN	—	—	—	X	—
+1-904	Florida	Alachua Free-Net	—	X	—	—	—
+1-904	Florida	PSINet	X	—	X	X	X
+1-904	Florida	Tallahassee Free-Net	—	X	—	—	—
+1-905	Ontario	Durham Free-Net	—	X	—	—	—
+1-907	Alaska	AnchorNet	—	X	—	—	—
+1-907	Alaska	FairNet	—	X	—	—	—
+1-908	New Jersey	Express Access	X	—	X	X	—
+1-912	Georgia	Worth County-Sylvester Ga. Free-Net	—	X	—	—	—
+1-913	Kansas	Databank	—	—	X	X	X
+1-914	New York	ANS CO+RE Services	—	—	X	X	X
+1-914	New York	PSINet	X	—	X	X	X
+1-915	Texas	Big Country Free-Net	—	X	—	—	—
+1-915	Texas	Rio Grande Free-Net	—	X	—	—	—
+1-915	Texas	West Texas Free-Net	—	X	—	—	—
+1-916	California	Davis Community Network	—	X	—	—	—
+1-916	California	Netcom	X	—	X	X	X
+1-916	California	Northern California Regional Computing	—	X	—	—	—

Tele-phone	Place	Provider	Type				
			Login Host	Free-net	Dial. IP	Dir. IP	CIX
		Network					
+1-916	California	Sacramento Free-Net	—	X	—	—	—
+1-919	North Carolina	Forsyth County Free-Net	—	X	—	—	—
+1-919	North Carolina	Triangle Free-Net	—	X	—	—	—
+27	South Africa	InfoTek	—	—	X	X	X
+27	South Africa	The Internet Solution	—	—	X	X	X
+27	South Africa	TICSA	—	—	X	X	X
+31	Austria	EBONE	—	—	—	X	—
+31	France	EBONE	—	—	—	X	—
+31	Netherlands	EUnet	X	—	X	X	X
+31	Netherlands	SURFnet	—	—	—	X	—
+31	Sweden	EBONE	—	—	—	X	—
+34	Spain	Goya-EUnet Spain	—	—	X	X	—
+353	Ireland	IEunet	—	—	X	X	—
+358	Finland	CSC	X	—	X	—	—
+358	Finland	DataNet	—	—	—	X	—
+358	Finland	Finland Free-Net	—	X	—	—	—
+358	Finland	Nordic Carriers	—	—	X	X	X
+38-41	Croatia	CARNet	—	—	—	X	—
+39	Italy	Venezia Free-Net	—	X	—	—	—
+41	Switzerland	SWITCH	X	—	X	X	—
+44	France	PIPEX	—	—	X	X	X
+44	United Kingdom	Demon Internet	X	—	X	X	X
+44	United Kingdom	EUnet GB	X	—	X	X	—
+44	United Kingdom	PIPEX	—	—	X	X	X
+44	United Kingdom	UK PC User's Group	X	—	—	—	—
+45	Denmark	DKnet	X	—	X	X	—
+46	Sweden	Medborgarnas Datanat	—	X	—	—	—
+46	Sweden	SWIPnet	X	—	X	X	—
+49	Germany	EUnet Deutschland	—	—	—	X	—
+49	Germany	Free-Net Erlangen-Nuernburg	—	X	—	—	—
+49	Germany	netmbx	X	—	X	X	—
+49	Germany	uropax.contrib.de	X	—	X	—	—
+506	Costa Rica	CRnet	—	—	—	X	—
+506	Costa Rica	InfoRISC	—	—	X	X	X
+506	Costa Rica	Proyecto HURACAN	X	—	—	X	—
+51	Peru	Red Cientifica Peruana	X	—	X	X	—
+52	Mexico	CONACYT	—	—	—	X	—
+52	Mexico	MEXnet	—	—	—	X	—
+54	Argentina	CCC	—	—	—	X	—

Tele-phone	Place	Provider	Login Host	Free-net	Dial. IP	Dir. IP	CIX
+54	Argentina	Proyecto Wamani	X	—	—	—	—
+54	Argentina	RECyT	—	—	—	X	—
+54	Argentina	UNdlP	—	—	—	X	—
+55	Brazil	Fapesp/CNPq	—	—	—	X	—
+56	Chile	PUC	—	—	—	X	—
+56	Chile	REUNA	—	—	X	X	—
+56	Chile	UDC	—	—	—	X	—
+56	Chile	UTFSM	—	—	—	X	—
+591	Bolivia	BOLNET	—	—	—	X	—
+593	Ecuador	ECUANET	X	—	X	X	—
+593	Ecuador	Intercon	—	—	—	X	—
+598	Uruguay	RAU	—	—	—	X	—
+61	Australia	AARnet	—	—	—	X	—
+61	Australia	Melbourne Free-Net	—	X	—	—	—
+61	Australia	Pactok	X	—	—	X	—
+61	Australia	Pegasus Networks	X	—	—	—	—
+632	Philippines	Philippine Public Telecomputing Network	—	X	—	—	—
+64	New Zealand	Actrix	X	—	—	—	—
+64	New Zealand	Wellington Citynet	—	X	—	X	—
+65	Singapore	Singapore Telecom	—	—	X	X	X
+81	Japan	IIJ	—	—	X	X	X
+81	Japan	InterAccess	X	—	—	X	X
+81	Japan	SPIN	—	—	X	X	X
+81	Japan	TWICS	X	—	X	—	—
+82	South Korea	Korea Telecom	—	—	X	X	X
+852	Hong Kong	Hong Kong Supernet	X	—	X	X	X
+886	Taiwan	DCI	—	—	X	X	X
+921	Germany	Free-Net Bayreuth	—	X	—	—	—
+972	Israel	Actcom	—	—	—	X	—
+972	Israel	Dataserve	X	—	X	X	—
+972	Israel	Goldnet	X	—	X	X	—
+972	Israel	Kav Manche	—	—	—	X	—

Appendix B

Software

Throughout the book we have mentioned various pieces of software that you may want or need. In this appendix we list places in the Internet where you can find such software. You can use ftpmail to retrieve it, or, if you have an Internet connection, anonymous FTP.

In the following table, the name of each software package is given in *italics*, followed by a line for each software source. Each line lists the platform (UNIX, MS-DOS, or Macintosh), the FTP server domain name (such as gatekeeper.dec.com), and the pathname (such as **/.8/mail/ua/pine/pine3.89.tar.Z**). The pathname may appear broken onto two lines so it will fit horizontally.

New versions of software appear frequently, so you should check to see if there is a newer version available than what we have listed here. In addition, remember that in many cases there is also commercial supported software to perform the same task.

We list software here that is current at the time of this writing. We list these software packages in alphabetical order by the name of the packages.

Software Package

For	Where	Pathname
archie		
UNIX	archie.unl.edu	/pub/archie/clients/ archie-1.4.1
	archie.unl.edu	/pub/archie/clients/ perl-archie-3.8.tar
DOS	archie.unl.edu	/pub/archie/clients/ archie.zip
Mac	mrcnext.cso.uiuc.edu	/pub/info-mac/comm/tcp/ anarchie-121.hqx
btoa/atob		
UNIX	dimacs.rutgers.edu	/pub/btoa.shar
UNIX	math.sunysb.edu	/programs/atob/
compress/uncompress		
UNIX	math.sunysb.edu	/programs/compress/
DOS	ftp.cc.mcgill.ca	/pub/ftp_inc/dos/compress/ comp430s.zip
DOS	ftp.uga.edu	/pub/msdos/compress.zip
Mac	mrcnext.cso.uiuc.edu	/pub/info-mac/cmp/ maccompress-32.hqx
FTP		
Mac	ftp.dartmouth.edu	/pub/mac/Fetch_2.1.2.sit.hqx
DOS	farces.com	/pub/visitors-center/software/ ms-windows/ftp/ws_ftp.zip
Gopher		
UNIX	boombox.micro.umn.edu	/pub/gopher/Unix/ gopher2.016.tar.Z
DOS	boombox.micro.umn.edu	/pub/gopher/PC_client/ pcg3bin.zip
Mac	boombox.micro.umn.edu	/pub/gopher/Mac-TurboGopher/ TurboGopher1.0.7g.hqx

Software Package		
For	**Where**	**Pathname**
gzip/gunzip		
UNIX	prep.ai.mit.edu	**/pub/gnu/**
		gzip-1.2.4.tar.gz
DOS	prep.ai.mit.edu	**/pub/gnu/**
		gzip-1.2.4.msdos.exe
Mac	mrcnext.cso.uiuc.edu	**/pub/info-mac/cmp/**
		mac-gzip-02.hqx
LISTSERV		
UNIX	sales@lsoft.com	
Majordomo		
UNIX	ftp.greatcircle.com	**/pub/majordomo/**
		majordomo-1.92.tar.Z
netfind		
UNIX	ucselx.sdsu.edu	**/pub/unix/netfind.tar.Z**
PGP		
UNIX	soda.berkeley.edu	**/pub/cypherpunks/pgp/pgp26/**
		pgp26ui-src.tar.gz
DOS	soda.berkeley.edu	**/pub/cypherpunks/pgp/pgp26/**
		pgp26.zip
Mac	soda.berkeley.edu	**/pub/cypherpunks/pgp/**
		MacPGP2.2src.sea.hqx.gz
Pine		
UNIX	ftp.cerf.net	**/pub/software/unix/mail/**
		pine3.89.tar.Z
UNIX	gatekeeper.dec.com	**/.8/mail/ua/pine/**
		pine3.89.tar.Z
POP		
UNIX	ftp.cc.mcgill.ca	**/pub/network-services/pop/**
		popper-1.831.tar.Z
tarmail/untarmail		
UNIX	math.sunysb.edu	**/programs/atob/tarmail**
		/programs/atob/untarmail
UUCP		
UNIX	gatekeeper.dec.com	**/.3/net/uucp/**
		taylor-uucp-1.02.tar.Z
DOS	nisc.jvnc.net	**/pub/MSDOS/uucp/**
Mac	mrcnext.cso.uiuc.edu	**/pub/info-mac/comm/uucp/**
Mac	pacific.mps.ohio-state.edu	**/mac/uucp/**

Software Package

For	Where	Pathname
uuencode/uudecode		
UNIX	ames.arc.nasa.gov	/pub/UNIX/uucp/uuencode/ uucode.shar
DOS	casbah.acns.nwu.edu	/pub/dos/uuencode.com /pub/dos/uudecode.com
Mac	mrcnext.cso.uiuc.edu	/pub/info-mac/cmp/ uu-lite-16.hqx /pub/info-mac/cmp/ uu-parser-172.hqx
WAIS		
UNIX	quake.think.com	/wais/wais-8-b5.1.tar.Z
	ftp.cnidr.org	/pub/NIDR.tools/ freeWAIS-0.2.tar.Z
	ftp.wais.com	/pub/wais-inc-doc/txt/ Price-List.txt
DOS	ftp.uga.edu	/pub/msdos/doswais.zip
Mac	mrcnext.cso.uiuc.edu	/pub/info-mac/comm/tcp/ wais-for-mac-11.hqx
whois		
UNIX	charon.mit.edu	/pub/whois/

Appendix C

Headers and Formats

Here is a list and brief description of the RFC822 mail headers. You may not see all these headers, nor use them, but here they are for your information. We divide the fields into the functional groupings defined in the RFC. See the RFC for further details.

Source Headers

From: who the mail is from

`Sender:`	the actual sender of a message
`Reply-To:`	address to send replies to
`Return-path:`	path back to sender
`Received:`	when message was received by each MTA
`Resent-Reply-To:`	who to send a reply for a resent message
`Resent-From:`	who resent the original message
`Resent-Sender:`	the actual sender of the resent message
`Resent-From:`	who resent the message

You will rarely see the `Resent-` form. These headers denote the message was resent or forwarded from another user. In most cases users simply forward a message with the forwarded message in the message body, headers and all.

Destination Headers

`To:`	primary message recipients
`cc:`	secondary message recipients
`bcc:`	blind carbon copy message recipients
`Resent-To:`	resent message recipients
`Resent-cc:`	secondary resent message recipients
`Resent-bcc:`	blind carbon copy resent message recipients

Date Headers

`Date:`	date and time the original message was sent
`Resent-Date:`	date the message was resent

Optional Headers

`Subject:`	topic of the message
`Message-ID:`	unique message identifier
`Resent-Message-ID:`	unique resent message identifier
`In-Reply-To:`	message being replied to
`References:`	other correspondence this message refers to
`Keywords:`	keywords in the message
`Comments:`	any additional comments about the message
`Encrypted:`	indicates the message is encrypted
`X-`	start of a user-defined field

MIME Headers

You don't usually have to deal with MIME directly, but you may see these headers, especially if your mail program is not MIME capable.

`MIME-Version:`	version number of the MIME system in use.

This is the only MIME header that actually appears in the RFC822 message headers. The rest of the MIME headers only appear in the individual MIME body parts.

`Content-Type:`	defines the content type of each MIME body part.
`Content-Transfer-Encoding:`	defines an auxiliary encoding of each separate MIME body part to allow it to transfer

	through the mail transport system
`Content-Id:`	defines a unique identifier for this MIME body part
`Content-Description:`	descriptive commentary on this MIME body part

X.400 Headers and Addresses

The long awaited OSI Message Handling System. You will see these, and may have to deal with them. However, as a proportion of total mail messages, X.400 messages are becoming increasingly rare.

An X.400 address is encoded in a binary format. The message address consists of a series of attributes. For convenience the common ASCII representation of a set of attributes is the attribute keyword followed by its value. The attributes are separated with slashes. An example X.400 address in this format is:

`/C=GB/ADMD=BT/PRMD=DES/O=UCL/OU=CS/S=sam`

There are many X>400 attributes. Here is a description of the more commonly found X.400 attributes.

`C=`	country code.
`ADMD=`	public administrative organization running the X.400 service. This is usually the abbreviation of a PTT.
`PRMD=`	private administrative organization that runs the X.400 service.
`O=`	organization.
`OU`	organizational unit.
`S=`	surname.

From the Internet you will normally send an X.400 address to a mail gateway. The common syntax for accomplishing this is to append the name of the gateway on the end of the address as in:

/C=GB/ADMD=BT/PRMD=DES/O=UCL/OU=CS/S=sam@gateway.org

This message would be forwarded to the machine **gateway.org** which handles translating the ASCII representation of the X.400 address into X.400's internal binary format.

Appendix D

Reading

So many books are available about the Matrix and the Internet that we can't even list them all here. Instead, let's just list a few of the ones that are most relevant to electronic mail.

For more details on how to get connected, see *The Internet Connection: System Connectivity and Configuration* by John S. Quarterman and Smoot Carl-Mitchell, (Addison-Wesley, 1994).

For more information about many of the networks and other systems in the Matrix, see *The Matrix: Computer Networks and Conferencing Systems Worldwide* by John S. Quarterman (Digital Press, 1990) and *The Online User's Encyclopedia: Bulletin Boards and Beyond* by Bernard Aboba (Addison-Wesley, 1993).

If you are deciding whether you want to connect to the Internet, you can find out more about what is available on the Internet by reading *The Internet Companion: A Beginner's Guide to Global Networking,* Second Edition by Tracy LaQuey (Addison-Wesley, 1994). If you want details of how to access Internet resources, try *The Internet Guide for New Users* by Daniel P. Dern (McGraw-Hill, 1993) or *The Whole Internet User's Guide & Catalog* by Ed Krol (O'Reilly, 1992).

If you have decided you want to connect to the Internet and you need software and advice on how to use it, you may find one of a trio of books by Michael Fraase useful: *The Mac Internet Tour Guide*, (Ventana Press, 1993), *The PC Internet Tour Guide*, (Ventana Press, 1994), and *The Windows Internet Tour Guide* (Ventana Press, 1994).

Glossary

accept   The moderator of a moderated mailing list may choose to accept a submission and then post it to the list.

address   A string of text used to identify the intended recipient of a mail message.

alias   A mail address that causes software to distribute a mail message to one or more addresses.

alphanumeric   Letters and digits, A-Z, a-z, 0-9, often plus underscore (_) and hyphen (-).

Anonymous FTP   A method for retrieving publicly available files across the Internet. See *FTP*.

AOL   A commercial conferencing system.

APNIC (Asia-Pacific Network Information Center)   An Internet coordinating body for the Asia-Pacific region.

archie   A directory service for files in anonymous FTP servers.

article   A USENET news message.

Asahi-net   A commercial conferencing system in Japan.

ASCII-net   A commercial conferencing system in Japan.

Asia-Pacific Network Information Center   See *APNIC.*

ATT Mail   A commercial mail network.

autoposted   A list whose submissions are automatically forwarded to the list by software, without human intervention.

autoresponder   A mailing list that responds to any mail message with a message of general information.

bang-path address   See *UUCP address.*

BBS (Bulletin Board System)   A BBS is a single computer that users dial up with modems.

BITNET (Because It's Time Network)   A large, but now shrinking, academic network, based on the NJE protocols.

BIX   A commercial conferencing system.

bounce message   When a mail message cannot be delivered by a mail system, the software that detects the problem ordinarily sends a bounce message back to the original sender, or to some appropriate address.

BTW (by the way)   An abbreviation of a phrase commonly used in electronic mail.

Bulletin Board System   See *BBS.*

cat   A UNIX command that concatenates files.

cc:Mail   A proprietary mail package.

Central Processing Unit   See *CPU.*

CIX (Commercial Internet Exchange)   A corporation that coordinates many commercial Internet providers.

ClariNet   A commercial news network using USENET news technology.

client process   A program that uses a network protocol to use a service provided by a server process.

client/server paradigm of computing   A client process on one computer uses a network protocol to communicate with a server process on another computer in order to use a service provided by that server. A single computer may be running one or more client processes and one or more server processes at the same time, and thus may be both a client and a server.

closed   Subscription requests to a closed mailing list must be approved.

CMC (Computer Mediated Communication)   The traditional academic term for media such as electronic mail, mailing lists, and news.

command line interface   An interface that permits users to type commands, usually one per line.

commercial conferencing system   A centralized host system (sometimes actually a tightly coupled network cluster) used to sell conferencing services.

Commercial Internet Exchange   See *CIX*.

commercial mail system   A network primarily intended to transport commercial mail traffic.

common courtesy   A relatively reliable guide to actions in electronic mail and mailing lists, but remember many different kinds of people are accessible.

common sense   Something to be wary of when first using electronic mail and mailing lists.

CompuServe   A commercial conferencing system.

Computer Mediated Communication   See *CMC*.

CPU (Central Processing Unit)   The chip in a computer that adds, multiplies, and performs other basic manipulations on data, and that also controls what other parts of the computer do.

cyberspace   The social space experienced by users of the Matrix.

daemon   A program that handles some system function automatically. The word is Greek, and originally indicated a spirit, not necessarily either malevolent or beneficient.

deferred bounce message   A warning bounce message.

Delphi   A commercial conferencing system.

digest   An online newsletter consisting of articles collected from a mailing list and grouped together into a single message.

Digital (Digital Equipment Corporation)   The computer vendor that makes FTPmail available to users in the Matrix.

distribution   An indication of which computers a USENET article should be delivered to.

distribution list   A synonym for a mailing list, or the actual list of addresses for a mailing list.

DNS (Domain Name System)   The distributed naming system used by the Internet community, both on the Internet itself and on related networks.

DNS name   A series of tokens separated by periods.

DNS tree   The tree formed by drawing lines from each domain to its parent.

domain address   Two sets of tokens separated by a single "at" sign (@).

domain addressing   Addressing using DNS domains.

Domain Name System   See *DNS*.

domain syntax   The style of addressing, such as mailbook@tic.com, required for use with the Domain Name System; used throughout the Internet, but also outside the Internet, and also even on some networks that do not otherwise support the Domain Name System.

domain_part   The part of a domain address to the right of the at sign (@); it typically denotes a host computer. See also *local_part*.

EARN (European Academic and Research Network)   The NJE network in Europe. See also *BITNET*.

EasyLink   A commercial mail network.

echoes   A category used to group FidoNet echomail articles into topics of discussion.

echomail   The distributed conferencing facility of FidoNet.

electronic mail   Messages sent asynchronously over a computer network to specific addressees or lists of addresses; also known as e-mail, email, or just mail.

email   A abbreviation for electronic mail.

End Of File   See *EOF.*

enterprise IP network   An enterprise network that uses IP.

enterprise network   An internal network within a company or other organization that is dedicated to support of company operations.

EOF (End Of File)   A marker for the end of a file.

European Academic and Research Network   See *EARN.*

e-World   A commercial conferencing system.

exploder   A subsidiary list that distributes mail to some of the subscribers of a mailing list.

FAQ (frequently asked questions)   A list of both questions and answers to them; a mailing list often has a FAQ associated with it.

fido   A FidoNet host.

FidoNet   A large BBS network, supporting electronic mail and distributed conferencing. Most FidoNet hosts run DOS.

File Transfer Protocol   See *FTP.*

filelist   The LISTSERV name for a filesystem directory.

firewall   Hardware and software that deliberately prevents use of certain network services while permitting others to qualified users.

flame   To send rude, irate, or otherwise inappropriate messages.

flame fest   An escalating series of flames going on for days or weeks.

flame retardant   Words intended to prevent further flames.

flame war   See *flame fest.*

flaming   Nasty, overly emotional, verbose, or just plain inappropriate messages.

followup   A USENET news article posted in response to a previous article.

FQDN (fully qualified domain name)   The domain_part of an electronic mail address, including all the domain parts from the specific hostname to the top level domain.

freenet   An Internet login host that provides services with little or no charge to the end user.

frequently asked questions   See *FAQ*.

FTP (File Transfer Protocol)   The standard TCP/IP file transfer protocol.

FTPmail   A server that accepts commands by electronic mail to retrieve files by FTP and return them by electronic mail.

fully qualified domain name   See *FQDN*.

FYI (for your information)   An abbreviation of a phrase commonly used in electronic mail.

gateway   A program or computer that carries messages or information between two networks.

GEnie   A commercial conferencing system.

GopherMail   A mail server for Gopher menus and information.

GUI (Graphical User Interface)   A user interface that displays icons and windows and expects a mouse to point and click.

GULFNET   The NJE network in the Persian Gulf. See also *BITNET*.

host   A computer that is connected to a computer network and that users use to send and receive electronic mail.

IMHO (in my humble opinion)   An abbreviation of a phrase commonly used in electronic mail.

implementation   An implementation of a network protocol is software that communicates with similar softare across a network according to the rules specified in that protocol.

information retrieval   Retrieving information once you have found its source. Information retrieval protocols include FTP, Gopher, WAIS, and WWW.

informational message   A bounce message indicating a transient condition that may correct itself.

the Internet   The largest group of computers and networks that use IP to provide direct interactive communication.

Internet access   The ability to use Internet services, including remote login (TELNET) FTP (file transfer), mail, and news, among many others. Beware of false claims of Internet access, since some providers use the term even though they only provide mail and conferencing between their users and the Internet.

Internet community   All the people and organizations that communicate with people or organizations on the Internet, by whatever means.

Internet Protocol   See *IP*.

InterNIC   An Internet coordinating body.

IP (Internet Protocol)   The glue that binds the tens of thousands of networks of the Internet together. IP provides a common address space and a suite of related protocols, including the application protocols WWW, Gopher, archie, FTP, TELNET, SMTP, and NNTP, and the transport protocols TCP and UDP.

IP address   A unique 32-bit integer used to identify a node on an IP network, so that data may be routed to and from it.

JPNIC (Japan Network Information Center)   An Internet coordinating body for Japan.

junk mail   Advertising messages sent to large numbers of people without asking them first.

KIS (Knowbot Information Services)   An Internet information service; not available by mail.

LAN (Local Area Network)   A network using a technology intended for short distances, such as within a building. Such technologies include Ethernet (thicknet, thinnet, 10BaseT, IEEE 802.3) and token ring (IEEE 802.5, FDDI). A LAN is used with a higher level network protocol, such as IP, Novell NetWare, AppleTalk, DECNET, or XNS.

list owner   The person responsible for maintaining a mailing list. For a related but different function, see moderator.

LISTSERV   A BITNET program that handles mailing list subscriptions and unsubscriptions automatically, and also provides access to list archives and other files.

local address   An address intended for delivery on the local host; recognizable by the lack of an at sign or by the domain_part matching the local host name.

Local Area Network   See *LAN*.

local_part   The part of a domain address to the left of the at sign (@); it typically denotes a user of the host computer given in the domain_part. See also *domain_part*.

login host   A system that sells login accounts to users so they can use the Internet.

mail   Electronic mail, also known as email or e-mail.

mail envelope   Addressing and other information used by the electronic postal system in delivering a mail message.

Mail Exchanger   See *MX*.

mail format   The common conventions for structuring a mail message.

mail program   Software that you can use to send and recieve electronic mail. Also known as a mail User Agent.

mailbox   A file used to contain electronic mail for a person.

mailer   Another name for a mail program.

Mailer-Daemon   The ordinary name of the mail system itself.

mailing list   A group of electronic mail addresses reached by sending mail to an alias; a discussion forum constructed from electronic mail.

mainframe   A very large computer, typically having a word larger than 32 bits and a rack-mounted physical installation.

Majordomo   A program that automatically handles mailing list subscription requests.

the Matrix   The largest group of networks and computers worldwide that exchange electronic mail. The Matrix includes the Internet, BITNET, UUCP, FidoNet, WWIVnet, and thousands of other networks. It does not include isolated BBSes, unnetworked mainframes, or disconnected LANs.

MCI Mail   A commercial mail network.

menu interface   An interface that permits users to select items from lists that appear on the screen.

message body   The part of an electronic mail message after the headers, containing the main message.

message header   A group of lines at the beginning of an electronic mail message that specify the addresses, subject, and other characteristics of the message, similarly to the header of a paper memo.

Message Transfer Agent   See *MTA*.

MIME (Multipurpose Internet Mail Extensions)   Extensions to the RFC822 mail message format to permit multiple fonts, graphics, video, and sound.

Minitel   The common name for Teletel.

mixed addressing   Combining different mail addressing formats to permit gatewaying mail from one network to another, perhaps through still others.

modem   A hardware device that translates digital signals from your computer into sounds that travel over an ordinary telephone line.

moderated   A moderated mailing list has all postings preapproved by a moderator.

moderator   The person who approves or disapproves submissions for posting to a moderated mailing list.

MTA (Message Transfer Agent)   Software to transfer mail to another computer. Normally, users use UAs, and UAs invoke MTAs as needed.

multi-process systems   Systems that can each run more than one process at a time. See also *multi-user system*.

Multipurpose Internet Mail Extensions   See *MIME*.

multi-user systems   Systems that can each have more than one user at a time.

MX (Mail Exchanger)   An MX record associates a domain name with another domain name that names a host that will handle mail for the first domain name. The first domain name may be a host like any other, or it may be inaccessible, either because it is not connected for other services, or because it does not exist.

National Public Telecomputing Network   See *NPTN*.

netfind   An Internet information service; not available by mail.

network   A group of computers that communicate using a common network protocol. Also used by some to refer to a BBS.

Network Information Center   See *NIC*.

Network Job Entry   See *NJE*.

news   A distributed many-to-many conferencing system. See *USENET*.

newsgroup   A category used to group USENET news articles into topics of discussion.

NIC (Network Information Center)   A group whose purpose is to supply information to network users.

NIFTY-Serve   A commercial conferencing system in Japan.

Nikkei Mix   A commercial conferencing system in Japan.

nixpub (public access UNIX system)   The name is taken from a list of such systems.

NJE (Network Job Entry)   The network protocols used by BITNET.

NPTN (National Public Telecomputing Network)   An organization of freenets.

the office   A traditional place of work; not as important when you have electronic mail.

online newsletter   A document compiled by an editorial process similar to that of a paper newsletter, but delivered online, usually through a mailing list.

online paper newsletter   An online newsletter that is designed to be printed before being read.

open   Anyone may subscribe to an open mailing list.

paper mail   Old-style messages using paper letters, envelopes, and stamps; sometimes called paper post or postal mail.

PC-VAN   A commercial conferencing system in Japan.

PEM (Privacy Enhanced Mail)   A protocol for using encryption to make electronic mail private.

People   A commercial conferencing system in Japan.

percent sign convention   The use of a percent sign (%) in the local_part of a mail address to cause a message to be forwarded to the host specified in the part of the local_part to the right of the percent sign.

PGP (Pretty Good Privacy)   A publicly available implementation of public key encrytion, which allows you to send and receive messages without the other person knowing your private key, and without needing a trusted third party.

Pine   A simple mail program.

pipeline   A series of UNIX commands manipulating data passed through pipes.

Point of Presence   See *PoP*.

point-by-point rebuttal   Quoting every single point of a someone's message and appending a rebuttal to each one.

PoP (Point of Presence)   A local access point for a network.

POP (Post Office Protocol)   An Internet protocol that you can use to pick up your mail from a server.

post   To send a news article over USENET.

Post Office Protocol   See *POP*.

postal mail   See *paper mail*.

poster   The person who posted a USENET news article.

Pretty Good Privacy   See *PGP*.

Privacy Enhanced Mail   See *PEM*.

private   Only subscribers may retrieve information about the list.

process   A program that is running.

Prodigy   A commercial conferencing system.

protocols   Agreements for how to exchange information; IP, NetWare, and AppleTalk are network protocols. Software may implement protocols. Such software usually has a user interface. Users use such user interfaces.

public Anyone may retrieve information about the list, including the addresses of its subscribers.

public access UNIX system See *nixpub*.

reject The moderator of a moderated mailing list may choose to reject a submission and not post it to the list, usually sending it back to the submittor with comments instead.

relay machine Any computer that passes mail onwards to another destination.

Request for Comments Number 822 See *RFC822*.

Reseaux IP Européens See *RIPE*.

resource discovery Finding sources of information or services. Resource discovery protocols include archie, Gopher, Veronica, WAIS, and WWW.

resource record A value stored under a domain name.

resource sharing Exchanging information. Resource sharing protocols include FTP and TELNET, among many others.

RFC822 (Request for Comments Number 822) The Internet standard for the format of electronic mail messages; also widely used on other networks.

RFC822 header lines Lines that can go in the header of an electronic mail message that conforms to RFC822.

richtext A format for encoding text styles such as italic and boldface in plain ASCII text.

RIPE (Reseaux IP Européens) An Internet coordinating body for Europe.

root node The top-most node in the DNS tree.

send/receive protocol A protocol in which the client sends a message to the server and expects to recieve a response each time.

server process A program that acts as a server by using a network protocol to provide a service to client processes.

shar A utility that makes bundles of files that can be extracted with nothing but a UNIX shell.

Simple Mail Transfer Protocol   See *SMTP.*

single-process systems   Systems that can each run only one process at a time. See also *single-user system.*

single-user systems   Systems that can each have only one user at a time. A single-user system can still be multi-process, as for example a UNIX workstation, but the most common single-user systems are also single-process.

smiley face   This is a smiley face. :-)

SMTP (Simple Mail Transfer Protocol)   The standard TCP/IP mail transfer protocol.

SMTP (Simple Mail Transfer Protocol)   The standard TCP/IP mail transfer protocol.

Sprint   Packaged dialup software and services.

SprintMail   A commercial mail network.

store-and-forward   When one computer stores messages it recieves and then forwards them to another. Electronic mail is a store-and-forward service, which may travel over either store-and-forward networks such as UUCP, FidoNet, and WWIVnet, or over interactive networks such as the Internet.

submission   A message submitted to the moderator of a mailing list for possible posting to the list.

subs   A category used to group WWIVnet articles into topics of discussion.

syntax   The rules for putting together characters to form a mail address.

telephone tag   Attempts by two people to catch each other on the telephone, leaving each other messages in the meantime.

Teletel   A network in France, run by France Telecom; the largest isolated network we know of.

TELNET   The standard TCP/IP remote login protocol.

Terminate and Stay Resident   See *TSR.*

Texas Internet Consulting   See *TIC.*

thread   A series of messages on the same subject, following a thread of conversation.

TIC (Texas Internet Consulting)   A company that consults in networks and open systems, with particular emphasis on TCP/IP networks, UNIX systems and standards.

time zones   Geographical zones within which clocks are generally set to the same time.

tokens   One or more alphanumeric characters.

TSR (Terminate and Stay Resident)   The mechanism by which even DOS can have daemons.

UA (User Agent)   Another name for a mail program.

UNIX to UNIX CoPy   See *UUCP*.

unknown host message   A bounce message indicating the system addressed by the domain_part is not known to the responding MTA.

unknown mailer error   A bounce message indicating some kind of internal mail system error.

unknown user message   A bounce message indicating the user addressed by the local_part is not reachable on the system addressed by the domain_part.

USENET   All computers that carry USENET news, which is a distributed many-to-many conferencing system. USENET is just a single network service, not a network, but it is carried over many underlying networks, including UUCP (where it started), BITNET, FidoNet, and the Internet.

USENET mail addresses   There's no such thing, since USENET is just news; however, the networks that carry USENET all support electronic mail and thus their users have mail addresses.

User Agent   See *UA*.

UUCP   1. A large network that support electronic mail and distributed conferencing (USENET news). Most UUCP hosts run UNIX, although many run DOS or other operating systems.
2. UNIX to UNIX CoPy. The network protocol that supports the UUCP network.

UUCP address   The address syntax used on the UUCP network, involving a series of hostnames separated by exclamation points and ending with a username.

UUCP addressing   The use of UUCP addresses.

UUCP Mail Network   A longer name for UUCP.

UUCP registry   A registry for UUCP hostnames, which guarantees registered names will be unique.

voice mail   Automated recording and playback of voice telephone messages; commonly used to play telephone tag.

WAIS (Wide Area Information Servers)   An information services that provides keyword search of databases.

WAISmail   A mail server for WAIS queries.

White Pages   Addresses for individual people, and sometimes also of organizations, are traditionally listed in telephone books on pages colored white, in contrast to the Yellow Pages, which traditionally list categories of services.

WHOIS   A centralized Internet directory service.

Wide Area Information Servers   See *WAIS*.

WorldLink   Packaged dialup software and services.

WWIVnet   A large BBS network, supporting electronic mail and distributed conferencing. Most WWIVnet hosts run DOS.

Zilker Internet Park   An Internet and Matrix access provider.

Index